The Drama of Russian Political History

NUMBER NINETEEN

Eastern European Studies

Stjepan Meštrović, General Editor

The Drama of Russian Political History

SYSTEM AGAINST INDIVIDUALITY

Alexander V. Obolonsky

Foreword by Vincent Ostrom

TEXAS A&M UNIVERSITY PRESS   COLLEGE STATION

First edition

The paper used in this book meets the minimum requirements
of the American National Standard for Permanence
of Paper for Printed Library Materials, z39.48-1984.
Binding materials have been chosen for durability.

∞

Library of Congress Cataloging-in-Publication Data

Obolonsky, Alexander V.
[Drama rossiyskoy politicheskoy istorii. English.]
The drama of Russian political history : system against individuality / Alexander V. Obolonsky ; foreword by Vincent Ostrom.
p. cm.—(Eastern European studies ; no. 19)
Includes bibliographical references and index.
ISBN 1-58544-224-0 (cloth : alk. paper)
1. Russia—Politics and government. 2. Soviet Union—Politics and government. 3. Political rights—Russia. 4. Political rights—Soviet Union. I. Ostrom, Vincent, 1919– II. Title. III. Eastern European studies (College Station, Tex.) ; no. 19. IV. Series.
DK61.02613 2003
947—dc21 2002012708

To my dearest ones

my wife Olga

and my late parents,

Valentine Obolonsky and Maria Bryantseva

They personified for me many qualities of the

different generations of the Russian intelligentsia.

Contents

Foreword

The drama of Russian political history is important to all humankind. The Russian Revolution, the Soviet experiment, and the collapse of the Union of Soviet Socialist Republics have occupied worldwide attention as critical developments of the twentieth century. No other events have stirred such far-reaching ramifications among the diverse peoples of this world. Nor have other events been marked by greater suffering and tragedies during the twentieth century. What began as heroic adventures turned into tragedies of global proportions.

Alexander Obolonsky's *The Drama of Russian Political History* is an effort by one who has lived with that drama to understand its deeper meaning as a struggle for the human soul, reaching to dimensions of personality, character structure, and the meaning of life. The struggle is one between individual freedom and responsibility and the requirements of the social order as a system that makes its demands for conformity. In one, individuals are presumed to be free to choose and to assume their responsibility in the social order. In the other, individuals take the place assigned to them in an order that is dominated by the requirements of the system and by one's status in the system. In one, human character structures are more strongly person-oriented in a general system of ethics consistent with more universal moral orders. In the other, an established status system is bound together by rituals associated with different estates in which the requirements of the system prevail in relation to that of the individual. One is *person-centered;* the other is *system-centered.*

Henry Sumner Maine, in a volume entitled *Ancient Law,* first published in 1861, conjectured that "the movement of the progressive societies has hitherto been a movement *from Status to Contract*" (italics his).[1] Rather than using well-defined status systems in stratified social orders, the shift to "contract" implies a shift to equality in assigning standing to persons as a legal concept, accompanied by freedom among individuals to enter into legally binding voluntary agreements with one another over increasingly large domains of human relationships. In this context, it is important to recognize that the freeing of individuals is an integral part of the drama of Russian history. During the 1560s and 1570s, even the nobility was reduced to serfdom, obliged to render compulsory service to imperial authority in the reign of Ivan IV, also known as Ivan the Terrible. Ivan IV had his counterpart in England's Henry VIII.

The importance of the drama of Russian political history for human civilization was highlighted by Alexis de Tocqueville in the paragraphs concluding the first volume of *Democracy in America,* first published in 1835:

> There are at the present time two great nations in the world, which started from different points, but seem to tend towards the same end. I allude to the Russians and the Americans. Both of them have grown up unnoticed; and while the attention of mankind was directed elsewhere, they have suddenly placed themselves in the front rank among the nations, and the world learned their existence and their greatness at almost the same time.
>
> All other nations seem to have nearly reached their natural limits, and they have only to maintain their power; but these are still in the act of growth. All the others have stopped, or continue to advance with extreme difficulty; these alone are proceeding with ease and celerity along a path to which no limit can be perceived. The American struggles against the obstacles that nature opposes to him; the adversaries of the Russian are men. The former combats the wilderness and savage life; the latter, civilization with all its arms. The conquests of the American are therefore gained by the plowshare; those of the Russian by the sword. The Anglo-American relies upon personal interest to accomplish his ends and gives free scope to the unguided strength and common sense of the people; the Russian centers all the authority of society in a single arm. The principal instrument of the former is freedom; of the latter, servitude. Their starting-point is different and their courses are not the same; yet each of them seems marked out by the will of Heaven to sway the destinies of half the globe.[2]

Obolonsky's *The Drama of Russian Political History* provides us with a critical assessment of the course of Russian history over the period of the last four centuries. The struggle over freedom and servitude is the central theme. The "system-centeredness of the anthill" has prevailed through the major upheavals that have followed since the principality of Muscovy came to dominance in the struggle for a Russian empire. The increasing significance of person-centeredness in those struggles is associated with the place of the intelligentsia in Russian society. The term *intelligentsia* applies to the learned members of Russian society. The intelligentsia is concerned with the work of the mind as that involves the exploration of new intellectual frontiers, including those associated with other civilizations, especially Western civilization. Features that assumed special significance in Western civilization—the independence of the church from secular authority, the emergence of free cities, the Reformation, and the development of market economies—did not have parallels in the Russian empire. The adoption of Western technologies by Peter I was not accompanied by development of the rule of law but by an oppressive system of command and control.

The struggle within the intelligentsia was marked by deep divisions between those who sought to undertake moderate reforms as responsible persons reaching out to others and those who sought to use secrecy and violence to destroy the existing autocracy and undertake a revolutionary transformation of society. The great irony of Russia in the twentieth century was the success of the radicals in destroying the autocracy of the Tsar to replace it with the autocracy of radical partisans associated with the Communist Party as a revolutionary movement dedicated to using the instrumentalities of the state to transform society. In Obolonsky's words, the autocratic pyramid was upturned; but the new autocracy was even more oppressive than the old. His analysis of the psychological dynamics that preserved the system of servitude is especially enlightening, enabling us to understand how a secretary general of the Communist Party could become another Ivan the Terrible four centuries later in the twentieth century.

Tocqueville's allusion to the place of the Russians and the Americans in relation to the future of human civilization involves a double irony in light of the second volume of *Democracy in America*, first published in 1840. Tocqueville's concern was whether a free, self-governing society could indefinitely reproduce itself across generations, centuries, and millennia. Human life is of limited duration, and Tocqueville proceeds on an assumption that a free, self-governing society is required to establish the moral foundations for self-responsible individuals to constitute the configurations of self-governing institutional arrangements on the basis of voluntary agreements, as implied by Maine's concept of contract. Tocqueville was aware of the basic problematics before Maine's *Ancient Law* was published.

We have a deep puzzle. Governments in some basic sense are involuntary associations. The Americans used a concept of *covenant* to undertake the formulation of constitutions as enduring agreements specifying both the prerogatives of governmental officials and limits to those prerogatives associated with the prerogatives of persons and citizens to order their relationships with one another. To make constitutions binding as covenants across generations requires standards of ethical judgment, moral responsibility, and an understanding of what it means to function as covenanting persons and citizens in a democratic society. These conditions are consistent with requirements of voluntary agreement as applied both to units of government and to the larger configuration of relationships in the affairs of everyday life that have bearing on the constitution of a self-governing society.

Tocqueville's conclusion was that if Americans, or implicitly citizens in any democratic society, act *naturally* without reference to the ethical conditions of a covenantal character, then the viability of democratic society is placed at risk. Democratic societies are unlikely to survive into the indefinite future unless persons and citizens are knowledgeable about the arts and sciences of association based on moral and ontological precepts. These are the foundations for building the institutional arrangements that enable people to resolve their problems by relying on principles of voluntary agreement, including those built on enduring principles of constitutional law and a due process of law compatible with the requirements of freedom and justice.

What might be identified as the strategies of partisan politics in modern democracies has all the manifestations that are likely to place democracies at risk. Constitutional arrangements typically allow for pluralities or majorities to prevail in taking electoral decisions to elect representatives and to take decisions in the enactment of legislation. Politicians have strong incentives to form winning coalitions in which majorities can prevail at the cost of those who are in the minority. Strong incentives also exist to build appeals to the electorate couched in slogans that serve as "glittering generalities" or "sonorous phrases." Partisan politics get built on deceptive and fraudulent promises. This tendency is exaggerated when individuals look on themselves as being like everyone else and view a uniformity of law to be the essential criterion associated with justice. Under these circumstances, Tocqueville anticipated that citizens will presume that a democratic people will come to view government as "a sole, simple, providential, and creative power."[3] This view is contrary to the requirements of the institutions of government, which can be bound by principles of constitutional law.

Tocqueville, thus, anticipated that the dynamics of building winning coalitions in partisan politics reinforced by a gullible electorate will create a form of democratic despotism that puts the requirements of a free civilization at risk. In volume 2 of *Democracy in America,* we find a description written by Tocqueville before 1840 that provides an uncanny statement of the basic characteristics of what we have come to call the welfare state:

> The first thing that strikes the observation is an innumerable multitude of men, all equal and alike, incessantly endeavoring to procure the petty and paltry pleasures with which they glut their lives. Each of them, living apart, is as a stranger to the fate of all the rest; his children and his private friends constitute to him the whole of mankind. As for the rest of his fellow citizens, he is close to them, but he does not see them; he touches them, but he does not feel them; he exists only in himself and for himself alone; and if his kindred still remain to him, he may be said at any rate to have lost his country.
>
> Above this race of men stands an immense and tutelary power, which takes upon itself alone to secure their gratifications and to watch over their fate. That power is absolute, minute, regular, provident, and mild. It would be like the authority of a parent if, like that authority, its object was to prepare men for manhood; but it seeks, on the contrary, to keep them in perpetual childhood: it is well content that the people should rejoice, provided they think of nothing but rejoicing. For their happiness such a government willingly labors, but it chooses to be the sole agent and the only arbiter of that happiness; it provides for their security, foresees and supplies their necessities, facilitates their pleasures, manages their principal concerns, directs their industry, regulates the descent of property, and subdivides their inheritances: what remains, but to spare them all the care of thinking and all the trouble of living?

> Thus it every day renders the exercise of the free agency of man less useful and less frequent; it circumscribes the will within a narrower range and gradually robs a man of all the uses of himself. The principle of equality has prepared men for these things; it has predisposed men to endure them and often to look on them as benefits.
>
> After having thus successively taken each member of the community in its powerful grasp and fashioned him at will, the supreme power then extends its arm over the whole community. It covers the surface of society with a network of small complicated rules, minute and uniform, through which the most original minds and the most energetic characters cannot penetrate, to rise above the crowd. The will of man is not shattered, but softened, bent, and guided; men are seldom forced by it to act, but they are constantly restrained from acting. Such a power does not destroy, but it prevents existence; it does not tyrannize, but it compresses, enervates, extinguishes, and stupefies a people, till each nation is reduced to nothing better than a flock of timid and industrious animals, of which the government is the shepherd.[4]

In undertaking to satisfy the requirements of life extending from the cradle to the grave, the welfare state creates the anomaly of promising to spare people the cares of thinking and the trouble of living. Self-responsibility in creating voluntary arrangements for constituting relationships among individuals in societies is not consistent with the dependencies of the welfare state. What has become known as affirmative action in the United States is a shift that emphasizes a law of status as having a superior standing to agreement among free and responsible persons. There are circumstances in which democratic peoples stimulated by envy, greed, and a sense of helplessness can bind themselves into a state of servitude, trampling a free civilization underfoot.

The role of the intelligentsia assumes critical proportions in the struggle for person-centeredness in Obolonsky's *Drama of Russian Political History.* The future of freedom in Tocqueville's *Democracy in America* depends on the development of a science and art of association grounded in basic religious precepts to be applied in the public affairs of everyday life. People need to know the standards of moral judgment and the science that enables them to put the doctrine of self-interest to use in addressing basic interdependencies that occur in human relationships. Unfortunately, a portion of the Russian intelligentsia who presumed to know the Truth chose to use systemic methods of command and control to destroy the old Russian autocracy and to create an even more vigorous system of autocratic dominance.

To understand the challenge facing both the Russians and the Americans as we enter the twenty-first century in the Christian era will require careful attention to what Obolonsky has to say in this volume, considered in light of the challenge presented in Tocqueville's *Democracy in America.* The creative potentials of freedom in constituting human civilization depend on learning the moral precepts that serve as standards of judgment and the sciences and arts of association by which individuals can combine their creative potentials in building the institutional arrangements for free societies by methods of voluntary agreement implying binding commitments that are subject to revision and change by covenantal methods. Basic religious precepts that form the foundations of Jewish, Christian, and Islamic teachings and similar teachings in the Brahmin, Buddhist, and Confucian traditions need to be combined with efforts to build the sciences and arts of association consistent with the requirements of self-governing societies.

The Russians and the Americans have indeed affected the destinies of peoples everywhere in this world during the twentieth century. If the struggle over freedom and servitude is to be resolved, the Russians and the Americans are required to give careful consideration to what they can learn from one another. Neither the dictatorship of the proletariat nor the welfare state provides the basis for constituting self-organizing and self-governing societies. The shift from status to contract offers potentials provided that the conditions of equality and freedom are grounded in moral precepts consistent with the self-responsibility for undertaking binding commitments with one another.

Peace, freedom, justice, knowledge, information, well-being, and free trade are universal public goods, which have the characteristic that the greater the number of people enjoying such possibilities, the better off everyone would be. The realization of self-governing potentials consistent with such requirements is vastly different than pursuing collusive strategies to create dominant coalitions and to war on one's adversaries. Fallible human beings can engage in a quest for knowledge, but the truth of universal assertions must always be applied to the variability of time and place exigencies. The Russians and the Americans have a good deal to learn from one another, and what they learn will sway the destinies of humankind for at least the twenty-first century. Alexander Obolonsky opens a dialogue that is worthy of careful attention and further response with regard to the drama of politics in the affairs of everyday life among self-governing societies. You are invited to join the community of discussants and engage in critical reflections about the place of the Russians and the Americans in the future of human civilization. The resolutions that ordinary people in everyday life reach about what can be learned from the experiences of the Russians and the Americans will have an important influence on the drama of human history in the new millennium.

Obolonsky's use of the metaphor of a "crossroads" or "junction" as being a challenge to people in different societies, in my judgment, applies to all human societies. The dynamics of normal politics in putting together winning coalitions, whether by elections or coups d'état, mean that governments in the course of making policy decisions have strong incentives to reduce their transition costs and to distort constitutional arrangements toward a system of command and control through the nationalization of law. The centrality of customary law, local law, and regional law is replaced by circumstances in which the details of life come to be controlled by administrative rules and regulations adopted by the bureaucratic apparatus of the most general political jurisdiction. Unless the dynamics of normal politics can be challenged through the development of reform agendas, people come to be governed not by reflection and choice but by accident and force. These are the circumstances that Alexander Hamilton saw as the fundamental challenge confronting the Americans in the 1780s. This is the challenge confronting the peoples of the world in the new millennium.

If such potentials are to be realized, those who devote themselves to the cultural and social sciences, the social professions, and the humanities have a special responsibility to develop the bodies of knowledge that apply to the arts and sciences of human association, as Tocqueville expounded in volume 2 of *Democracy in America.* In short, we all face crossroads as we deal with the changing human condition through time. The dynamic of normal politics relying only on principles of one-person one-vote majority rule will yield to majority tyranny and the dependency of people who turn to the government to spare them the cares of thinking and the troubles of living.

The collapse of the Soviet system, the crisis of governance in Africa and much of the rest of the world, and the vulnerability of American democracy to the patterns of normal politics and the administrative state present a serious challenge for humanity. Harold Berman indicates in an article on world law—correctly, in my judgment—where we are at the dawn of a new millennium: "In the twentieth century, for the first time in the history of the human race, most of the peoples of the world have been brought into more or less continual relations with each other. We speak without hesitation of a world economy, a world technology, world-wide communications, world organizations, world science, world literature, world scholarship, world travel, world sports. We speak almost as confidently of an emerging world society, despite the forces of ethnic and territorial disintegration that threaten it. May we not speak also of world law?" [5]

The new world order cannot be constituted by autocratic heads of states. Instead, Berman sees the system of world law as being worked out in human conventions that turn on mutually agreeable working arrangements as people deal with one another in ways that transcend boundaries of nation-states.

Obolonsky's concern with how people approach the crossroads of history applies to all of us. We all face the challenge he presents. American corporate farms may produce more eggs, chickens, and other agricultural products than Soviet collective farms, but can they produce responsible citizens? Obolonsky's concern about personality and character structure, social ethics, and the moral order as being at the foundations of the multidimensional character of human societies poses basic questions about how people draw on knowledge and resources in human understanding to reflect on the meaning of human experience and on how to prepare ourselves to confront the future with fundamental respect for human individuality in a world that reaches to global proportions. The Russians, the Americans, and other peoples of the world have the opportunity and the responsibility to relate to one another on the basis of reflection and choice in light of what we can learn about our respective successes and failures.

Vincent Ostrom
Indiana University, Bloomington

Preface

"God bless us, we live in interesting times," the wise old Confucius said. As if in response to Confucius across twenty-five centuries, contemporary Russian poet Alexander Kushner has observed that "the times are not to choose, but just room to live and die." Russians living in the last decade of the twentieth century had the questionable fortune of living in times that were probably too interesting. Now the country has reached a difficult and troubling crossroads in its history. The choice of one path or another will determine the future for each of us; and the lives of our children and grandchildren will depend on the choices we make. Times of political choice—the crossroads of history—occur only at infrequent intervals.

Many years of my life have been devoted to work on this book. The first version was written in the late 1970s and early 1980s during the most hopeless and stuffiest period of the post-Stalinist era. I wrote not about contemporary events but about earlier periods in Russian history. However, the possibility of publication was not available then, nor during the era of *perestroika.* The main reason was that my work was not about victories and successes but about errors and lost opportunities in the sad and tragic history of my country, about possibilities that had not been realized. Errors and lost opportunities require critical reflection if they are not to be repeated. Ironically, when I suggested the book to some of the Russian emigrant publishing houses, it was rejected for a similar reason—I was too critical of pre-revolutionary Russia! So I found myself between two passions: the fires of Soviet and anti-Soviet editors burned for opposing orthodoxies.

Fortunately, times have changed in my country. In the fall of 1994, an updated version of the book was published in Moscow. Many things have happened since then. The flow of events carries and rolls us along. To stay oriented, to understand the direction of flow and the true meaning of events, no matter where you are—in the middle of the stream or apparently on the bank (nobody is really on the bank of historical processes)—

you need to keep in mind some basic landmarks. Having been in various places both as an oberver and participant of political events in Russia during these years, I have acquired certain confirmations of the validity of the keystones of my concept of historical process, at least for Russia. In the same period, we—the people on both sides of Atlantic Ocean—are witnesses to neglect of basic questions or lack of understanding of where we are and where we are headed. We are at once still under the ruins and debris of old myths but also captivated by a new mythology. That prospect is not very encouraging because specific answers to questions about who and what were responsible for the course of events in relatively recent times do not release us from a duty to search for answers to the basic questions about the whys and hows, questions that run through both historical and modern times. Neglecting those questions means we risk failing to take the steps needed to open our way to a new destiny rather than repeating the tragic cycles of history.

Being directed by this concern, I reconsidered many of my earlier perspectives, seriously revised some points of my concept, and wrote this book specifically for English-language readers. It departs in certain respects from standard academic practice. First, I not only use traditional academic sources but also draw in places from poetry and belles lettres, because this brings sometimes deeper and more essential understanding of core problems. Second, although employing a range of sources, both Russian and Western, I have not tried to be comprehensive. My colleagues in Russian studies whom I have not mentioned or cited will forgive me, I hope. This volume is by no means a textbook but rather an attempt at a new reading of Russian history in a modern context, offering a new concept of that history. The real choice was either to be consistent in unfolding these ideas or to include so many reservations to almost every even insignificant point as to risk having readers lose the thread of my logic. I preferred to take the former route, leaving more room for further discussion and critique, which I hope will follow. Moreover, in using a variety of sources, I have deliberately emphasized the introduction of some Russian ones, finding this a more valuable course for my Western colleagues and more informative for a broader circle of readers. Third, the genre of this book is a philosophy of history, not in the archaic sense but in the postmodern meaning of that phrase, whereby probabilities and the subjunctive mood are not forbidden, and the so-called value-free approach (one of the greater self-deceptions of twentieth-century social science) is not synonymous with "pure" or "true" science. Yes, I am a liberal and consequently anti-Communist in my convictions; I am not going to conceal it. I am convinced that it did not harm my research in terms of methods or approach and may serve to enhance its worth in terms of a broader conceptual context.

This is not a book on political or economic history. My main purpose has been to retrace the origin and development of two opposite but basic moral-psychological cultural paradigms, looking at their evolution and inherent struggle so as to identify crucial points and junctions in the course of Russian history, moments when alternative options for further development were revealed. To the extent that the concept of historical process offered is original, most Russologist and Sovietologist literature is tangential to my approach. This is one more reason why I needed to be selective rather than comprehensive in my references and bibliography, and it is also a point on which I anticipate a critique by academic colleagues who have a more positive vision of the twentieth-century Russian drama. To avoid abusing the attention of readers, I decided to be brief concerning such matters of common knowledge as the Bolshevik coup in 1917 and the detailed evidence of the malicious, antihuman character of Bolshevik regime measures like mass terror, coercive collectivization of the peasantry, purges, deportations of millions people based on ethnic social criteria, and other multiple crimes of the Leninist-Stalinist party directed against its own population. I know that there are some people, in both East and West, who still cannot accept the terrible truth of the scale of these atrocities, despite the existence of a myriad of publications about the events, including documents from the KGB and its precursors' archives, Lenin's secret letters to other members of the party leadership, the testimony of witnesses and victims, scholarly studies, and renderings in belles lettres. At bottom, the problem is not lack of reliable evidence. As we know, there are some people who still do not believe that the Nazis deliberately killed Jews. Apparently no amount of additional evidence will convince them. I must accept the existence of this pluralism as empirical fact, but I believe that pursuing discussion of these themes is beyond the realm of logic; such denial is a matter of human psychology and symbols of faith. It goes without saying that I acknowledge a full variety of views. However, we are sometimes inclined to underestimate the importance of the specific vision deriving from inside and outside a situation. Some things that seem obvious to Russian scholars need detailed argumentation if they are to come into clear focus for Western readers, and vice versa. Ideally, we have to be complementary, and we need to work more closely on and in a regime of dialogue. The present work, I hope, will prove a modest contribution to the process of building bridges between Russian studies scholars of the two shores.

I hope my inquiry is pertinent beyond the Russian situation and applies in some degree, as an investigation of human experience, to any setting where people are confronting the challenge of choosing among different patterns of order in the constitution of societies. The search for answers to questions about Russian history and its relationship to different scenarios of the country's future is important for Russia but also for other countries, particularly for the United States of America, a significant democratic power in the modern world. Russia is destined to be an important factor in world politics; and the course of events there will have a great influence on the world situation. That is why I present this work in English, and substantially revised since the Russian edition, as a contribution to the discussion needed not only in national and international contexts but for the human dimensions of civilization as well.

Acknowledgments

In the process of work on this book, I had the happy occasion to spend the academic year with the Workshop in Political Theory and Policy Analysis at Indiana University. In my opinion, this workshop is the place in the American academic world where the unique intellectual climate of an international community of scholars provides the best possible combination of intensive theoretical exchanges concerning basic problems of human civilizations, a stimulating atmosphere of joint scientific inquiry about practical ways of resolving those problems, and a friendly working spirit. I am grateful to Professors Vincent and Elinor Ostrom, codirectors of the Workshop, for making this possible.

It would be impossible to overestimate the meaning of the intellectual partnership, many-sided help, and support of Vincent Ostrom for this book and for me personally. Vincent carefully read, edited, reread, and commented on various versions of individual chapters and the complete manuscript. His critical remarks, his provocative and sometimes puzzling questions, and our multiple stimulating discussions in the process of our joint work constantly pushed me to consider the Russian case within broader theoretical and comparative contexts. Readers can judge the results of our common efforts; my own conclusion is that work with Vincent is one of the most important intellectual events in my life.

I also greatly appreciate my many years of discussions with Professor Darrell Hammer concerning the different aspects of Russian, Soviet, and post-Soviet political history and realities. Other colleagues at Indiana University—Yuri and Lucya Bregel, Robert Byrnes, Mary Dakin, William Edgerton, and Roman Frackowski—gave me various kinds of help during my work in Bloomington. Special thanks go to Gayle Higgins for her editorial help and numerous practical activities at different stages of manuscript preparation. I am very thankful, too, to many other people in the workshop, at Indiana University, and in Bloomington. They are too numerous to mention individually, but I recognize and appreciate their contributions. I must also acknowledge the stimulating challenge of those at Texas A&M University Press whose helpful suggestions gave me the opportunity to update and strengthen the book in the concluding stages of the work.

This book would never have been written and published without the invaluable moral, intellectual, and practical support and help of my wife Olga. She shared with me all the difficulties, discouragement, and even dangers during the long years of work and conspiratorial efforts to forward it to the West much earlier than could be done overtly. Unfortunately my parents, Valentine Obolonsky and Marya Bryantseva, left our world before the book was published in Russia and were not able to share that occasion. But I shall never forget their intellectual lessons and practical help for my work. The younger generations of my family—Sergy, Marina, Tolya, and Mika—stimulated my thoughts about the future of human societies and provided me with a good deal of optimism.

And last but not least, I must mention as an important part of both my personal life and Russian intellectual culture in general, the informal, so-called kitchen disputes with my Moscow friends. These numerous, mostly nighttime talks were helpful and provocative in shaping the basic ideas in this book.

The Drama of Russian Political History

CHAPTER ONE

On Methodology and General Concepts

Russian history and life are full of paradoxes. Most of them are, unfortunately, rather sad. Basic questions are: Why has the Russian nation—endowed by nature with huge amounts of natural, human, and intellectual resources; having developed a great literary and scientific heritage; and having made significant, sometimes crucial contributions to many aspects of the larger world civilization—proven unable to arrange the conditions of its own existence in accordance with the great potential that it possesses? What fundamental deficiency made possible this great anomaly?

Like many of my compatriots, I have spent the major part of my deliberative life contending with a feeling of deep troubles as adverse states of affairs have prevailed in my homeland. Individuals react to these feelings in different ways. I made perhaps not the best but the most suitable personal choice and began many years of analysis and reflection about the reasons for and consequences of the tragic destiny of my country and the historical course it had taken at different junctures, each determining its direction until it approached the next juncture.

To a certain degree, I faced the necessity of writing the story of a pathology that has prevailed in my own country. That task is difficult and painful in many respects, especially in its moral character, because one is compelled to describe the disease of an organism that is native to oneself by the circumstances of one's birth, regardless of one's disagreements with its way of life. Moreover, it was not simple to ignore the unavoidable reproaches of "antipatriotism," "vilification," and "Russophobia." If I coped with all these difficulties, it was only because I understood clearly the dirty tricks that historical idealization and mystification have played in Russian history—who gained political and other advantages from those myths, and who suffered the calamities endured by the people and the country.

On the other hand, rather than concentrating on current political events, I had to plunge into the deeper levels of national thought, morality, and psychology in terms of continuities and discontinuities in attitudes and standards of public consciousness and public behavior. To resolve these problems in an immense historical panorama, I had to restrict myself to concentrating on key historical periods and selective aspects of those times. Certain methodological issues have had to be resolved.

THE POINT OF DEPARTURE

As a point of departure, I rejected one-dimensional, monistic conceptions and interpretations of history. In the nineteenth and twentieth centuries, that "devil of one-dimensionalism" had manifested itself first in forms of economic determinism and the Marxist conception of class struggle as an ultimate universal explanation of human history.[1] Another variant of monism—the political one—focused on the state and the people and groups in power as responsible for all the catastrophes and all the gains of human societies. The third variant of monism—the scientific-technocratic one focusing on technological modernization—has created sweet illusions; but the collapse of these illusions brought painful disappointment to many developing and developed countries. One more version of monism, potentially aggressive and even less adequate than the rest, gained ground and unfortunately still maintains its ground in nationalistic conceptions stressing ethnic factors, the "voice of blood," and nationalistic identity as a key motive power of civilizations.[2]

I presupposed that a multidimensional conception of society would be a better cognitive construction for the purposes of analysis in both historical and contemporary research. This conception allows one to describe any society by means of several groups of relatively interdependent factors viewed as variables—economic, technological, moral, political, psychological, and aesthetic. By joining appropriate considerations of these factors, we can assess a society's condition at any period of time. As major independent variables, I consider the economic, moral, psychological, and aesthetic to be the most fundamental. Others, like the political variables, I consider to be derived from the most fundamental.

I realized that such a framework, like any other formulation, inevitably simplifies the true situation to some degree, particularly because these factors are never completely independent or precisely measurable. However, they do have a certain degree of autonomy, and interaction among them is not constant either in the direction of influence or in the way they are bound together. In some societies or at some times, an economy actually affects all the other spheres of life. In other cases, an economy is in turn derivative, perhaps from moral factors. For example, an expansion of Islam in the Arab world during the later centuries of the first millennium A.D. provoked modifications in all other aspects of life, including the economy. In some societies and eras, we see an intensive development of one or two factors while others remain in the shadows. For example, the unique blossoming of cultural and political life in ancient Greece took place in the context of rather ordinary patterns of economic and technological conditions. The effort to pick out some single dominant feature of social development, which is presumed to be valid for all countries and times, is, as a rule, artificial and arbitrary.

During recent decades we can observe an encouraging shift in the minds of people in many countries. Different models of the one-dimensional man—the economic, technocratic, political, nationalistic ones—have begun to concede their positions in favor of more balanced views. More universal, integral characteristics of personality—the ethical, cultural, and psychological—have come to the forefront. The well-known American historian of social thought Frank Manuel described this reversal of social perspective, which has occurred over a century and a half, in the following way: "To promote his idealistic theory of Spirit as the essence of human existence, Hegel had written with the greatest contempt about an 'alimentary' history. Currently, when we, in spite of Hegel, recognize the place of arms and stomach in human history, we should be ready to bring into history's temple the other, more hidden features of the human soul."[3]

I presume that the current condition of post-Soviet society is determined, to a certain extent, not only by economic but also by moral factors. Moral factors prevail despite a very unstable economic situation.

The moral degradation of society over several decades and the cultivation of a defective system of moral values have evoked cultural conditions in which even the most radical economic and administrative reforms could not achieve positive results unless accompanied by the reconstruction of a normal work morality. The failure of a work morality can create many unexpected negative consequences.

The primary purpose and task of my inquiry is to reach a deeper understanding of the phenomenon of the Russian spirit, to use a romantic cliché; or to describe the history of Russian collective consciousness, to use more "scientific" language. For that purpose, I relied on two main aspects of analysis, socio-ethical and socio-psychological, supposing that the political aspect is mainly derivative from those cultural and psychological features. In my opinion, this approach gives me the possibility of penetrating fundamental aspects of the Russian tragedy that remain hidden to economic or political interpretations of history.

In terms of general theory, I proceeded from the assumption that human history can be represented by two opposite "ethical genotypes" that have had a considerable influence on the character of life and the historical destiny of different nations. To conceptualize these ideal types: all varieties and differences in the concrete historical and cultural forms of human civilizations can be considered as a development and transformation of two opposite traditions—two opposite views of the social world. I identify these views as *system-centeredness* and *person-centeredness.* The fundamental difference is in the polarity of their scales of values.

In a person-centered scale of values, individuals are the primary focus of attention—"a measure for all things," as the ancient Greek philosopher Protagoras said. All phenomena in both the natural and social worlds, including the internal spiritual world of the individual, are considered in light of respect for the human person.

In a system-centered scale, an individual as such is not given any attention at all or is considered only as a means to achieve certain super-individual purposes. Such a system depends on a more general worldview. In several systems, such as Hinduism, this purpose is placed beyond the human world. In those cases, one could speak about variants of "cosmocentrism." We face different variants of "sociocentrism." The main idea is a total dissolution of the human ego to the transcending interests of empire, regal person, cult, custom, ideology, state, or cosmos. The common denominator in all these variants is the justification of some ultimate authority in the absence of an idea about the fundamental worth of human personality as a self-sufficient value. The meaning of human life is thereby reduced to its contribution in maintenance and development of some general system of order. In such an approach, the individual is always a tool and never an end. The way of thinking corresponding to the person-centered tradition is substantially the opposite. The ethos of this way of thinking is a personal orientation, a recognition of the uniqueness, autonomy, and self-sufficiency of each person. The role of individuals cannot be reduced to their function in social, natural, or any other system of order.[4]

We can see the first bursts of a person-centered way of thinking and life during the times of classical antiquity. I by no means subscribe to an uncritical idealization or romantic view of Hellenic Greece. We need to keep in mind the tragedies and degradation of life in the centuries that followed. But we cannot remain indifferent to the spirit of the Hellenic personality. Through the souls and shadows of one hundred generations, the spirit of the free citizens of those Greek polities sends us a message about the self-consciousness of persons who perceived for the first time in human history the dignity and value of one's own person.

The next impulse to a person-centered way of thinking and way of life came from early Christianity. The trajectory of human destiny would have been completely different if Christian morality had become a practical code of social life. But the real history of the institutions of the Christian Church, and especially the interpretations of them in most cases, proved to be far from the genuine Christian ideals.

Those transformations evoked a system of order that was still mainly system-centered, with the presumed dominance of an external ultimate authority. Nevertheless, a small light of person-centeredness was never extinguished from the beginning of the Christian era.[5] Sometimes it was hardly noticeable; sometimes it grew a little brighter; but it was never completely extinguished. And paradoxically, it displayed itself in circumstances that, superficially viewed, were absolutely hostile to it. *We should not equate person-centeredness with humanity. The relations between them are more complicated.* We can remember, for example, the inhuman activity of the Inquisition. Its purpose was to subordinate an individual's conscience to the prescriptions of contemporary clerical doctrine or, on an occasion of disobedience, to destroy an individual physically. But the paradox is that inquisitors, who spent much sophisticated energy on cruel tricks in the struggle for a human soul, served to confirm the importance and uniqueness of the human soul as manifest in individual conscience.

The outstanding twentieth-century Russian philosopher Nikolai Berdyaev specifically identified this peculiarity of religious persecutions in comparison with other forms of tyranny: "The old tyranny associated with the fires of inquisition left more room for human individuality, paid it more attention. Even extreme intolerance can be, nevertheless, a sign of respect to human individuality, to the spiritual life of man. When the church excommunicates and denounces heretics, it recognizes an interminable value of the human soul and pays attention to the uniqueness of individual destiny. . . . It is not so horrible, when a personality is a subject of limitations, oppressions, even torments, as when the very principle of human individuality is denied and impersonal considerations are substituted."[6]

A new history of the person-centered way of thinking began with the Reformation but took its initial steps by a process of Renaissance assimilation of the ancient moral heritage. This triumph of the new type of consciousness has provided unprecedented progress in many fields of social life. I call this type of mind *energetically individualistic.*

Now let me portray the system-centered types of order. A traditional orientation toward stability of relationships within the system of order is the supreme value. An orientation to a perpetual reproduction of the same human condition yields the denial of individualism, the neglect of the very idea of human personality, and a tendency to identify personal interests with the interests of a social whole—whether that be kin, tribe, community, or a broader system, including the state or a more extended system of order for all humankind. For the member of such a collectivity, a balance in one's personal life can be achieved only by means of total harmony with the system. The system keeps its stability only through the submission of its members.

Paradoxically, this way of thinking does not guarantee against revolts and other social cataclysms. History is marked by many bloody riots in traditional societies. But all these movements are directed not against the system as such but against particular people and groups inside the system who are presumed to abuse their own privileged positions and have therefore become dangerous to the stability of the system. Such popular uprisings carry the banner of the "just," "enlightened," or "benevolent" ruler. When the smoke of battle gradually clears, one can see that the main bastions of the system have remained untouched or have been made even more secure than before. Individuals come and go, but the system remains. The same pattern prevailed after the revolution of 1917 in Russia. To avoid misinterpretation, I need to emphasize that I use the word *system* here in a sense broader than that of a political system. One of the major tasks of this inquiry is to demonstrate how the substitution of governing officials did not bring any basic change in the character of the system in my country.

There are two main forms of system-centered societies: so-called primitive societies and the societies of an Oriental type, representing two kinds of traditionalism as a way of thinking. They can be conventionally designated as primitive and sophisticated. The European system-centered societies, including that of Russia, belonged to the Oriental or sophisticated form of system-centeredness.

A question arising is how to consider these types in relation to the standard opposition of West and East. The temptation exists to identify the West with person-centeredness and the East with system-centeredness. Generally speaking, there is some rationale for identifying person-centeredness with the western side of the Eurasian landmass and system-centeredness with the eastern side. But the notions of West versus East are too ambiguous. I hope these two types can be investigated to allow for a fuller clarification of their problematics. The opposition is not confined to any one geographical area and need not persist across eras in human civilizations.

Now let me try to formulate the main difference between these two polar types of social ethics. Where they seem to be diametrically opposed approaches is in efforts to resolve the moral tensions that inevitably develop between personality and different types of social order. The system-centered tradition presumes that the interests of a social whole (some group or society) are indisputably supreme, while person-centeredness proceeds from assumptions that individual considerations and the standing of persons have priority over the interests of social collectivities.

It was natural that the relationships between the two ethical prototypes almost always had a conflicting character. Historically, the system-centered type was the earlier one; later person-centeredness "germinated" from it. Since then, the two have developed in parallel ways. Each system perceives the existence of opposition as a threat and takes the attitude of either absorbing or submitting to the other rather than viewing the two as complements to each other. This is why the wars between representatives of these two systems have been marked by such great hostility. The emotional bitterness and the ideological manifestations of the struggle have not ceased even during relatively peaceful periods. Trade and cultural contacts have not been seen as mutually profitable cooperation but as efforts to weaken and place increasing pressure on the other.

These modes of relationships have remained as invariants through the course of human history. The forms, tactics, and ideological symbols have changed but never the deep-seated anxiety and hostility. The same situation still prevails in spite of objective conditions that work in the opposite direction toward a worldwide civilization and in spite of the timid but persistent attempts by human beings to move closer to one another in cooperative endeavors.

We cannot broach these huge and multifaceted problematics in their global dynamics. We can only suggest that the crises of the twentieth century have brought us to the threshold of a new type of social ethics. This type has its history as a philosophical construct. But beginning in the 1960s, one could see its symptoms and manifestations in patterns of social behavior.

My guess is that, as a result, this new ethical type has the possibility of taking on the form of a more or less balanced combination of system-centered and person-centered patterns of ethics as an integration of principles applicable to both communal and individualistic patterns of morality. In ideal form, it might be a combination of the better elements of both types and could provide for a harmony of interests for both individuals and society. Such a system needs to recognize individuality as an essential complement to social systems, and social arrangements as essential complements to individual creativity. I presume that this new meaning is to be identified with the development of what might properly be called a democratic civilization.

But any such fruit takes time and effort to mature. The events in Russia at the beginning of the twentieth century have become a tragic consequence of impatience for some "great leap forward." Radical ideologists attempted to bypass whole periods of socio-ethical development and to move directly from an archaic traditionalism to some utopian collectivism. Such neglect of continuities in historical processes can only crash. And so it happened. Instead of the ideal of a new kind of humanity, we got the strange hybrid that combined the worst traits of Russian traditional political culture and the groundless ambitions of socialism.

The struggle for democracy yielded a new version of Leviathan, or Ivan the Terrible, rather than the withering away of the State.

The greatest intellectuals of earlier Russia warned of this danger. In politics and philosophy, they were represented by S. Y. Witte and a group of philosophers (e.g., Nikolay Berdyaev) called the *vekhovtsy,* named for the famous volume of their articles titled *Vekhi,* meaning "The Landmarks." In literature, they were represented by many writers, beginning with F. M. Dostoevski. For instance, D. M. Merezhkovsky, a very popular writer in the early twentieth century, expressed his presentiment about the "reign of the coming Boor." This fatal feeling became rather common in the last decade before the Revolution. But history moved along the path proclaimed by the radicals. As a result, we got a society organized on the basis of despotism pretending to be the "highest form of social organization." It actually proved to be no more than a different variant of collective slavery in the form of "mechanical solidarity," as described by Emile Durkheim, in which an individual is only an object belonging to and serving society.[7]

The socialism that developed from that system-centered foundation relied on an extreme form of ethical relativism, draped in the rigorous ritualism of a revolutionary morality. It was based on the false belief that one social class, one political party, or even, in the end, one group of people inside the revolutionary party could express and achieve the demands of "social progress." Hence a kind of monopoly over progress was created. The main ideology of this approach was: We know better than anybody else what the Common Good is and you'll get this Good by any means, whether you want it or not.[8] Ironically, this drive to impose by all possible means a particular vision of historical processes has been camouflaged by deterministic phraseology, manifested on the part of only one "progressive" class of proletarians. The series of tragic events in Russia since the Revolution of 1917 unfolded from this source.

Now we need to consider briefly the socio-psychological aspect of our analysis. It offers an opportunity to consider the mechanics of how stable, multigenerational communities of relationships evolve and how they relate to other communities of relationships.[9] The participants in these groups perceive themselves as "we," as opposed to "they." In terms of this approach, the whole of human history looks like a chain of continuities implying patterns of isolation and collisions between different "we's" and "they's."

The persons, styles, direct motives, and forms of conflict change on the stage of history, but deeper sources of conflict and mutual suspicions strive either to screen off or to oppress those who do not belong to the group with whom we identify. These features of ethnicity do not offer a universal explanation for all historical intergroup conflicts, but they do serve as a good base for analysis in many cases.[10]

As is well known, the nineteenth century became an era for constructing an approach to economic relationships in which the human personality was to be identified with classes associated either with producers who usurped material resources and were viewed as exploiting others or with those who have been exploited themselves. Human personality was considered mainly within that important but limited dimension, almost ignoring the spiritual aspect of life. In the framework of our multidimensional consideration, which is opposed to a one-dimensional approach, we shall emphasize three aspects of socio-psychological theory: (1) national stereotypes of political behavior, reproducing, in their stability and continuity, dead generations' attitudes and reactions in new conditions and situations, (2) the psychology of social crises, and (3) the psychological basis for the maintenance of stability in periods following crises.

Certainly, not only the past but also the future exercises an influence on us, especially in the current epoch, when the future practically breaks into our present life and insistently demands being taken into account in the decisions being made. Nevertheless, we rely largely on the past in approaching the dawn of the future. The current scale and speed of change only emphasizes the tragic feeling of anxiety that modern human beings experience because we find ourselves in the zone of two simultaneous forces—past and future.

This approach to the cultural characteristics manifest in a way of life is not fatalistic. The past is multilayered and ambivalent in its meaning; we perceive a foreground, an intermediate vista, and a background. In any culture elements of tradition and innovation, continuities and discontinuities are intertwined. Such a view gives us opportunities to clarify for ourselves factors that enter into our ancient history, recent history, and current events in light of alternative probable scenarios for the future. We are not enslaved by our past. However, if we are to create our today and tomorrow sensibly, we need to conceive clearly which roads our ancestors followed at particular points in history and why they may have stumbled and fallen in their efforts to shape their future.

Where are we coming from and where are we going? Or are we lost in the course of history, wandering around in circles? Every nation has its own unique historical experience. The differences in historical experiences create some of the differences among nations. Sometimes these differences are deep; sometimes they are superficial. But once more, the socio-psychological opposition of "us" and "them" reveals universal aspects of all human history from prehistoric times until today and, I fear, into the tomorrow of civilizations.

One last methodological remark: I presume that political aspects, like competition between socialist and liberal political ideologies and their intransigent struggle in the political arena, are to be considered as a derivative from cultural aspects viewed through socio-ethical and socio-psychological perspectives. Even revolutionary changes in political regimes are not necessarily accompanied by radical changes at the more fundamental levels of life manifest in the fields of social ethics and psychology. A chronology of political changes does not usually coincide with a chronology of changes in national character. We will try to examine the interplay of these groups of factors belonging to different levels of analysis in the process of our historical journey. This is one of the differences between my inquiry and standard political and historical-political studies. Comparisons require attention to constants that accompany variants.

We turn now from methodological details to our main purpose, the effort to scrutinize the Russian cultural genotype in terms of political dynamics and stasis, in continuities and discontinuities, and in similarities and variations among different social groupings. We shall also try to mark the main historical stages, bypasses, and crossroads of its evolutionary path. All of that is important not only for history's sake but also as a key to understanding our recent past and present times. At this point, we should follow Tocqueville's advice: "To those who study it as an isolated phenomenon the French Revolution can but seem a dark and sinister enigma; only when we view it in the light of the events preceding it can we grasp its true significance. And, similarly, without a clear idea of the old regime, its laws, its vices, its prejudices, its shortcomings, and its greatness, it is impossible to comprehend the history of the sixty years following its fall. Yet even this is not enough; we need also to understand and bear in mind the peculiarities of the French temperament."[11]

THE CONCEPTION OF RUSSIAN HISTORY

Analysis of the Russian cultural prototype in its dynamics, stability, differentiation, and partial transformations is the main subject of this study. First, I will disappoint those who expect to learn some unknown sensational facts or disclosures about the terrible mysteries of Russian history and the Russian court from this book. I do use several new sources and a number of rare, little known sources, but revealing new "facts" is not the major emphasis in this research. This is not a historical study in the purist meaning of the word. That which is a primary purpose of inquiry for the "pure" historian is only a point of departure for me.

This is why I use many of the classic texts and why in the analysis of a rather considerable period of Russian history, I mostly confine myself to *A Course in Russian History* offered at the end of the nineteenth century and beginning of the twentieth by an outstanding Russian historian, V. O. Kliuchevsky. Oddly, A Course of Russian History is extremely valuable and at the same time its meaning is not well understood for subsequent patterns of development.[12]

In this work I attempt to conceptualize some key events in Russian history from the seventeenth century to the present. Our purpose is to understand and explain in terms of certain theoretical logic some of the tragic paradoxes of Russia's past, in order to reach an understanding of our present time and gain some standpoints for prognosis. The philosophy of history is concerned not only with the past but also with the relationship of the past to the future. In other words, we can say with some degree of simplification that our purpose is to reconsider the "enigma of the Russian soul," while rejecting any romanticizing, so that we can comprehend its essence and consider it in light of our recent past and present situations.

The magnitude and character of this purpose forces us to make our analysis as brief as possible. That is why we concentrate first mainly on questions that are most significant for this aspect of analysis. Second, as we approach the present time, we shall scrutinize each passing period in more and more detail. Third, I deliberately omit here any substantial review of and challenge to most works on Russian history and politics. I am familiar with the most important studies in these fields and rate some very highly; I understand that omitting them from discussion opens opportunity for easy criticism by academic purists and "Brahmins." But, I hope, this is a lesser evil and an appropriate price for the opportunity to present my general concept briefly and consistently. Otherwise, if we neglect these self-constraints, there is a danger that readers will lose the main points and drown in an ocean of facts about certain historical epochs.

However, partially for personal reasons, I cannot skip mention of two talented authors who established two approaches to the course of Russian history. When I began this work more than twenty-five years ago, I had before my eyes a manuscript by Alexander Yanov, later published in the United States.[13] He undertook a considerable and impressive effort to build a universal theory of Russian political life. He covered a period of three and a half centuries—from Ivan III (1462–1505) to Paul I (1796–1801). His construction of the historical cycles of three repeating elements has substantial similarities with the famous conceptions of Arnold Toynbee, despite his disagreement with some interpretations offered by Toynbee. Yanov argued against the treatment of Russia as a variant of the "Asian" cultural/historical type: "Similarly to Asian despotism, the Russian autocracy also reproduced itself again and again after each new 'Time of Troubles.' But different than the Asian type, the Russian reproduction always introduced *some new level of complexity.*"[14] Another difference between Russian and Asian despotism, in Yanov's opinion, was the existence of an opposition counterculture that persisted and manifested periodic challenges. He also recognized that the direct expression of oppositional ideas was always an intellectual matter. That is why the major theme of his book is a collision between two crucial forces in Russian culture—autocracy and intellect.

To my mind, Yanov's work as a whole has considerable value despite the fact that particular, debatable arguments exist. I certainly disagree with some of his basic conceptualizations and proceed with a somewhat different conceptual approach to historical analysis. I shall express my doubts and, to some degree, disagreements with Yanov in the process of considering particular periods in Russian history.

My approach is also different from the conceptual approach of Richard Pipes, in spite of similarities in the interpretation of many particular questions.[15] His core concept is based on the idea of a "patrimonial-despotic regime," potentially totalitarian. From the early beginning of the Russian state, its patrimonial-despotic character is identified in his study as the basic difference between Russian and Western patterns of relationships concerning power and society. I doubt that we have sufficient reasons to consider the early patrimonial Russian *knyazhestva* (principalities) as a kind of totalitarian regime. Second, I try to avoid the usage of the word *West* as an ultimate answer, an ultimate elucidation, without particular contextual explanations. In my opinion, the concept of the West as the penultimate elucidation of the course of human development is an unjustified simplification. I do appreciate Pipes's research for many of its qualities. My concept, however, is based not on the state and the political realm but on historical-cultural invariants, which I consider to represent a deeper level of historical processes. I proceed with the following conceptual scheme.

The dominance of the system-centered ethic among the main branches of the Russian peoples has been indisputable through most of its historical existence. The opposition of "society" and "personality" did not initially emerge as a practical problem. The reason was not a harmony between these two levels of social life, nor a lack of contradictions between the individual and the social whole, but a completely dominant, a priori conception in favor of the social whole. The system-centered prototype in the sphere of social ethics, the respective traits of national character in the sphere of social psychology had completely determined the social, including the political, modus operandi and style of relationships. It blocked the development of any alternative tendencies with a high degree of reliability and consistency. The "system" had a well-developed instinct for self-preservation and reacted sensitively to potentially dangerous trends.

The sources of this extreme "vigilance" are ambivalent. On the one hand, the reserve of the system's endurance allowed it to remain stable even after the heavy blows of historical fate that were triggered by external threats and internal cataclysms. On the other hand, any historical chances that might have allowed Russia to alleviate the pressure of despotic rule had been paralyzed and were doomed from the very beginning to be destroyed as soon as they came into opposition with the national stereotypes of political behavior and the moral foundations of social relationships. As a result, the Russian people found themselves in the firm grip of misfortune and humiliation requiring an extreme sacrifice to save themselves from further misfortunes and humiliations.

Small movements of countercultural tendencies have slowly gnawed away the system-centered foundations. The historical winds of change began to reach the Middle-Russian plain as well. It brought the seeds of another form of life. New sprouts have grown from those seeds. At the same time, the "guardians of purity" became more and more neglectful in plucking out those weeds.

Moreover, fruit that was very tempting from a pragmatic standpoint grew from some of these sprouts. Temptations evolved to save some of these innovations under strict state and "ideological" control. The most common form of this control relied on the barriers of sociocultural estrangement. Sometimes these barriers had very exact borders. For example, the borders of the so-called *Nemetskaya sloboda*—a sort of ghetto or strangers' settlement—were usually in an isolated part of town. Foreigners were not allowed to settle outside these areas. Sometimes it was only a psychological border created by distinctions between "pure Russians" and "apostates" who picked up the foreign subtleties. The key problem was not the forms of isolating of people at home from the danger of foreign influence but that such barriers laid the foundation of a split between the different parts of the nation. The split grew to the size of an abyss between the Russian intelligentsia and the rest of the Russian people in the nineteenth century. This abyss, which proved to be unbridgeable, persisted as one of the most important reasons for the tragic evolution of Russian history.

The beginning of this process was slow and proved rather insignificant. This "greening" of an alternative, person-centered type of relationship looked weak, not presenting a threat by its possible competition with the dense and overpowering jungle of system-centeredness. All it could do was survive by establishing minimally stable roots in the traditionally system-centered soil of the country. But from one generation to another, the changes accumulated, until one could speak about the emergence in Russia of a new ethical and psychological type: person-centeredness. The great abyss took a long time to emerge.

Apparently, the first decades of the nineteenth century were the period when person-centeredness in Russia became a rather significant part of the social landscape. We can see some signs and even temporary explosions of this tendency during the two preceding centuries. But the principal difference in the nineteenth century was that for the first time, person-centeredness announced itself as a definite force that could not easily be destroyed. Such an attempt to destroy was made during the reign of Nicholas I; but the person-centered approach possessed a certain social base among the gentry and educated persons who developed a strong self-consciousness feeling of self-responsibility for the conditions of life in Russian society. Thus, a "new species of people," as Denis Diderot said, emerged in Russia at that time. And the whole nineteenth century passed under the signs of accommodation to the cultivation and propagation of this species.

By the beginning of the twentieth century, the person-centered genotype had become fully legitimate in Russian society. Belonging to this genotype, certainly not by name but by essence, even proved to be the core criterion for a major subdivision within the Russian intelligentsia—a group almost unprecedented for its role and significance in the social life of the country.[16] The influence of person-centeredness grew to such a degree that the very basis of the system-centered pattern of order was placed under serious threat. The base on which the pyramid of Russian system-centeredness had stood for centuries began to quake, and the person-centered mentality began to spread into broader and broader circles of Russian society. If Russia had had a couple of decades more for undisturbed development, nothing could have prevented the country from an irreversible move toward a person-centered way of life.

But alas, the abyss between the different parts of society had not yet been bridged well enough. Russian system-centeredness demonstrated once more its incredible capacity to survive. Energized by this threat, it managed to perform a desperately radical maneuver. By a complete outward transformation, it obscured the situation, destroyed once more its historical person-centered alternative, and saved the predominant position of system-centeredness in society. This transformation was achieved at a very high price. Many traditional symbols and attributes, including the interests of a privileged stratum of society, were sacrificed.

If we return to the image of the pyramid, we can see that it was turned on one side, and the dark mud of deep national system-centeredness simultaneously swamped both the old autocratic system-centered regime and most representative features of the alternative person-centered counterculture, because unfortunately they had mostly been concentrated within only one segment of society. Many changes occurred at the surface of events, certainly, but it was the same pyramid. The same pattern of social order remained practically intact.

The so-called October Revolution misled many observers and participants in those events, even the most attentive and perspicacious of them, with only a few exceptions (e.g., Berdyaev). When the smoke of revolutionary battles dispersed, it became apparent that system-centeredness had prevailed with only modest changes in its ideological and political slogans. Defeating its person-centered opposition, system-centeredness continued to enjoy its predominant historical position. Moreover, it managed to do it more skillfully, with a firmer grasp over the spreading territory of the former Russian Empire, and in the name of liberation. *So the antireformist line, camouflaged behind radically different masks, won.*

In the process of further analysis, I shall try to demonstrate this point in detail. For now we can restrict ourselves to one rather dramatic example. Vasiliy V. Shulgin was one of the most conservative, even reactionary political actors under the Tsar's regime. He was a convinced monarchist, a strong opponent of any social modernization, who consistently supported traditionalism. Through his long political life he was devoted, before the Revolution, to struggles against the liberal "bourgeois" parties. After the Revolution, he struggled against the Soviet regime. He paid for that with two decades of imprisonment. At the end of the 1950s, he was released and lived quietly in city of Vladimir some 190 kilometers from Moscow. He retained his absolutely clear intellectual and analytical capacities, as is reflected in his latest books. But his political "ideology" has changed dramatically. He found that the extreme conservative ideals of his youth had been inherited by the current rulers of Russia using the name of the Soviet Union; and he blessed them.[17]

All of these questions are a subject of more than academic interest. The traditional Russian cultural genotype completely dominated the country at least until the last decade of the twentieth century. In 1990s, for the first time in more than one hundred years, real hope of overcoming system-centeredness has again emerged. After the completion of our retrospective analyses, I shall apply the same approach to the current situation in Russia and consider the possible future course of Russian civilization. But we turn now to centuries past.

CHAPTER TWO

The Time of Troubles

1606–1612, and the Rest of the Seventeenth Century

The question of where to begin our historical journey poses some complexities. One popular opinion is that the Mongol and Tartar yoke decisively determined the course of Russian history and is therefore the place where we need to begin to establish the roots of subsequent problems. I do not agree with that position. First, even if we recognize that the Mongol invasion was crucially important for the future course of Russian history, we can hardly consider the more than five centuries after Tartar dominance had practically ended as a simple continuity of tendencies formed in the thirteenth century. Second, viewing the Tartar military invasion, and the exacting of tribute from Russian lands, as a confrontation between two different cultural systems seems arguable. Actually the different socioeconomic structures—nomadic and agricultural—collide as competing systems. That pattern of conflict was a common historical situation among the Eurasian peoples. There is no evidence indicating the existence of an embryonic person-centered scale of values in the conquered and devastated Russian lands.

On the contrary, all known evidence indicates otherwise. *The Russian-Tartar conflict took place in the context of a similar system-centered archetype.* It would be incorrect to consider the Tartar yoke as a "fatal breakdown" in Russian history. Moreover, attention should be given to the judgment of the historian L. N. Gumilev, who attempted to demonstrate that the relationship with the Tartars was a military and political alliance between two unequal partners, a sort of suzerain-vassalage relationship.[1]

In this alliance, Russian princes as the weaker party paid for their security and mandates to rule by rendering tribute. But I believe that Gumilev's explanation exaggerates the allied nature of this relationship. Gumilev was strongly influenced by his own romantic theory of "nomadic civilizations," which had many advantages when compared to "European" civilization but which failed to realize their cultural and moral potential.

The point of view expressed by V. O. Kliuchevsky seems more balanced. He used the term *yoke* but supposed that the influence of the Tartar yoke was not such a great burden that Russia could not realize its own historical potential. Moreover, he recognized that Tartar suzerainty over Russia had its positive side:

> Few of Vsevolod's thirteenth-century successors gave a thought to old clan or territorial tradition, while still fewer honored them, seeing that those successors were lacking in all sense of kinship or duty to society at large. . . . Social consciousness so atrophied that a king was incapable of rising beyond the mere instincts of self-preservation and plunder. . . . Indeed, had those rulers been left to themselves, they would soon have torn their patrimony of Rus into petty shreds of appanages between which the sword was never sheathed. Fortunately the principalities were not independent units. . . . The Khan's authority invested those various petty, mutually hostile appanages with at least a semblance of unity. . . . More than once the threat of that potentate's wrath served to deter squabbles, or his discretion [served] to forestall or arrest a disastrous feud. In fact, the Khan's authority was the blunt Tartar knife which cut the knots of the tangled skein in which the stupidity of Vsevolod's posterity frequently bound the affairs of the country.[2]

Russia had no Tartar garrisons on its soil. Tartar *baskaki* (governors-general) committed no greater excesses than did native tribute collectors. The Orthodox religion—one of the most important components of Russian life—was well respected by the Tartars. They nearly adopted it as their religion. Conflicts of a religious character emerged only later when Tartars, after a long hesitation, made a choice in favor of the Islamic faith.

In any event, it does not make sense to go so far "upstream" in the course of Russian history. To choose the fifteenth or sixteenth century as a possible point of departure for our analytical pilgrimage would have greater justification. The temptation to consider the parallels between Ivan IV (the Terrible) and Stalin is obvious. But that temptation is countered for other reasons. That era was too long ago, when people's feelings and thoughts were too different from our own. We cannot find in that era any vestige of a person-centered character.

The seventeenth century is another matter. Kliuchevsky in his periodization of Russian history began "the whole span of modern Russian history" from there: "The ideas and attitudes which had evolved throughout those years were familiar to, and influenced the social awareness of, a nineteenth-century Russian in his belief that, in so far as they were characteristics derived from the past, he was scrutinizing his own personality and values."[3]

Following Kliuchevsky, I also suppose that studying the seventeenth century can be of great significance for the development of Russian national self-consciousness. The knots of Russian historical destiny had been tied by that time, and we can also observe great similarities, sometimes amazingly so, in processes and events of the seventeenth century and of those following, including the twentieth century. This revelation of traits characteristic of one's own life and social environment in the minds and ways of life of one's far distant ancestors is an important and exciting matter. However, Kliuchevsky's *A Course in Russian History,* in my opinion, still did not reveal the basic differences that gradually emerged in their true character.

Before we begin to consider systematically the mainstream of the Russian cultural archetype, it is necessary to sketch, at least briefly, its lateral branch manifestation—the subculture of the Russian free cities: Novgorod, Pskov, and, partially, Vyatka. During the last two centuries of its existence, the Novgorod republic became, in liberal consciousness, a sort of "Golden Age" symbol of lost Russian freedom and of the destruction of democratic potential. What were the reasons for that view?

In my mind, this view has a certain degree of reasonableness but also a great deal of a historical idealization. During its approximately three hundred and fifty years of sociopolitical existence, Novgorod differed substantially from other parts of country. The City Republic had contractual relationships with princes who were invited from other places to act as managers, subject to multiple legal constraints on the prince's jurisdiction experienced through independent township meetings *(veche)* with their own executive bodies, and a customary mode of conflict resolution between rich and poor people based on the so-called fist law. All of these features demonstrate that some unusual patterns of political culture and some innovative ideas concerning the meaning and role of personality had already arisen in Russia.

Much less is known about the negative traits of the Novgorod republic—an extreme and cruel clash of group interests, which were not constrained by common standards of political processes and moral judgment. Certainly, Novgorod was not the only state in medieval Europe where such conditions prevailed. We can recall, for example, the mores of the Florentines as described by Niccolo Machiavelli in *Florentine History.*[4] What is more puzzling is the circumstance that the enslaving of the peasantry began in this "free" part of the country a couple of centuries earlier than in other regions of the country.

The city of Pskov, located approximately one hundred miles from Novgorod and treated as its "little brother," was much more stable and better organized. In medieval Russia, Pskov had the best-developed code of civil law. Pskov was the only place where one could find no sign of serfdom during that time. Thus, in political respects, we can consider Pskov as an "improved" variant of the Novgorod republic.

Unfortunately, history gave this city too short a time and too few chances for free development. Like Novgorod, it was absorbed by Muscovy. In the perspective of our dichotomy, both cities can be considered to represent an embryonic phase of a person-centered pattern of order—a "pre-person-centeredness"—which did not become acclimatized to Russian soil.

It also seems remarkable that during the last battle between Moscow and Novgorod, the affections of all the rest of the Russian lands proved to be on the side of the obvious aggressor—the principality of Muscovy. The people of Novgorod were treated as arrogant and recalcitrant because they had managed to avoid the Muscovites' rule. The standard feature of system-centered logic works in the following way: "If I am in trouble, so be it; but I won't let my neighbor live better than I do."

THE RUSSIAN MENTALITY

Let us leave this brief excursion into the story of the Novgorod-Pskov failure and come back to the mainstream of Russian history, particularly to Moscow of the seventeenth century. At the beginning of this period, we can see a complete mastery of system-centered ethics in all of the social strata—on all of its social "floors." In the clearest way, it manifested itself in ideas about the essence of the state and the character of relationships binding Tsar and people. "The state had no other meaning than the hereditary domain of the sovereign, who belonged to a certain dynasty. If an average Muscovite citizen of the day were told that a sovereign's power was also a duty, an office, and that, in governing his people, a ruler served the common welfare, such words would have seemed to him incoherent, a mere confusion of thought. So we can understand how the Muscovites of the time conceived of the sovereign's and the people's relation to the state. They thought that the Muscovite state in which they lived was the property of the sovereign, and not of the Muscovite or Russian people. . . . They could more easily imagine a sovereign without a nation than a state without a sovereign."[5] The state was conceived of "not as the people's union administered by sovereign power, but as the Tsar's property, which included, as a part of its economic resources, the population settled within its boundaries."[6]

For that reason, "even law had the character of administrative orders issued by the Kremlin estate office. Law regulated the activities of the subordinate and the manner in which various civic duties were discharged by the inhabitants."[7] An idea of law in the Western sense did not exist at all because, as Kliuchevsky noted: "Before the seventeenth century we find in Muscovite legislation no enactments that could be regarded as constitutional laws, defining the structure and rights of the sovereign power and the fundamental rights and duties of the citizens."[8] The Muscovites of the sixteenth century saw in their sovereign "not so much a guardian of the popular welfare, as the proprietor of the State territory. They viewed themselves as mere temporary sojourners in that territory—mere political accidents. The personal will of the Sovereign was the one mainspring of the State's life, and only the personal or dynastic interest of that Sovereign could convey the State's life as a *raison d'être*. In short, beyond the Sovereign, neither the State nor nation existed."[9]

This view of the state is one of the basic causes for the tragic development of Russian history. The socio-psychological stereotype that accompanied this concept was a fatal obedience to destiny, a lackey's servile position as subordinate to a higher authority, an obsequious willingness to play as supernumeraries in the scaffolding of a political lottery that power had arranged from time to time.

In addition to these ethical and psychological "pillars" of the regime, the machinery of political police and compulsory indoctrination were relied on periodically. This need emerged in cases when for some reason the sanctity of power weakened temporarily. For instance, it happened under the reign of Boris Godunov because his legitimacy as heir to the appanage of Muscovy was not as indisputable as that which his predecessors had enjoyed. For that reason, "he wove a complicated net of secret police supervision, in which the chief part was played by house serfs who informed against their masters and by thieves who when released from prison flitted about Moscow streets listening to what was being said about the Tsar and grabbed anyone who dropped an incautious word. Denunciation and slander soon became a great public evil." Beyond that, "he dispatched everywhere a special form of prayer that had to be recited in every house at dinner when the health of the Tsar and his family was hailed."[10]

Only one form of social criticism was tolerated in that servile society. It was the criticism of an idiot, true or false. "God's fool" could overstep the rational bounds and constraints of ordinary life and, therefore, became invulnerable to any punitive action. Any punishment supposes deprivation of something valuable, but if a person had voluntarily relinquished everything in advance, that person could be deprived or effectively punished. Such a person acquired the privilege to speak "the whole truth" to the faces of others who were enslaved by secular values and temptations. A person who called out the names of those who were the sources of social vices was presumed in Russia to be mad.

All others, who had at their disposal only tacit forms of protest, were reduced to self-isolation from their world. This could mean either going to a monastery or emigrating. "The Muscovite people developed a peculiar form of political protest. Those who could not put up with the existing order did not rise against it, but "wandered away"—"escaped from the country." Kliuchevsky treats this kind of negative reaction to authority relationships as a sort of "servant" or "lodger" syndrome: "When the relationship between people and government fails to secure their welfare, the people become dissatisfied with their rulers and rise against them. When servants or lodgers, whose relationship to the house owner is determined by a temporary agreement, find that they are not receiving the promised benefits, they leave the house."[11]

So it was with the Russians.

A significant portion of the "emigrants" became Cossacks. It seems appropriate to say a little about this rather special social group. The opinion exists that Cossacks were a kind of "island of freedom" in an ocean of slavery and had a freedom-loving orientation. But that is no more than a historical idealization. To those who have a special interest in this question, I recommend an interesting recent publication by Marina Razhbaeva and Vadim Semenkov on the roots, literary sources, history, and consequences of this mythology.[12] The so-called Cossack outlaw settlements were typical societies of highwaymen. The economic base for their way of life was organized brigandage and mercenary service. A sense of profit was what motivated their annual decisions concerning the direction of their military raids and the lands to rob during the next "hunting" season. These lands could be Poland, Muscovy, Crimea on the outskirts of the Ottoman Empire, or even other Cossack lands, such as in the Ukraine. A Cossack's mode of life could be compared with the early Viking way of life, with Arabian and later Turkish pirate states in the southern Mediterranean, and with the filibustering republics of the seventeenth and eighteenth centuries—but with one important exception: the Cossacks' practice of selling and reselling their military services as mercenaries.

Morally, Cossacks differed for the worse from the other social classes of Russian society. The latter were bound up with the norms of a traditional and communal morality. The Cossacks were "moral-free"; they did not have ethical constraints. They rejected one system of moral norms but did not adopt an alternative one. They proved to be in a kind of moral vacuum. It was Cossacks, not Poles, who were the main disintegrating and debilitating force during the Time of Troubles.

Later, in the eighteenth century, Cossacks found it more profitable to sell their services on a permanent basis to the Russian Tsar and to continue their "entrepreneurship" under the aegis of the Russian state. As a result of that deal, they gradually lost their freedom of maneuver and were forced not only to conduct military functions but also to undertake punitive actions against insurgents inside the Russian Empire itself; that is, to serve its domestic police needs. To the end of the nineteenth century, special Cossack detachments earned the dubious glory of being the cruelest oppressors of any political unrest, including peaceful actions such as student demonstrations.

To return to description of the moral and psychological stereotypes of the obedient subjects of the Russian Tsar, since civic or political activities were practically closed to them, the human potential sought other modes of expression and found these, sometimes in very bizarre ways. Sublimation occurred, for example, in the form of heavy drunkenness and debauchery.[13] Success in these activities presumed a vestige of daring—of manly dignity. And what is really interesting is that the authorities closed their eyes to the multiple negative consequences of popular drunkenness, not only for financial reasons—because it was a reliable source of restocking the state's budget—but also for political reasons: as a reliable way to stifle any embryo of civic self-consciousness. Generally speaking, *an appreciation of the dignities of freedom was very low.* For example, voluntarily selling oneself or one's children into serfdom was a common thing. By contrast, in ancient Athens the famous lawgiver Solon prohibited committing a debtor to slavery in 594 B.C.

In Russia, the interests of the state were always conceptualized as something self-contained, almost divinely transcendental, immeasurably more important than the interests of people. The Russian people had only obligations to the state, and the state had all the rights. The various estates or classes differed not by their rights but by their obligations to the state. Everyone should either defend the state, work for the state, or feed those who defended the state. Hence there were soldiers and workers but no citizens. As a result, a political strengthening of the state yielded not improvements but, quite to the contrary, deterioration of people's conditions of life. Measures that might be viewed as progress gave the state new opportunities to oppress its subjects and to enslave them more effectively. Leviathan absorbed people's blood and flesh and became stronger and more demanding. Thus the state waxed, and the people waned.

Furthermore, there was a dramatic lack of consideration of social and political questions, of deliberation about the problems of a true social order. Before the seventeenth century, one can find in the Russian literature only a few sources concerned with the question of social order—the conditions for the population. Most were apologias for the unrestricted power of the sovereign. The classic and almost the only example of "dissident thinking" on this topic was an exchange of letters between Ivan the Terrible and Prince Kurbsky, who escaped from Russia to Livonia. A few grains of interest in the problematic of the people can be extracted from religious disputations concerning a righteous way of life for the true Christian, but not much more. The image of the Christ figure was the suffering Christ who accepted His fate on the Cross. The princes Boris and Gleb were elevated to sainthood for their humble submission to a comparable fate at the initiation of their brother, who succeeded to his father's prerogatives as sovereign. As a matter of fact, we find an almost blank page on the problematic of the people in the Russian literary tradition before the eighteenth century.

This contrasts markedly with Western traditions. In Europe we see a considerably different situation, even several centuries earlier. For instance, in the twelfth century, "in Germany, even in the marketplaces and workshops, people read [or got others to read for them] works written in the heat of controversy by clergymen, wherein they freely debated such subjects as the ends of the State, and the rights of kings, popes, and peoples. Other countries had not been involved to the same degree in these polemics, but nowhere were they without effect. Human affairs were newly emerging as subjects for reflection."[14]

As early as the eleventh century, the imperial chaplain Wipo wrote that in Italy "all the young men"—referring to those of the ruling classes—"were sent to the schools to work with the sweat of the brow; the barbarian laws and the Carolingian capitularies, as well as the Roman law, continued to be studied, summarized and glossed." In Anglo-Saxon England, "where the language of the laws was the common language, there developed in the island, from the beginning of the twelfth century, a thing unknown in the same period on the other side of the Channel—a legal literature which, though written in Latin, was based essentially on Anglo-Saxon sources."[15]

In the first half of the fourteenth century, the English philosopher William of Occam, who had the personal experience of constant contacts with a potentate during his many years at the court of Bavarian duke Louis, clearly defined the idea of authority as an obligation of sovereign to people. He wrote that free people under the Holy Roman Emperor's power were not slaves because they obeyed voluntarily; that the power of the emperor was not unlimited and should not be opposed to the principle of the common weal; and that if it were, the people had a right to transfer imperial power to a more appropriate person. That construction was radically different from the concept of the state as the Tsar's patrimony. The centuries that followed—the epochs of Humanism and the Renaissance—further expanded this abyss between the Russian and the European political consciousness.

In Russia, until the eighteenth century, any independent intellectual thought was a priori under suspicion and was treated as an indication of "Latinism," of questionable loyalty to the "True Faith of the Fathers." Opposition to the temptations of Latinism was viewed almost as a sign of virtue and patriotism. The Orthodox clergy ordered their congregations, as we can read in an ancient Russian moral treatise: "Everyone who loveth geometry is an abomination unto God. It is a spiritual sin to learn astronomy and Hellenic books. Following this reason, a believer easily falls into various errors. You must love simplicity more than wisdom. Do not seek that which is beyond you, do not try that which is too deep for you, but hold to the ready-made doctrine that has been given you by God." A text in school copybooks included the following instructions: "Brothers, do not indulge in high-flown reflections! If you are asked, Do you know philosophy? answer: I have not run Hellenic races, have not read the rhetoricians' astronomy, have not kept company with wise philosophers, and have not set eyes on philosophy; I am learning the books of gracious law in order to know how I may cleanse my sinful soul of sins." Such a view encouraged the complacency of ignorance. "I am unskilled in words but not in reason," an ancient Russian scribe wrote about himself. "I have not been taught dialectics, rhetoric, and philosophy, but I have the mind of Christ." The old Russian ecclesiastical community was thus losing the means of correcting its errors and indeed of having any incentive to do so.[16]

Embracing ignorance and especially enforcing a lack of tolerance for dissidents were certainly not a Russian peculiarity in that epoch. The Counter-Reformation gathered in a sinister harvest in many countries of Western Europe. However, in contrast, this period was also the beginning of the Age of Enlightenment, based on the existence for at least five hundred years of universities and of a rooted tradition of free discussion of burning questions, as already noted. In Russia such a critical intellectual subculture still did not evolve.

Such negativism in science and education displayed a traditionalist fear of Latinization. This fear was supported and nurtured by the Orthodox Church. For the same reason, any changes in a habitual order of manners were presumed to be dangerous and suspect. Both the secular and the ecclesiastical authorities well understood the meaning of these traditional cultural stereotypes. They tried to reinforce them and constantly manipulated them for their own purposes. An orientation to stability as the highest value is the main feature of the traditional type of mind. At this point, we have completed a description of the Russian genotype that provided us with our point of departure—the beginning of the seventeenth century. The next task is to trace its historical destiny.

THE ODYSSEY OF THE SEVENTEENTH CENTURY

We can only speculate about how long a national consciousness can maintain unshakable confidence in its own exceptionalism unless provoked by extreme circumstances. The male branch of the Rurik dynasty left no successor at the end of the sixteenth century, and as a result an uncertain situation emerged. Historians call the period between 1598 and 1613 the "Time of Troubles." A unique combination of historical circumstances planted in Russian national consciousness some seeds of doubt concerning the infallibility and supremacy of the Russian way of life. For the first time, a real chance for political choice had evolved.

At least three traditional political stereotypes were challenged in that period. First, the nation discovered that neither sovereign nor state could exist even for a day without the people—whereas a people without a sovereign could survive, at least for a while. Second, it became clear that the state was not a Tsar's patrimony to be settled by accidental circumstances; on the contrary, Tsars could find themselves to be accidental and powerless figures. Third, a more incredible and revolutionary circumstance revealed that these "bond slaves" possessed some political will when in certain situations; and, expressed in particular ways, this will could become a source of power for sovereign authority. This frightening but alluring perspective opened the way for challenging a one-dimensional system-centered consciousness.

In 1606, a supreme authority for the first time made an act of self-limitation. Prince Vasili Shuisky, while mounting the throne, swore and kissed the cross and had recorded in official documents sent to the provinces that he renounced three of the prerogatives of autocratic power: (1) the power to "ban without cause"—that is, the Tsar's authority to ban someone purely for personal indiscretion and without sufficient reason; (2) the authority to confiscate the property of the relatives of banished persons; and (3) the authority to conduct criminal trials on the basis of denunciations and torture alone, without confronting the witnesses of the accused and without other attributes of normal judicial processes. But these prerogatives had been an essential part of the power of the Muscovite Tsar. As Ivan III had put it at the end of the fifteenth century, "I shall give my realm to whomever I like." And his grandson Ivan the Terrible said, "We are free to show favor to our servants and free to put them to death." By swearing to renounce these prerogatives, Vasili Shuisky became a constitutional sovereign governing his country in accordance with law, instead of being a master over slaves.[17]

This was a very remarkable event in Russian political history. A supreme sovereign, in acceding to the throne, had not only placed some limits on his own authority but had also formally and publicly proclaimed the conditions of these limitations.

We should not idealize the person of Shuisky. He was liar and intriguer who would go through fire and water to attain his political purposes. The main reason for his "liberal" promises was lack of personal legitimacy. This document was forgotten during subsequent turbulence. But the very fact of its appearance should have impressed the people living at the time as a revolutionary event.

Four years later, during the climax of the *Smuta* (disturbances or Troubles), the first true constitutional document was discussed and approved. In was a draft of a covenant between a Russian mission headed by M. Saltykov and the Polish king Sigismund III concerning conditions for the accession to the Moscow throne of the Polish prince Vladislav. It was certainly no formal constitution.

> We are not speaking about juridical formalities but about the essence of the document. In the first place, it safeguarded the inviolability of the Russian Orthodox faith. Then it went on to formulate the rights and privileges of the Muscovite people as a whole and of the supreme power of the State. Indeed, the very idea of personal rights, scarcely noticeable in Russian political thought before, was for the first time more or less definitely expressed in the agreement of February 4, 1610. Everyone had a right to a legal trial; and no one should be punished arbitrarily. Two other conditions, relating to an individual's personal rights, are striking in their novelty: men of high rank should not be degraded without cause; and men of humble rank should receive promotion according to their merit; everyone in Muscovy must be free to go to other Christian countries for the sake of study, and the Tsar must not punish them for such actions by confiscating their property. The agreement actually contained a suggestion of religious tolerance and freedom of conscience.[18]

However, the latter two conditions were deleted from the final version of the treaty by Muscovite boyars. Obviously, they considered the right to travel abroad and promotion of men according to merit as too dangerous for the habitual Muscovite order. Instead, a new and very remarkable paragraph was included, intended to provide special privileges for native-born people, noting that "the Muscovite princely and noble families should not suffer any detriment to their honor or titles from foreigners coming into the country."

The most revolutionary event during the Time of Troubles was the appearance on the Muscovite throne of the so-called False Dmitry I or Pretender I. The conservative tradition in Russian official historiography originated from that time and stigmatized him as not being the rightful successor; the Church anathematized him. Ironically, the issue of "pretending" has been reiterated by many Soviet historians and has survived into post-Soviet times.[19] But we can leave this psychologically interesting phenomenon behind; whether he was or was not a "rightful" successor of the Rurik dynasty is not important for our analysis (although from genetic point of view, it is better if he was not a descendant of Ivan The Terrible). However, other things are significant for us. Dmitry's crucial features were: (1) his personification of a definitely different cultural archetype; and (2) the historical role that he played.

> The throne of the Muscovite Tsars had never had such an occupant. . . . He was highly gifted and had a quick mind which easily solved the most difficult questions before the Boyars' Council. He was of a lively and even sterling temperament; at moments of danger he displayed courage that bordered on rashness, and he was easily carried away by his feelings. He was a fine speaker and had a good deal of all-round knowledge. He completely changed the ceremonial routine observed by the former Tsars in daily life, and simplified the cumbersome and oppressive court etiquette, . . . addressed people simply and courteously, all quite unlike a Tsar. He proved himself from the first to be an active administrator, avoided cruelty, saw to everything himself, was present every day at the Boyars' Council, and personally trained the soldiers. . . . He occasionally pointed out to his advisers in the Council that they had not seen anything, had not studied anything, and ought to go abroad for some education, but he did it politely, without giving offence.[20]

In foreign affairs, Dmitry chose a pro-Western but flexible policy that he combined with attention to the military defense of the country "on all azimuths." None of his successors, for at least 150 years after him, had wisdom enough to adhere to this style. He tried to adapt Russia to Europe not as a "poor provincial relative" but in the respected role of leader of the struggle against Asian threats. For that purpose, he promoted a plan to raise all the Catholic powers, headed by Orthodox Russia, against the Turks and the Tartars. Like Kliuchevsky, several other prominent Russian historians of the nineteenth century—Nikolay Kostomarov, Sergey Soloviev, Lev Mechnikov—considered the Pretender to be an outstanding political actor offering important innovations for Muscovy, especially when viewed against the backdrop of his predecessors. Among the first to note this was Russian historian Nikolay Ustrialov, who in the 1830s published five volumes called "Accounts of Contemporaries on Dmitry the Pretender." An interesting publication on this subject is Lev Mechnikov's contribution in the late (Geneva) emigrant edition of Hertzen *Kolokol.* In more recent literature see, for example, Ruslan Skrynnikov's *Time of Troubles.*[21] But this was not a mainstream view. Paradoxically, most of official Russian historiography, both Tsarist and Soviet, presented False Dmitry only negatively—as a "traitor," "Polish protégé," etc. Both Tsarist and Communist mythology created the same image of an enemy out of the person who made the first attempt in Russian history to turn the country toward another way of life. This kind of reaction was natural: for any variant of system-centered orientation, someone like False Dmitry embodied a challenge and a threat.

Alas, *the political reorientation was too sharp.* Dmitry's popularity among the people did not help much. Mostly it was a reaction to the high human qualities of this young Tsar; people considered him not as a reformist leader but as a personified ideal of the "kind Tsar"—an ideal for which they had yearned during the tyrannical sixteenth century. His political attitudes and program proved to be inappropriate both for the nobility and for all the other strata of society. They were completely unprepared for that shift. Dmitry came too early. An additional negative circumstance was that he was accompanied by armed Polish soldiers and mercenaries, who comported themselves in Russia as conquerors, with demonstrative contempt for the "Russian savages." Dmitry became the victim of a palace plot. He was killed. Thus the first person-centered sprout was lost before it could blossom. It could not survive in the severe Muscovite political climate.

During the Time of Troubles, the Russian people had for the first time an opportunity to sense themselves not as subjects of an absolute monarch but as citizens. Unfortunately, they abandoned this opportunity because none of the social classes had achieved the appropriate level of civic consciousness. All individuals, not to mention larger groups, acted on the basis of narrow self-interest. In that uncertain if promising situation, they sought only personal gains and privileges, not guarantees for the constitutional standing of individuals and estates. The Russian nobility—the boyars—were no exception. This distinguished them from the British aristocracy, for example, who often had the political wisdom and skills to sacrifice their own narrow interests in favor of public consensus. The Russian aristocracy was more like the French aristocracy—a closed caste highly sensitive about its pedigrees. We might recall Tocqueville's analysis of the consequences of that difference in *The Old Regime and the French Revolution.*[22] The French aristocracy gained the privileged status of being exempt from royal taxes, while the British aristocracy adhered to a principle of balance in assuming its burdens on behalf of the commonwealth.

The major weakness of Yanov's conception lies in his treatment of the boyars as the main bearers of the progressive counterculture. Instead, the boyars demonstrated many times their complete inappropriateness for that social role. They were never able to realize either the potential feed-through benefits of their status or their potential role as carriers of social responsibility.

One more discouraging detail was discovered during the Time of Troubles. When state power grew weaker, all moral restraints ceased to work as a general social consciousness. That is why, to borrow Alexander Pushkin's words, "the Russian rebellion was senseless and merciless." For example, at the climax of the Time of Troubles, Ivan Bolotnikov, leader of one of the strongest competing parties, who managed to establish a temporary hold on spontaneous popular riots, appealed to these base popular "reflexes." Vasili Kliuchevsky reports that "proclamations from his camp were disseminated in Muscovy, calling on the serfs to kill their masters and take as a reward the masters' wives and estates, and to slaughter and plunder tradespeople. Thieves and rogues were promised noble rank, governorship, honor and wealth."[23] The Cossacks acted in an especially ruthless way. During several years of riots, they managed to overrun almost the whole country. As a result of these destructive raids of pillaging and plundering, people sought a "strong ruling hand" and came under the yoke of a new autocratic dynasty for another three hundred years. The first era of political choice was marked by a return to despotic authority.

We should also recognize that the lack of any national political consciousness meant that the Russian people were completely unprepared for the idea of exercising choice about the nature of political authority. Only royal kinship could be accepted by the Russian vernacular political culture as a legitimate source of supreme authority. This was the era in which the Dutch republics and the Swiss confederations were being founded, when struggles over the Reformation were dominating the Western scene, and shortly before the Puritans and other religious dissidents began to establish colonies in New England.

Andzhej Frych-Modzhevski, a Polish philosopher of the sixteenth century, in his treatise bearing the remarkable title "On a Correction of State" (*De Republica Emeranda* in the Latin original) wrote the following in a chapter title "About the King":

> The Poles believe that being born a King's Son is not enough: chosen [elected; *eligi* in the Latin] should be the one who possesses the supreme authority. For what a Helmsman is on the ship, a King needs to be in the Kingdom: surely, those of wisdom choose the Helmsman not for his noble heritage but for his skills and proficiency of steering. And so it is with the Kings who are being chosen [the same term—elected] not for their noble descent but for their skills to govern the Republic. Because the Polish Kings are not of royal lineage but chosen [the same term] with the consent of all the estates. Therefore, they do not exercise power to proclaim laws, or levy taxes on their subjects, or make eternal decrees at their own discretion. Whatever they do they follow either the advice of all the estates or prescriptions of the laws, and this is better than in the nation whose Kings arbitrarily impose taxes, declare wars on neighboring countries, and perform other acts: and although they do it because of and for the good of the Republic, being not subordinate to the law, they easily fall back on the odious tyranny which makes permissible everything they do: but it is the King who ought to obey the mores and laws of the homeland and govern according to their prescriptions.[24]

This conception is expressed in the style of Montesquieu; but it was written and published two centuries before him on the frontiers of European world. Poland is not crucial to our analysis; but in the context of the system-centered tradition prevailing in Russia, such a view was impossible.

Turning back to Russia at the beginning of the seventeenth century, for the first time in their history people were in a position to exercise a critical decision about public authority. They could have chosen between the old, well-known way and a new, unknown, risky but alluring way. At that crossroads of choice, Russia was practically unanimous in favor of the old way. In 1613, the crown was placed on the head of a sixteen-year-old boy—a distant relative of the previous dynasty and the beginning of the Romanov dynasty. That is the story of the first lost opportunity for a different way of life in Russia.

Nevertheless, the Time of Troubles left a legacy in Russian society. The Muscovites became more familiar with the example of an alternative cultural archetype that reached them through a Polish formulation. Certainly, that first formulation was not yet an expression of a true person-centeredness, but some traits of its features were expressed. The Muscovites rejected the formulation then, but they did not forget it.

In the seventeenth century, Poland proved to be the main transmitter of Western culture to Russia. The Polish language fulfilled in Russian society at that time the same functions as French would do in the following two centuries. People in educated circles in Russian society could speak and read Polish. Polish books prevailed among the few private libraries in Moscow.[25] This was not a unique circumstance. French, for example, was the language of common communication among the British aristocracy, at least until the sixteenth century.

It should also be noted that the Russian residents of the southern and western parts of Russian lands who lived under Polish jurisdiction during the sixteenth and seventeenth centuries were better educated than were Russians who lived within the borders of the Russian national state. Tsar Alexis the Calm was compelled to hire a tutor for his children—Simeon Polotskii—from those "occupied territories" in the western portions of his domain.

The era of expansion of the Polish kingdom with its republican traditions provided an opportunity for drawing comparisons between the different patterns of social order. These comparisons were not favorable for the native Russian order. After a century of stress and privation, Russia proved to be more backward than during the reign of Ivan III. So an idea about the advantages of an alternative way of life gained some psychological foundation: "The Western influence gained ground as we recognized our material and spiritual poverty, brought out more and more clearly by wars, diplomatic relations, and commercial transactions with other countries. Comparison with the resources of the western European states made us aware of our own backwardness."[26] The seeds, brought by a Western wind, had not been lost.

The reign of Alexis the Calm, the second Tsar of the new Romanov dynasty, needs to be considered in that context. People with a reform orientation prevailed among Alexis's retinue, such as the Tsar's tutor, B. Morozov; his close advisers F. Rtishchev and A. Ordin-Nashchokin; and their spiritual successor Prince V. Golitsin, adviser to Alexis's daughter Sofia. Prince Golitsin was the author of many reform ideas that not only anticipated but considerably exceeded the *perestroika* of Peter I. Despite their many differences, these people had several common moral and psychological features: respect for the governed; a critical attitude toward customs and traditions; a pro-Western, particularly pro-Polish, orientation in politics and culture; clear attitudes in favor of education, which were rather unusual in Russia at that time; striving for rationalization of administration by increasing its effectiveness, including at the urban and local levels; and striving to emancipate the administration from the personal influences and interests of the nobility. It is also important to emphasize that these pro-Western orientations were not a simple imitation of alien experience. These people tried to combine European achievements with Russian national originality. Alas, their efforts were not able to undermine the predominant cultural type seriously. The system-centered swamp absorbed the footprints of the reformers. Not many practical steps were taken in the direction of reforms under Alexis the Calm. Most plans were abandoned. "The Russians of the seventeenth century kept taking a step forward, and then stopping to think about what they had done, and whether the step ahead was not too long."[27]

This pattern of cautious consideration can be partially explained by the personal character of the Tsar. In discussions between reformers and conservatives, his priority was to moderate, to calm both parties. He had not been estranged from reformist plans until faced with active resistance by the champions of the ancient regime. Since the latter were the more aggressive, Alexis was frequently inclined to take their side or, at least, took highly compromised decisions or put decisions off entirely. He wished to realize changes but at the same time was frightened by these changes. He reminds one of Gorbachev in that respect.

> Tsar Alexei Mikhailovich was the kindest of men, a good Russian soul. I am prepared to say that he was the best representative of ancient Russia—at any rate, I know of no other who produced a more pleasant impression—but certainly not on the throne . . .

> He was willing to follow all that was good, but only to a certain point, so as not to disturb the comfortable equilibrium either in himself or in his surroundings. . . . Should Russia remain faithful to her native past, or take lessons from foreigners? Tsar Alexei settled this question in his own fashion. So as to choose between antiquity and innovations, he did not break with the old and did not reject the new. . . . He was not averse to plucking the flowers of foreign culture, but he did not want to soil his hands with the rough work of planting it in Russian soil.[28]

One more peculiarity of Russian modernization was displayed then for the first time. State authority instinctively felt a mortal threat to itself from the uncontrollable spreading of Western conceptions of mind and patterns of behavior among the Russian population. But since it was not able to stop this process, it created preventive mechanisms, counterbalances to keep cultural change under control. First, it tried to restrict the process to only a few selected fields, where it would presumably work for the benefit of state politics—for example, in improving the military discipline of the army. Second, it tried to compensate for innovations by means of ideological levers emphasizing Russian "uniqueness" and by monopoly of the "true Orthodox faith" that opposed Western "perversities"; it treated Europe as a dangerous and insidious tempter. Actually, this was exploitation of a perpetual human trait—"we" versus "they."

In various guises, this political strategy has been pursued by Russian (and later Soviet) authorities for centuries. For a long time, the main symbols of Russian uniqueness were identification with the Orthodox Church and, to a certain degree, with the image of Tsar-Father, the patriarch. After the revolution of 1917, other symbols were substituted but not the key principle: a readiness to take the fruits of Western civilization but not to allow the spirit that created those fruits to spread—no peaceful coexistence in the field of ideology.

But pursuing this policy of selective modernization, as I call it, was not a simple matter. From the beginning, the process displayed a tendency to slide out of control. This should have been expected, because the very concept contained a logical discrepancy: it attempted to disassociate ideas from deeds—causes from effects. As a result, opposition emerged at both poles, among the causes and among the effects, in Russian society. On the one hand, during the seventeenth century, the potentially liberal political dissent and analytical critique of indigenous ways evolved as a social phenomenon—remember that Prince Kurbsky, the opponent of Ivan the Terrible a hundred years before, was the only exception. In the seventeenth century, there were many more exceptions, which could even be classified by the directions of their dissent. On the other hand, even the very moderate and cautious course of Alexis's government toward selective modernization faced fanatical resistance from the conservative opposition. The spiritual leader of this opposition, archpriest Abbacoum, had the outstanding personal qualities of being a decisive and uncompromising person. Partially for that reason, the movement for the defense of purity of "the sacred faith of our forbears" adopted from the beginning the character of a crusade *(jihad)* against traitors and "revisionists."

What at first glance looked like a mosaic of developed political parties turned out to be mostly religious conflicts between so-called Old Believers, who conceived of themselves as keepers of the true Christian faith, and their opponents. All this fighting hardly touched the depths of national consciousness and had no significant influence on social mores or socio-psychological perspectives. And all the changes that took place occurred within a small social stratum. Most of population remained obedient subjects.

Nevertheless, *the possibility of a divergence in Russian society resulting from different cultural stereotypes appeared for the first time.* That point is important for an adequate comprehension of later developments. "Western influence destroyed the spiritual wholeness of the ancient Russian society. . . . Just as a pane of glass cracks when its different parts are unequally heated, so Russian society, unequally affected by the Western influence, broke apart."[29]

But in fact, over the long term the Russian government promoted this fracturing of society both by its initiatives in trying to take advantage of Western innovations and by its slowness and inability to pursue a coherent policy. In particular, the regime showed little concern about the people's education. The imported technological and cultural innovations were introduced to a social and cultural milieu that was not prepared for the necessary adaptations.

Paradoxically, a whole program of societal transformations was formed and even began to be realized during the two decades between the death of Alexis the Calm and the coming of Peter I to absolute autocratic power. The seven-year-long regency rule of Princess Sofia was especially important. The Soviet historical mythology that inherited many clichés from official Tsarist historiography treated that period between Alexis the Calm and Peter I as one of conservative dominance. But in fact, it was a time when the concept of comprehensive reforms, much broader than Peter's perestroika, had been formed. Beyond the military, fiscal, and administrative policy innovations, this concept of reform also emphasized the fostering of trade and industry, the establishment of urban self-government, the opening of general and technical schools, and the liberation of serfs by endowing them with land. Prince Golitsin, head of the foreign ministry and Sofia's closest adviser, was the main author of these efforts. The "Great Golitsin" conceptualized the design for Alexander II's reform to liberate the serfs—but almost two centuries earlier.[30] Golitsin formulated the concept of free farmers owning their own land and making annual tax payments. Unfortunately, he and Princess Sofia lost political sway after the palace revolution that brought Peter to power.

I will not digress to discuss the achievements of Golitsin and the practical accomplishments in the country at that time beyond mentioning one remarkable example that occurred during Sofia's reign. Moscow was a city consisting almost entirely of wooden houses. During seven years, more than three thousand masonry houses were constructed in the city.

A program of Russian modernization had already been established in its main characteristics before the appearance of Peter on the stage of historical significance. Moreover, this program included certain democratic measures that were completely opposed to the general direction of Peter's efforts and were, therefore, more progressive than Peter's reforms. Of course, even under favorable circumstances, the task of overcoming the system-centered archetype would have been difficult. Resolution would probably have required a long historical period. Nevertheless, the possibility of moving gradually toward a person-centered way of life seems at that time to have been favorable for Russian society. Peter not only appropriated the idea of reform from his predecessors but completely perverted it. In my judgment, it was a great misfortune for Russia that it was Peter who headed and conducted his perverse reform efforts.

I understand clearly that my judgment is contrary to the long-standing tradition of treating Peter I as the greatest reformer and as the key symbol of progressive Russia. I do not deny some collateral positive consequences of his politics, particularly his military and administrative reforms. My next task is to consider his historical role only in the context of my main analytical effort—to trace the dynamics of struggle between system-centered and person-centered principles in Russian national consciousness. We now turn directly to Peter's time.

CHAPTER THREE

The Devastating Course of Peter's "Modernization"

The Eighteenth Century—Age of Lost Opportunities

The true meaning of historical events and their reflection in the public's view are sometimes quite different things. The historical legends about Peter I depict the Great Reformer as a farseeing and wise politician, the father-founder of modern Russia, almost as "the first Tsar-democrat." These are among the most widely held and stable but false stereotypes of Russian national consciousness, in both their popular and scientific manifestations. The myth of Peter's political concept as "barbarian ways to overcome barbarism" remains quite influential among most Russian and a majority of Western writers on this subject. One needs to recognize, however, that some Western scholars, even though captured by the same stereotypes, present a more balanced approach.[1] I presume that the reason is not only their lack of ideological blinders, which gives them some advantage over Russian authors, but also that they have grown up in another kind of political culture, with another measure of how much coercion is acceptable.

The cult of Peter's personality is also widely held among the Russian population. In every place that he visited, even momentarily, the myths exist, associating crucial moments in history with Peter's orders or actions. Peter appears to be the god who created the Russian world. It is amusing how this cult permeates well-educated groups in society as well, even though such people are normally much more skeptical and cautious about idolizing historical personages. The almost religious worship of Peter has some similarities to the adoration of Napoleon in France. Criticizing Peter in Russia is like cursing Napoleon in France or Jefferson in America.

Accordingly, a negative judgment of Peter's regime is usually associated with either extreme conservatism or antipatriotism. Who else but reactionaries or enemies could speak out against a canonized hero?

But in fact, others have prevailed among Peter's critics. Princess E. R. Dashkova, for example—one of the most brilliant and progressive Russians in the eighteenth century, president of the Academy of Sciences, and someone who can by no means be classified as conservative or antipatriotic—in describing in her memoir a conversation in Vienna with Austrian prime minister Caunits, depicted Peter very negatively: "Brutal and rude, he trampled everybody under his power like slaves born to suffer. If he had the wits of a great legislator, he would have followed the examples of the other nations and allowed industrialization to occur by means of gradual reforms to attain the same improvements which he provoked by violence. . . . Both slaves and slave-owners were victims of his unbridled tyranny."[2] The horror of Pushkin's Eugenii, who was chased by the ghost of the Bronze Horseman in a poem of that title (evoking the famous monument of Peter in St. Petersburg, symbolizing the autocratic character of the Russian monarchy) but could not escape wherever he ran, also reflects a negative perception of Peter.

It was not by chance that Leo Tolstoy, who intended to write a prose poem about Peter's era, abandoned this project when he learned more about his "hero."

> The personality of Peter the Great disappointed him and he felt an aversion to the whole era. He found nothing great either in the person or the actions of the czar and he could see nothing but his faults. His so-called reforms, he said, were not for the good of the state but for his personal profit. . . . He had borrowed his reforms from Saxony where the laws were the cruelest and the mores the most licentious. For Tolstoy this explained the friendship between Peter and the Great Elector of Saxony who was one of the most debauched sovereigns of that time. If the czar was friendly with men such as the pastry maker, Menchikov, and the Swiss deserter, Franz Lefort, it was because,

> among the nobility who despised him, he had not found any friends willing to share his dissipated way of life. . . . Tolstoy was especially indignant about Peter's cruelty to the czarevich, Alexsey.[3]

Kliuchevsky's attitude is also remarkable. In his general phrases and judgments, he does not depart far from the prevailing tradition of honoring Peter and paying him all the usual ritualistic tribute. He gives Peter all the standard signs of respect, naming him "Great" and "Reformer" in discussing Peter's reforms. But in his concrete analysis he practically refutes his own compliments and portrays the image of an almost monstrous Tsar, who hardly stimulates any sympathy or admiration but provokes the opposite feelings and judgments on the part of the reader. Under the conditions of censorship and the expression of official opinion in the press, these tactics reflect an author's cunning as a way to gain publication and avoid trouble.

As usual, Kliuchevsky combines an abstract theoretical analysis with rich descriptions of this historical personage. He pays considerable attention to Peter's personality, his character, and the mores and habits of his cultural milieu. We can see Peter, as it were, with his court, among his relatives, and against the background of his relationships with others from his childhood to his death. And these pictures evoke only negative impressions.

PETER'S CHARACTER AND CULTURAL MILIEU

During Peter's childhood, the main factor in Moscow's political life was an embittered struggle between different clans of the nobility for Alexey's legacy, for top positions in the power hierarchy. In that struggle, one cannot observe any moral constraints. Neither progressive nor reactionary, neither new nor old parties prevailed; but barbarous and power-loving instincts predominated. Peter was an eyewitness to those horrible clashes and scenes.

In the process of his education, Peter acquired a strong technical orientation devoid of moral considerations. In modern terms, he emphasized an applied social engineering approach. He sought out technical marvels from overseas that could be used for military purposes. His ethical and political ideas were impressed with a horrible indigenous political reality.

> It is not surprising, therefore, that Peter's tastes and ideas were somewhat one-sided. . . . His attitude to civic affairs was colored by a hatred for the clergy, the Boyars, the Streltsy (a kind of troops who twice—in 1682 and 1698—rebelled in Moscow), and the Old Believers. He was more occupied with soldiers, guns, fortresses, and ships, than with people, political institutions, popular needs, or civic relationships. For a long time Peter completely ignored the problems of society and human relations to which responsible people usually devote so much attention, so that before Peter could even realize that there could be any relationship between society and himself, he had stopped thinking about it. . . . As a ruler, Peter knew neither moral nor political restraints, and lacked the most elementary political and social principles.[4]

In other words, Peter's immorality was already formed in his early childhood and adolescence.

Probably this partially explains his extremely cruel and even sadistic character. An extraordinary brutality marked Peter's relationships with his playmates during his early years. One can hardly call those years childhood. These characteristics were displayed clearly in his "games." For example, the military games Peter conducted regularly in the years of his youth left many dead on the "battlefield" at the village of Preobrazhenskoe on the outskirts of Moscow, including Peter's own friends. He never showed compassion. Human life, not to speak of human dignity, had no meaning for him. In Peter, we have an extreme example of a ruler using human beings only as tools for achieving personal goals. He reached perfection in the skill of extracting from people all their potential but not caring at all about their fate.

As a whole, Peter's character—active, curious, chaotic, extremely rude, and despotic—displayed the very style of his life. Throughout his lifetime, spent in motion among different activities, Peter manifested these characteristics wherever he went and in whatever he built, in waging war against people, or in punishing or executing people, including his own son. He was highly controversial. His behavior abroad displayed his attitude clearly: an active cognitive orientation and constant efforts to appropriate foreign techniques went hand in hand with rude boorishness, barbarism, and complete contempt for a host's way of life and way of thinking. For example, when he visited England, the king ordered that a private estate be put at Peter's disposal and redecorated especially for the eminent visitors. When Peter and his entourage left after three months of residence, the owner presented the government with a bill for damages: "the floors and walls were liberally bespattered and smeared, the furniture smashed, and the curtains torn; the pictures were riddled and ruined because they had been used for target practice; and the lawn had been utterly ruined, and looked as if a regiment of soldiers in iron shoes had drilled on it."[5] Even if we admit the probability of some exaggeration in the extent of the damage, that list leaves a strong impression of Peter's character.

His entertainment at home was marked by an unconstrained lifestyle of compulsive rollicking, debaucheries, and obscenities where buffoonery was molded in the form of bureaucratic institutions: "In this way the 'Most Drunken Synod of Fools and Jesters' was created. Meetings were held under the presidency of a chief buffoon called the 'Prince-Pope,' or the 'Noisiest, all-jesting Patriarch of all Moscow, Kokua and Yauza.' There was a college of twelve cardinals, all tipplers and gluttons, who were attended by a large suite of bishops, archimandrites, and other dignitaries, whose coarse and obscene nicknames were too disgusting to print. . . . The first commandment was that members were to get drunk every day, and might never go to bed sober. . . . In short, it was a most indecent parody on religious rites and ceremonies."[6] Members of the real clergy also indulged in these feasts.

It is curious that in their character and even in concrete jokes, these modes of entertainment have many similarities with Stalin's feasts at his country estates, as his daughter S. Allilueva has depicted them. Thus historical continuity can sometimes be observed not only in the essence of processes and forms but in their details.

One more note about the early period of Peter's political life: There is extended treatment in the literature about the continuity between the Preobrazhensky regiment of Peter's childhood and his later victorious armies. Much less attention has been paid to the other continuities—his childhood "model" court became an important prototype for the Ministry of Political Police. This Preobrazhensky *prikaz* (headquarters) actually contained all the main elements of that punitive agency—interrogators, agents-informers, an investigative department, and torture cells—where the young Peter personally conducted interrogations and beheaded members of the disloyal Streltsy regiment.

All procedures and processes involved in political trials had been applied in his Preobrazhensky prikaz. These features placed his headquarters at the top of the structure of government. The prikaz exercised the power to administer any central or local agency, regardless of its scope or place in the hierarchy, if it was connected with political crimes. The meaning of political crimes was broadly construed. The head of the Preobrazhensky prikaz could arrest, imprison, and torture practically any person regardless of social or official position.[7] From this experience, Peter established the prototype for the Soviet KGB with its omnipotence and ability to penetrate into all fields of life. It was not by chance, I believe, that when Peter traveled to Western Europe, he designated the chief of the Preobrazhensky prikaz, F. Romodanovsky, to "rule Moscow." Now let us turn to Peter's political ideas.

PETER'S CONCEPTION OF POLITICAL ORDER

The basis of Peter's conception of political order was an almost Pharaoh-like conceit and ambition. "[He] had no coherent political understanding, but only a vague, confused notion that he had unlimited power and that somehow this was a menace. . . . As a ruler, Peter knew neither moral nor political restraints, and lacked the most elementary political and social principles. . . . To the end of his life he never understood the logic of history or the nature of the life of his people."[8]

To be fair, we should recognize that Peter, unlike his predecessors, considered his mission to be a type of public service. He conceived the purpose of the state not as a dynastic interest but as a commonwealth. But his practical actions severely contradicted this purpose: "His devotion to his people led him to overstrain their resources and waste their lives recklessly. He himself was honest and sincere, and did not spare himself; he was also just and kind to others. But, owing to his interest, he was better with inanimate objects than with people, whom he treated as if they were merely tools. He quickly found out who was useful, but he could neither learn not to overtax people nor put himself in another's place. In this respect he differed greatly from his father. Peter knew how to manage people, but either could not or would not try to understand them."[9]

The guidelines of his behavior were determined by two mistaken political prejudices—a strong "belief in the creative power of the Sovereign's authority, and an absolute reliance upon the maxim that nothing can exhaust either the strength or the patience of a Sovereign's people.... Nothing, he considered, could not be effected by force, could not, through compulsory methods, be initiated amongst the masses."[10] It seems, however, that Kliuchevsky exaggerated to some extent Peter's conflict with mass psychology and a sense of justice. Peter did not destroy the dominant psychological stereotypes of the people of Muscovy—the recognition that they are enslaved and that power is omnipotent. Moreover, he exploited those stereotypes in many ways.

Peter's political ideas, in their decisive parameters, were completely within the mainstream of Moscow's political traditions. To speak seriously about his innovations, one can only think of them in terms of new forms and methods in his efforts to achieve the same autocratic purposes. Specifically, his innovations in the forms of governing were displayed in his understanding of the potentials of bureaucratic organization. In 1718–20 serious structural reforms of administration were undertaken. The Swedish style of bureaucratic administration was established. The bureaucratic model of governing presumes an impersonal and formalized set of rules and procedures; that is, an alternative to personal discretion and arbitrary action by officials. But arbitrary rule continued to prevail. For that reason, the attempt to bureaucratize the government resulted only in its being bound by arbitrary edicts from the top. Red tape prevailed, revealing the negative side of bureaucracy. Its effectiveness was presumed to increase somehow, but the idea of bureaucratic perestroika has never been realized. As a result, an additional barrier—quasi-bureaucratic offices—emerged between the people and the state. The purposes of the state machinery did not change.

PETER'S REIGN

What, then, were the social and political purposes of Peter's reforms? "Peter's reforms did not aim directly at changing the political, social, or moral order, nor did they aim at forcing Russian life into an alien Western European pattern. The reforms only aimed at providing the Russian State and people with Western intellectual and material resources, so that Russia might take its just position in Europe, and its people might increase their productive capacity."[11] As noted in the preceding chapter, this kind of orientation was not something new. It merely continued the political pattern of previous reigns. The core of Peter's innovations was the same traditional, harsh, oppressive treatment of subjects, just in more skillful, extreme forms.

Only one component was really new—the considerable increase in demands on subjects. They were not only expected to be obedient to all the orders but now they should also take the initiative in fulfillment of these orders. "He also wanted the serf, while remaining a serf, to act responsibly and freely."[12] In this respect, Peter was ahead of his time. Neither his predecessors nor his successors were smart or energetic enough to make their subjects into "slaves with initiative." This idea was revived in the twentieth century, accompanied by considerably improved forms of "industrialized" technology for manipulating human beings. Thus the real purpose of Peter's policy was not to destroy or alter the old regime but to improve it, to make it more viable by increasing its functional efficacy. As internal tools to achieve this purpose, the reform measures became the means of "squeezing" the people to compete better with the West.

The question of Peter's relationship to the West is an important part of the mythology surrounding his personality. That mythology conveyed heroic-romantic images of the great Tsar who personally, by his own hands, "cut a window to Europe" and "joined Russia to European civilization." Let me put aside for now the problematical character and ambiguities of the general notion of European civilization. For the moment, let me reiterate that Peter did not turn to Europe for its civilization. He had a much narrower and more pragmatic goal: to assimilate Western technological achievements, quickly. He did this first in the fields of military and shipbuilding technologies, and then immediately proceeded to turn those capabilities against his own people and against the West. It is not by chance that Peter spent almost all his life waging war and struggling against the West. He sought in Europe not culture, not civilization in the genuine meaning of the word, but only technology. The voyagers and missions that Peter sent to Europe had definite instructions dominated by the main idea of stealing science from Europe and gathering all that was useful for the Russian empire.

Peter was no Westernist trying to modernize or Europeanize his country. He once said to his close associate Osterman: "We need Europe for a few decades; later on, we must turn our back on it."[13] Moreover, he understood that appropriation by his subjects of the genuine foundations of European culture could become a threat to his own autocratic regime. Hence he treated ties with Europe as a necessary but dangerous enterprise.

A concrete analysis of Peter's politics undermines the myth concerning the existence of any more or less coherent plan of reforms. His actions were chaotic and followed a single dominant idea: to enforce and expand his own autocratic authority. There was no other logic, no other strategy at any time during his reign. Peter's so-called plan of reforms is no more than a retrospective use of the imagination long after his death, an assessment that later served the purposes of apologies and propaganda—not the clarification of historical truth.

The quality of the Great Reformer's team was also remarkable. In his court, there were no people as capable intellectually as those found in the court of his father, Alexey—no one with civic feelings, with high moral standards, or with noteworthy levels of cultural achievement. All were essentially climbers, self-seeking adventurers, and malcontent intriguers who viewed their service as a means to feed their power-seeking ambitions and to make a fortune by fishing in troubled waters. Only this type of person could adjust to Peter. Even the positive features of Peter's innovations were inevitably distorted when implemented by such people. The supposed social base of Peter's rule—the gentry—were hardly the appropriate agents of his reforms. Therefore, Peter's policy tended not to ameliorate but to magnify the regime's negative qualities.

We need to consider briefly how Peter treated his human resources. Human life was valued in Russia just a little higher than in the Pharaohs' Egypt. The number of victims of any particular project depended more on the volume of activity than on the personal qualities of the ruler: the more wide-ranging the activity, the greater the number of victims. The percentage of human "wastage" remained more or less stable. It would be unjust to blame Peter specifically for the extremely high human price of his efforts without taking into account the volume of the activities he pursued. He was extremely active, and he buried more of his compatriots than did any prior Tsar, not because of his unusual brutality but mostly because of the scale of his operations. Nevertheless, the huge sacrifice, not exceeded until the twentieth century, requires attention.

The terrible toll in human life paid by the Russian people in building the new capital city at St. Petersburg is well known. That capital city was Peter's pyramid, so to speak. "It would be difficult to find anywhere in military history a massacre which accounted for more men than St. Petersburg and Kronstadt. Peter called his new capital his 'paradise,' but for the people it was a mass grave."[14] It is a sad twist of irony that even in our "enlightened" age, so many people consider such loss of life an appropriate price to have been paid for this classic and magnificent imitation of a southern imperial capital on the cold and windy reaches of a northern swamp. This city-monument, erected upon a countless number of builders' bones, was designed, first of all, to immortalize the name of its founder. Much less is known about the human cost of Peter's other constructions—seaports, roads, mines, etc.—not as "epochal" or famous, and some of them never finished, but as paved with hundreds of thousands of human bodies. According to the census data for 1710, the roster of taxpayers over a thirty-year period had declined by 20 to 25 percent. The year 1710 was only the midpoint in Peter's reign. In the second half of his reign, the population continued to decline at about the same rate.

Like any cruel despot, Peter had a fear of his own people that verged on panic. For instance, in 1705 at the city of Astrakhan, a distance of more than a thousand miles from the capital, riots broke out when local authorities mocked the population for resisting the process of coercive "Europeanization"—compulsory cutting off of beards and the imposition of "Germanic" clothes. These matters involved no threat to Moscow. Moreover, the rebels appealed to the Tsar for justice. However, the "Great" Tsar was so frightened that he urgently diverted troops from the Western border in the midst of a war against the Swedes and ordered the state treasury to be removed from Moscow and buried in a safe place. The atrocities of his emissary Sheremetev in the subjected city can be compared with the actions of Stalin.

The political police machinery treated each infraction with the same cruelty regardless of the kind of challenge it represented—whether arising from disturbances among military conscripts; political plots, real or imaginary; or the eradication of long beards and traditional clothing. A special institution of informers about assets supposedly being concealed from tax obligations was established in 1711. This institution comprised both official and volunteer sycophants. If denunciations were confirmed, informers received half of the fine as their reward; if not, an informer bore no responsibility. Thus denunciation became a form of wages secured and protected by the state. Such opportunities for arbitrary actions, extortion, and moral corruption had their usual effects on the character of a people.

Peter viewed the people as inert, amorphous, and slow-moving—like paste—capable of resisting a reforming hand but having neither their own will nor any value in themselves. He believed in only one way to govern human beings: by exercising bodily force and evoking an instinct of self-preservation. In the language of social psychology, this process uses manipulation at the lowest level of human needs.

In his tax collection policy, Peter also acted with his usual brutality. The method he introduced in the later years of his reign was especially extraordinary: he placed the burden of tax collection on regular army regiments located in different regions of the country and used them like administrative instruments to collect taxes. These troops, who had no ties with the local population and were probably easily provoked by remnants of enmity for the residents, acted like conquerors in occupied territory:

> The presence of the military caused greater hardship than the tax itself. Armed visitations were made three times a year and each visitation lasted for two months: for six months of the year the towns and villages were in a state of panic. Moreover, the inhabitants had to maintain the soldiery while they carried out searches and even executions. It was hardly likely that the Tartars under Batu Khan behaved worse when they conquered Russia. . . . The regiments had hardly settled into their permanent quarters when it was noticed that the number of census-souls had greatly diminished, partly as the result of increased mortality, and partly because many of them had fled. Soon after Peter's death an infantry regiment in Kazan found it could only account for half the number of taxpayers responsible for the regiment's upkeep—thirteen thousand census-souls were missing. . . . Peter transformed the army into one hundred and twenty-six police posts which then terrorized the population of ten provinces.[15]

Later, similar uses of the army became habitual. Similar practices were followed by NKVD (KGP precursor) detachments during collectivization of Soviet agriculture during the 1930s, also with disastrous results.

All these horrible fiscal practices were counterproductive. They reduced the number of taxpayers, undermined the people's incentive to create wealth and improve their own well-being, and allowed the fiscal agencies to waste the bulk of funds collected (up to 70 percent) by legal and illegal means. The annual budget deficiency reached 20 percent and the real purchasing power of money was reduced by half during Peter's reign. This was an enormous decline compared to most of contemporary Europe.

One might attempt to justify some of the brutality and maladministration by successes in the field of national industrial development, as allegedly occurred under Peter's rule. Indeed, 233 factories, mines, and other workplaces were established. Alas, the despotic methods of rule distorted this field of activity as well and doomed it as the wrong way to accomplish development. Peter's approach made use of the purely technological side of industrialization and completely rejected the moral and psychological foundations of the Industrial Revolution represented by the spirit of free enterprise and the protection of human rights, particularly property rights. Russian entrepreneurs—the only social class who had some elements of civic feelings and political common sense—were oppressed by excessive taxes, suffered from unscrupulous competition by landowners and monasteries, and operated with their hands bound by extraordinary governmental tutelage and regimentation. A potential stronghold of civil liberty was transformed from its very beginning by an opposite tendency: a routine system of bureaucratic dominance. Under those conditions, it was natural that "Russian enterprise did not meet Peter's expectations; hence, the capitalists were to build factories, form companies, and appoint partners by *ukazy* (decrees).... The method Peter introduced to organize his companies and factories was to grant a monopoly and compel people to undertake the new enterprise. This method of industrial promotion in a Treasury-controlled hothouse naturally led to government interference throughout which, with its detailed regulation, cavilling supervision, and lack of experience, frightened people away. There was yet another obstacle to industrial progress: private owners of capital were unwilling to take risks. The lack of common justice, and the excessive power of people in arbitrary authority, made timid people unwilling to put their savings into circulation."[16]

The first phase of Russian industrialization—like the second, which took place under Stalin—resorted excessively to forced labor. For instance, by his Decree of January 18, 1721, Peter extended to factory owners the privilege held by the nobility of acquiring villages with their serfs, on the condition of locating factories at these villages, where the serfs were required to work full time. Serfs were not the only people caught in these nets of coercive industrialization. Peter, like Stalin, ordered in his decrees that people "guilty" of crimes be assigned for "behavior correction" to the different sites of industrial enterprises; it is incorrect to credit the Bolsheviks with invention of the gulag. This "fruitful" idea had been tested and put into operation more than two hundred years earlier. "Patriotic" minds can be proud and happy: this was accomplished on native Russian soil, in accordance with imperial traditions. The Russian poet M. Voloshin appropriately named Peter "the first Bolshevik."

Peter's legislative activities were also opposed to the concept of law as a set of mutual restraints and obligations applying to state agencies just as to other entities. Peter never had any doubt that laws were only for regulating the behavior of subjects and had no binding effect on state authorities. Laws could be canceled or changed at any moment by the sovereign's personal discretion. He ignored the rules of legal formalities: his decrees were a chaotic mass of diverse, frequently contradictory regulations that were directed only by the logic of unlimited despotism. Russia did not acquire a concept of law in the proper sense of that word under Peter's rule; there were only commands, regulations, and instructions; not laws.

His efforts to institute compulsory education had some special characteristics. First, he followed the same style as in the conscription and training of soldiers, which created antipathy and provoked resistance. Second, his massive effort to send people abroad for education, when they were completely unprepared for that experience, failed to realize its potential. Many of these travelers had neither the attitudes nor the skills and habits for education; they did not understand what was to be learned; "they merely stared open-mouthed at the manners, governmental systems, and public regulations of Western Europe without learning . . . to distinguish between culture and rubbish, or to derive any clear-cut idea from what they beheld." As a result, when they returned home, "their newly imbibed customs and scientific impressions blew off them like dust from a turnpike road, and left only such an admixture of alien vices with native shortcomings as once moved a foreign observer to remark that, so far from that admixture helping to promote virtue and godliness, it simply hastened both moral and physical degeneration."[17]

Nevertheless, a certain positive effect was achieved. Fortunately, it was completely different from what Peter expected. Some travelers learned that social order can be sustained without autocratic authority, police coercion, and compulsive obedience. They realized how people can live by their own will, how children can learn without being beaten, how autocracy cannot deprive others with impunity, how a sovereign need not be allowed to command resources from subjects without the consent of the people's representatives. *A fuller comprehension of these peculiarities of the European way of life took almost a century. But this process opened, in the end, a real possibility for transition to an alternative road to development in Russian society.*

Alexander Yanov, who concentrated mainly on the political side of social processes, assessed Peter's historical role as extremely negative. In Yanov's three-stage conception of historical cycles, he depicted Peter's reign as the "high noon of autocracy" and supposed that Peter contributed to the "Tartarization" of Russia, not its Westernization. In contrast to the "unlucky" Ivan the Terrible, Peter was a winner who contrived to embody his pernicious ideas in social reality and for that reason brought much more evil to his country. I agree with the main direction of this judgment, but I have some reservations about the concepts on which the judgment is based.

In my judgment, in Peter's case, we are dealing with a type of pseudomodernizer. He managed to exploit those features of modernization that were cleansed of all elements of free thinking and devoted them to traditional autocratic purposes. His political purposes involved expanding the uses of technology without any change in the character of authority relationships. The tools devoted to autocratic purposes were quite different than those of his predecessors.

The human cost of his politics was horrible and his methods were pathologically cruel, even by the standards of that not very merciful era. But the main negative significance of Peter's historical mission was that he destroyed the seeds of true modernization and Westernization at the level of a cultural genotype and substituted its products in the form of superficial technological changes. As a result, he sterilized the dynamic psychological, ethical, and cultural features of national life because he prevented Russia from joining the more creative forms of organization associated with a more person-centered European way of life.

Peter's politics were new only in outward appearance; in their essence they completely corresponded with the basic system-centered stereotypes and attitudes of the Russian mentality associated with servitude. This was the basis for a cruel paradox in which Peter functioned as a grim despot who ravaged his own country and yet who was also canonized in popular consciousness as Peter the Great rather than Peter the Terrible. The habit of bowing down and submitting to a powerful hand became a major factor in charismatic leadership in Russia. Turning to the dynamics of socio-ethical and socio-psychological changes, in moral dynamics, we can observe a change in the influence of two different versions of traditional morality. *The role of communal morality diminished and the place of imperial morality increased.* In other words, the patriarchal (patrimonial) system of vertical relationships built mainly on class bonds collapsed and was replaced by formalized, impersonal relationships marked by estrangement. Alienation between the centers of power and the people grew. This gap was filled by a Russian-style quasi-bureaucracy—that is, officialdom characterized by arbitrariness more or less effectively restricted to a top-down rather than a bottom-up relationship. All of this took place within the framework of a traditional type of system-centered morality.

The changes in socio-psychological patterns followed the same style. The paternalistic feature of relationships between ruler and ruled was considerably weakened. The image of the Tsar-Father withered and yielded to the image of the omnipotent Tsar-Master. In other words, the emergence of "serfish" stereotypes of mind took place. The domination of this sort of psychology allowed Peter easily to overcome a more person-centered orientation, which was also associated with an Orthodox fear of Latinism. People learned to adapt to the master's will in their own way—to behave differently in public and in private. Thus a double morality—duplicity, hypocrisy—became a part of the Russian national character, thanks to Peter's efforts.

Many of the traditional vices in the national character persisted, and at the same time new ones emerged. The imperial authorities discredited the old system of moral values along with demands for changes to Western styles of clothing, manners, and appearance; but no new Russian pattern appeared. As a result, a sort of moral vacuum emerged. One symptom was the unprecedented growth of brigandage in the country: "Bands of pillagers, commanded by deserters, joined together in well-organized and well-armed cavalry groups, who attacked 'in regular formation,' destroying well-populated villages, impeding the collection of taxes, and even penetrating into the towns."[18] The country was both paralyzed and terrorized. In terms of social psychology, this situation can be depicted as a vicious growth of lawlessness and arbitrariness from the top of society and brigandage from the bottom. An increasing level of brutality from both sides accompanied the process. Something similar, on an even grander scale, could be observed in Russia two hundred years after Peter during the October Revolution.

The historical reality of Peter's reign and the myth of the First Reformer both found their places within the pyramid of the traditional Russian system-centered cultural genotype. We see in Peter a kind of second edition of Ivan the Terrible—unfortunately more successful in terms of enforcing system-centered order and prolonging its historical dominance in Russia by making it more effective in functional respects. To complete the assessment of the historical meaning of Peter's epoch, we now need to consider its immediate aftermath.

THE AFTERMATH

There are two more features in eighteenth-century Russia that need to be considered as essential elements in this analysis. One was an attempt by two aristocratic families—the Golitsins and Dolgorukhis—to place restraints on autocratic rule and to create in Russia something like a constitutional monarchy. In January of 1730, fifteen-year-old Peter II, the grandson and successor of Peter the Great, suddenly died after ruling for three years. The immediate male line of the Romanov dynasty was broken. The Privy Council gained an opportunity for choice and decided to enthrone Peter's niece, Princess Anna, but under conditions of considerable restrictions on her authority in favor of the Privy Council. She lived in Mitava, a small town in the territory of modern Latvia, and she would have had no opportunity to succeed to the Russian throne apart from these circumstances. A top-ranked delegation from Moscow brought her an offer and presented her with a document specifying the conditions of her rule. Anna signed this document and left for Moscow. (Peter II had restored the capital to Moscow.)

The gravity of the situation and uncertainty of the moment were generally understood. First, the very idea of placing limitations on autocratic power was a source of confusion to people who had acquired their political education under Peter's heavy hand. Second, the way that this limitation was to work seemed suspect. Six of the eight members of the Privy Council belonged to two ancient families. Other boyar families felt themselves disadvantaged. The phantom of tyranny by several persons instead of one autocrat emerged. The gentry not represented on the Privy Council did not see any benefits in this arrangement.[19] The leader of the Privy Council, Dmitri Golitsin, changed tactics and suggested that the gentry offer their own proposals for the state structure. He attracted attention, in this way, to the circumstance that the question had not yet been decided. Members of the gentry submitted several proposals. The Privy Council began to bargain, make concessions, and secure support by the creation of representative institutions, including a Chamber of Gentry and Chamber of City Representatives. All legislative power was to reside in the Privy Council. This plan only agitated political passions. Those supporting unlimited autocratic power became more and more active.

When Anna reached Moscow, she enlisted the support of the Imperial Guards and publicly tore the conditions agreement to pieces. The Guards stood by her and demonstrated their readiness to suppress any discontent. The members of the Privy Council kept silent and bore witness to their own failure. The illusion of limited monarchy existed in Moscow for ten days and was then destroyed. One of the darkest periods of arbitrary autocratic rule began.

These events have attracted the attention of many analysts at different times. The pre-revolutionary official historiography of Russia depicted the "councilors' plot" as an effort to undermine the foundations of the monarchy, an effort foiled by providence in alliance with the people. Ironically, Soviet historiography followed this same interpretation to support its strong autocratic power and, consequently, renounced any efforts to restrict autocratic power as "reactionary."

Contrary interpretations also exist. Yanov, for example, viewed the councilors' failure as the collapse of efforts to establish an "aristocratic republic," which he presumed to be the single realistic way to progressive development. In 1918 one of the leading Russian intellectuals of both the pre- and post-revolutionary eras, Peter B. Struve, wrote in his section of the famous collective work *Out of the Depths (De Profundis):* "Vladimir Il'ich Lenin-Ul'ianov ultimately was able to destroy the great power of Russia, and introduce on top of its ruins the bloody, fanciful Soviets of Deputies, because, in 1730, an offshoot of the Romanov dynasty, a niece of Peter, Anna Ioanovna, the Duchess of Kurland, defeated prince Dmitrii Mikhailovich Golitsyn and his fellow aristocrats, along with the middling gentry, who strove for freedom but feared the 'magnates.' With that defeat the foundation was finally laid for the tradition of a Russian monarchy established on the political submissiveness of the cultured classes before an independent mon-archial authority. In their basic content and character, the events of 1730 had a fatal predetermining influence on the political destiny of Russia."[20]

Struve developed his logic of consideration as follows: "The autocracy, having denied the cultural classes participation in ruling the state, again bound those classes to itself by chains of material interest, thereby weaning them from political strivings, and the means, and the training to protect their interests, apart from the raising and resolving of *political questions*."[21]

I do not consider the events of 1730 a crucial or fatal moment in the history of Russia. There is not sufficient reason to view the contending parties as either the forces of progress or the forces of reaction. Such an explanation seems a rather artificial and exaggerated way of explaining the differences that existed. None of the political groups was able to raise its sights beyond the desire to dominate political power. Except for Prince Golitsin, most of the actors neglected even to look around for political allies beyond their narrow group or kinship ties.

This shortsighted egoism can be contrasted to the political thinking of the privileged estates in England, who understood from ancient times the importance of self-restraint, taking others into account as a way of sharing in the exercise of political power. Alexis de Tocqueville in *The Old Regime and the French Revolution* recognized this characteristic when he observed: "The English aristocrats were haughtier by nature than the French and even less disposed to demean themselves by hobnobbing with persons of lower rank; nevertheless, they were compelled to do so by circumstances. No sacrifice was too great if it ensured their power."[22] Tocqueville considered this strategy of the English aristocracy as applying to tax policies: "For many centuries the only inequalities of taxation existing in England have been those successively introduced in favor of the poorer classes. . . . The English aristocracy voluntarily shouldered the heaviest public burdens so as to be allowed to retain its authority." Moreover, he supposed that ignoring the principle that "those who don't vote don't pay" could serve as the starting point on the road to the disintegration and collapse of society: "It was on the day when the French people . . . permitted the King to impose a tax without their consent and the nobles showed so little public spirit as to connive at this, provided their own immunity was guaranteed—it was on that fateful day that the seeds were sown of almost all the vices and abuses which led to the violent downfall of the old regime."[23] But as early as the thirteenth century, the English barons realized and recorded in the Magna Carta the principle of balance among the distinct interests of the different estates.

The "constitutional episode" of 1730 can hardly be considered a crucial point in Russian history. The attempt to find in it some form of democratic striving seems to represent historical idealization and a search for a turning point in Russian history. But those events developed within a pattern that was rather typical of intergroup struggles for power and privilege based on gaining preemptive advantage rather than on the sharing of power. The councilors' plot can be added to a growing list of failures to move toward the realization of a culture that is compatible with the responsible exercise of power commensurate with a recognition of the political standing of others.

CATHERINE II'S GREAT EXPERIMENT

The destructive influence of Peter's reign on public morality had long-term negative consequences. The attempt by an enlightened empress to ameliorate the national cultural stereotypes by decree, on a top-down basis, was made four decades after Peter's death. Catherine II, also known as Catherine the Great, undertook that attempt at the beginning of her reign.[24]

This effort was remarkable and significant as probably one of the grandest experiments in introducing social theory directly into political practice. Serving as the basis for the experiment were the starry-eyed ideas of the French philosophers about human nature, including what they presumed to be an innate inclination of human beings to strive to be good, and the opportunity for enlightened intellectuals in alliance with an enlightened ruler to create the Good Society. Catherine was especially susceptible to these delusions because she imagined that Russia was a cultural *tabula rasa,* a kind of virgin soil for the seeds of new progressive ideas to sprout. The empress decided to act "scientifically." She summoned a special legislative commission for the elaboration of a new universal code of law. This code was to cover the spheres of constitutional, civil, and criminal law with appropriate provisions for structures and procedures. The members of the commission were drawn from two categories of people: the heads of major administrative institutions, or their representatives, and delegates elected from different social classes, including merchants and some categories of peasants. The total number of deputies chosen was 566.

Catherine also personally prepared a draft of the code *(nakaz)* to guide the commission in its proceedings. She worked on this document regularly during the morning hours for two years. About three-fourths of its contents were compiled from Montesquieu's *On the Spirit of the Laws* and Beccaria's treatise *On Crimes and Punishment.* These were considered the most current and progressive works of the time. The main idea of the nakaz was to establish the rule of law as the foundation for the whole social structure and to address the duties and responsibilities of those who governed. In other words, it expressed the idea that a state exists for the people, not the reverse. Originally the nakaz comprised 655 articles; but after "preliminary censorship" by deputies of the commission, the length of the code was reduced by half. The empress had allowed representatives of the commission to read her draft before publication and to cross out whatever items they wished to remove. The chapter concerning serfdom suffered the most: the censor-deputies struck out twenty articles on abuses by serf holders and on ways to liberate serfs. The cleansing eliminated many "liberal" provisions; but the code still included many innovations that posed a challenge to the Russian system-centered tradition. Such innovations were made, for example, in the fields of criminal investigation and court trials and in provisions for religious tolerance. The code was published after deletions and revisions by the commission.

All of this was absolutely new for Russian society. The first reaction was emotional. The society experienced a type of sentimental pathos. People wept when they met the empress, they wept during official dinners, they wept during the reading of her manifests and the nakaz. These were political tears of joy and hope that the terrible past would never return. For the first time in Russian history, the supreme authority addressed people not like slaves but like free people who could fashion their own lives, and she invited them to cooperate in the hard work of social construction.

One more sentiment was also expressed by the deputies—servility. After the first sessions, they begged Catherine to adopt the title of "the Great, Wise Mother of the Fatherland." Her initial reaction was negative. She declared that she had called upon them to make the law for the Russian Empire, not to compliment her for her qualities. But later she could no longer resist these temptations. When the time for practical discussions came, sentimental and servile feelings yielded to primitive egoistic struggles for narrow group interests, for the expansion of group privileges, and for favorable solutions to practical questions of group interests. The deputies of the commission revealed themselves as absolutely unprepared to consider such provisions in light of the common public good. The members of different social classes proved to be irreconcilable in their aspirations and wishes.

The most discouraging aspect of Catherine's effort to formulate a just code of law was the almost total opposition to the abolition of serfdom. The gentry considered serfs to be their assets, which should not be lost—they should be defended against any challenge and, if possible, increased by way of any opportunity. The representatives of other classes also expressed claims to gain their share of such assets. Cossacks, merchants, and even the clergy demanded rights to possess serfs on their estates. Behind a screen of sophisticated demagoguery, a shameless effort to gain the opportunity to hold slaves prevailed! On other points the legislative commission, as a constitutional convention, was not able to achieve any substantial progress. The effort proved to be a complete failure.

The empress retreated from her original intention of giving the country a sort of constitution in the form of a just and rational code of law. She realized the public mood that prevailed and the risk that faced her if she persisted. She preferred to turn to other, less dangerous ways of realizing the image of the Great Empress and Wise Mother of the Fatherland. She conducted long-term, intensive correspondence with Diderot, Voltaire, and other French philosophers in which she spoke of her achievements in improving the people's life and of her own "purely Republican soul." She arranged her court in a refined French style and took some superficial liberal steps in politics; but the promise of revolutionary reform was forgotten.

Moreover, the milieu gradually corrupted her. Step by step, she began to take recourse in traditional autocratic methods of rule. She also accommodated public policies to the serf-gathering aspirations of the gentry, and as a result, by the end of her reign the overwhelming majority of country's population—the peasantry—found themselves even move enslaved than when she became empress. The attempt to remake egoistic lackeys into free people with a sense of civic responsibility had failed. And we can repeat once more our refrain about lost opportunity. What the empress had proposed was rejected by the society!

Russian society, however, had modified its image of Europe. We can see a basic shift during this period from one extreme, complete repudiation of all alien influences, to the opposite end of the scale, indiscriminate acceptance of everything that came from the West. Many superficial observers described this phenomenon as a true break in Russian cultural perspectives. For that reason there are great ambiguities in Russian historical literature. But our main guides in this period of Russian history are Kliuchevsky and some other serious analysts who shared his conclusions. They realized that the only change that had taken place was in the thinking among the gentry. *In their deep ethical and psychological foundations, the gentry, not to mention the other classes, retained their traditional system-centered perspectives.*

> As the dvorianstvo [gentry, nobility] entered upon a process of being relieved of compulsory service (in 1762) and scented the approaching of liberty, they felt a need to fill the void of leisure with the fruits of intellectual and moral labor which others had produced, of borrowing the flowers of culture for which that class had itself lacked the material. So more and more there grew amongst that class a demand for a life of elegance, for aesthetic interests... France's fashions, clothiers, manners, and tongue came to permeate dvorian society, and to serve as adornments to dvorian existence. . . . As a result, the nobleman became a gentleman for whom anything Russian had no existence, or only an existence that served as a butt for ridicule. . . In fact, he wished to remain wholly ignorant of Russia.[25]

In one comedy of that time, such gentlemen talked about the empress's nakaz in the following way: "What strange beast is that? Of Russia's laws I desire to know nothing whatever. Oh, that I did not know even the Russian tongue! How vile a speech it is! Whence comes I to have been born a Russian at all!"[26]

During Catherine's reign, the education of the gentry expanded beyond questions of fashionable dress and salon etiquette. It comprised French literature as well. But the ideas of French social philosophers remained abstractions that did not correlate in any way with the gentry's native experience and, thus, did not help people to formulate positive, practical ideas as explanations for their own actions and deeds. Kliuchevsky depicted a typical representative of that "lost generation" in the following way: "With some book of Voltaire's in hand, he ended his days in his Muscovite, or his manorial, study. Truly he presented a strange phenomenon, seeing that his every manner, his every habit, his every taste, his every sympathy, his every faculty, even to his speech was a thing alien, imported. At home, devoid of any living, organic ties with his surroundings, he saw himself left with absolutely nothing to do in the world. And though, as he was a stranger amongst his own [people], he strove to become his own [self] amongst strangers . . . European society always looked upon him as an immigrant, as a Tartar in disguise, even as his people in Russia looked upon him as a Frenchman born upon Russian territory. Much tragedy was bound up with his position as a nondescript, historical superfluity."[27]

However, this horrible gap between the world of the mind and life in the flesh was filled in one way or other. The mechanism of psychological defense worked itself out most frequently in the direction of isolation of the different spheres of life—separation of speculative philosophy and morality, on the one hand, from "practice" on the other; of commentary from real behavior; salon form everyday mores; ideology from reality. As Kliuchevsky notes: "Liberalism of that sort was neither bound to anything nor taught anything. There always lurked behind the new words, behind the new tastes and ideas, the old harshness and crudity of civic and moral consciousness." As an extreme, pathological example of this pseudo-unification of antagonistic principles in one person, we have the example of a poet and top provincial official, Struiski, who "was an almost fanatically enthusiastic jurist, when, in judging his peasants, did so in strict accordance with the jurisprudential rules of Europe by both reading the act of indictment, and delivering the speech for the defense. But, unfortunately, this highly civilized jurisprudential routine was accompanied with a purely Russian, barbaric method of interrogation. That is to say, torture. And in his cellars, to that end, Struiski kept a regular arsenal of instruments of torture. He was a true son of Catherine's age."[28]

THE EMERGENCE OF A NEW ORIENTATION

This picture leaves a rather sad impression and does not appear to offer much promise for the immediate future. But the grandchildren of Catherine's gentry entered the Senate Square in December, 1825, in the first heroic effort—and most tragic attempt in all of Russian history—to struggle not for group or caste but for common civic interests. Hence I see historical merit in Catherine II's contribution to the process of transforming the traditional Russian mental orientation in a significant part of society.

Within educated circles in Russian, some people did adopt true person-centered principles: Panin, Radishchev, and Fonvisin are examples of this new ethical phenomenon. The positive historical meaning of eighteenth-century Russia was, to my mind, the shattering of the traditional orientation toward stability and unquestioning obedience as the highest values and the resulting *formation of the ethical and psychological preconditions for possible changes in the future.* Some significant persons who adhered to individualistic values emerged in the society. But they lacked other crucial components of a reformist program: skills and experience in republican rule and self-governance. This gap continued to reveal itself later in many bitter experiences during the nineteenth century.[29]

CHAPTER FOUR

Romantic Decembrists and Pessimistic Philosophers

The Dualism of the First Generation Russian Intelligentsia

The second half of the reign of Alexander I (1801–25), from the end of the Napoleonic wars and until Alexander's death at the end of 1825, had been marked by a rather new phenomenon in Russian political life—the emergence of a relatively broad anti-autocratic movement, inspired at least partially by liberal ideals. It originated mainly among officers in the Imperial Guards who had marched across Europe in the campaign against Napoleon and reached Paris on the first day of 1814. Most of these people belonged to high social classes. In the beginning it was mostly a moral movement for peaceful, gradual change, despite taking the organizational form of secret societies. They were secret mostly in name, at least in the capital; in 1822 the Tsar issued a decree imposing a special ban on state servants taking part in these quasi-secret societies. This peculiarity had been influenced by the tradition of Masonic Lodges. However, the movement turned soon to the elaboration of constitutional projects that under an autocratic regime by definition amounted to antigovernmental action. It subdivided into more moderate northern and more radical southern societies. But the course of events would bring all movements together in an attempt at immediate violent resolution. Alexander's sudden death triggered a coup on December 14, 1825.

Ill-prepared, it was doomed to defeat by the new emperor, Nicholas I. The coup scared him and resulted in a conservative line for his thirty-year reign. Our point, though, is not events or politics but the moral meaning and consequences of Decembrist movement.[1]

Mikhail Lunin was probably the most analytical participant in the Decembrist movement. A collection of his letters written to his sister contains profound analytical reflections. He wrote in one of these that the spiritual revival of a nation must precede any changes in the political order if that new order is to be stable and fruitful. In principle, I am not inclined to underestimate the role of political institutions. But in considering the Russian case, I presume that the place of spiritual revival is one of the key features that must precede reform. In any event, we Russians still pay an incredibly high price for neglecting the priority of spiritual revival. Lunin's precept was both the key lesson learned through bitter experience and a philosophical comprehension of the role played by the first generation of person-centered Russian thinkers in the drama of Russian history.

This generation appeared in Russian public life during the first decade of the nineteenth century. The process of shattering the anticivic, traditional system of moral values and orientations, which had begun two centuries before, started then to produce positive but tragic results. The main social product of this process was the so-called gentry intelligentsia.[2]

In principle, an intelligentsia should not be identified with the people who adopt a person-centered consciousness. In modern Western countries, for example, such notions permeate varied segments of society. In some countries, the person-centered consciousness prevails among all social strata. In other words, a person-centered individual need not be an intellectual in social status. Moreover, intellectual capabilities have often been used within a system-centered scale of values, as we shall see later. But among the first generation of the Russian intelligentsia, the preeminent intellects were strongly person-centered. What were the prerequisites for the emergence of this new species of people from the inhospitable soil of Russian sociopolitical life?

A SPIRITUAL AWAKENING

Among the objective factors, *the freedom of the gentry* was the most significant. The Decree of 1762 emancipated them from compulsory service to the state and, in spite of the anecdotal circumstances of its appearance, created important long-term consequences. For the first time in Russian history, *an estate emerged that was protected by law from state arbitrariness.* This became the base of an aristocracy relatively independent from the state and thus politically free. Tocqueville considered this condition to be crucial for the social progress of feudal society. The Decree of 1762 also banned corporal punishment for members of the gentry. Thus by the first decade of the nineteenth century, two "unflogged" generations of nobility had created a social milieu with a well-developed sense of its own dignity—the generation of Pushkin and his contemporaries.

The second objective factor was the *success of enlightenment.* The country had long had serious troubles because people resisted education. Under Peter's rule, the excuse emerged that Russians were too lazy and, for that reason, were incapable of being educated. This idea no longer applied when people were free to decide where to invest their energies. By the end of the eighteenth century, the Russian gentry had recognized the utility of education. Next, during the reign of Alexander I, an operating system of education emerged, following steps taken by his mother, Catherine the Great. This system soon began to bear fruit.

The most important subjective factor was the gradual *development of the capacity to penetrate superficial aspects of European culture and to appreciate its core in a philosophical and spiritual sense.* Instead of noncritical, eclectic imitations of Western civilization, a deeper analytical understanding of Western realities arose. Moreover, the intelligentsia began to view some European and American experiences as suggestions for the reform of the Russian culture and way of life. These circumstances indicate the principal difference in basic values and orientations between the thinking Russians of Catherine's and those of Alexander's generation. While the Voltaireans of Catherine's era had looked for ways to escape from Russian reality, their children considered their main task to be the *transformation* of a genuinely Russian way of life, rather than its rejection. "So this was where the historical difference between the Decembrists' generation and the generation of their fathers lay: whereas those fathers had been Russians educated to become Frenchmen, the fathers' sons were French-educated men longing to become Russians."[3] What were the practical implications that followed from this shift in orientation?

As we have seen, a long tradition existed in Russia whereby people who could not be reconciled to servitude sought to escape. Depending on the circumstances, they became Cossacks, emigrated to Europe, imitated European life at home within their own circle, or escaped by an internal spiritual retreat. These escapist behaviors had been reproduced by succeeding generations. But the new generation of Pushkin and his contemporaries sought to remake the Russian way of life.

Peter Chaadaev, one of the most productive intellectuals and outstanding persons in the first half of the nineteenth century, was the embodiment of this "way from Russia to Russia through Paris." A. Lebedev, one of Chaadaev's biographers, has suggested that Chaadaev was the first Russian who really comprehended the Western modus vivendi and pattern of social order; and who, equipped with this knowledge, found his own way back to Russia. His contemporaries grasped Chaadaev's insights instinctively and appreciated his presence among them.[4] It seems to me, however, that this was not exceptional but characteristic for Chaadaev's generation, particularly among so-called secret societies during Alexander's reign. Those societies mainly comprised people who shared the cultural aspirations of that generation.

V. Kukhelbeker, for instance, was a representative member of that generation. Before he became a Decembrist, he made a long journey to Europe and kept an interesting traveler's diary. Every page of this diary is full of feelings of deep curiosity and, frequently, admiration for the spiritual heritage of Europe. However, he wrote in a letter from Dresden: "You can imagine, my friends, how often I visit M . . . and can understand that we talk only and solely about Russia, and we are never satiated with these talks; the current condition of our fatherland, the measures which the government undertakes for removal of some abuses, the warm faith in Providence, the heartfelt conviction that Holy Russia will achieve the highest degree of prosperity, . . . that Heaven determined Russians to become a great and beneficial phenomenon in the moral world, all that makes our conversations so vivid and warm."[5]

This fragment shows us that the author's friends and contemporaries were not surprised that two Russians meeting abroad should speak about the destiny of Russia as their most important personal concern. However, it is difficult to imagine their parents spending time in Europe in this way. This change can be defined briefly: the better part of Russian nobility had morally and psychologically made a considerable shift from the role of subjects to the role of citizens in their country. Yes, they still lacked political rights, but they had acquired a feeling of personal responsibility for improvement of the social and political order in their own country.

Some external circumstances were also conducive to this shift. During the war against Napoleon, the Russian army had twice crossed the whole of Europe. Thus, many young Russians had the opportunity to observe, compare, and consider. At the same time, their gains through victory and their sense that their role in that war was morally right allowed them, unlike their fathers, to view themselves in Europe not as poor provincials who had come to the capital city from some God-forsaken place but as noble partners among European nations whom they had liberated from a despot. The French invasion and related events cured Russian society of its uncritical Francophilia—the typical Russian affliction of Catherine's age.

This new sense of patriotism became another important subjective factor in Russian cultural life and especially in political life. For the first time, *patriotism became distinct from loyalty to a dynasty,* from personal deference to an august regal personage and to royal authorities. Patriotism was transformed into a feeling of duties to the people of a nation, to the country, in the civic, humanistic sense of these words. Patriotism was no longer a synonym for servile obedient allegiance to the empire or the state. The process of "de-subjectization" or "de-estatization" of personality and of becoming citizens in a civic culture and civil society had begun.

Consequently, the patriotic hurrah began to yield to patriotic grief; Russian reality gave many more reasons for grief than for joy. These feelings of pain and offense with regard to one's own country were particularly felt by army officers—participants in a great patriotic war who returned to Russia from France full of impressions about the European way of life. The Decembrist Ivan Yakushkin, for example, remembered many years later his extremely negative emotions when he had just returned to his native land; the police cruelly beat people who tried to approach the troops, and the respected Tsar Alexander charged with the cutting edge of his drawn sword when a peasant crossed the line of march in front of his horse.[6]

A remarkable symptom of the de-estatization of personal aspirations was the widespread rejection of official careers. Paradoxically, that step was taken by people whose outstanding talents opened excellent prospects for an official career. Their rejection of state service was not a form of escapism. This generation of gentry was not at all lazy. Resignations were motivated by just the opposite impulse—to be free from state service and to promote the public good in other ways.

Lunin, for instance, commented about his personal decision to resign from an official position in the following way: "Only one kind of career is opened for me—the career of freedom. None of the titles, even the highest ones, make sense for that. You're telling me that I have considerable talents and want me to bury it in some office for the vainglorious desire to get ranks and orders which Frenchmen truly call "crachat" [spittle]. . . . I do not wish to be dependent on my official position; I'll serve people by the way my mind and heart inspires me."[7]

Chaadaev recalled two motivations for his resignation: a wish to shock the authorities by rejecting their favors and perquisites ("toys"), and his intention to pursue his "true ambitions." Thus, he undertook constant intensive intellectual work in search of the deeper meaning of Russian history and reality. By his understanding of his patriotic duty, Chaadaev renounced biological, irrational, obedient servitude to a native country; he gave "love of truth" a higher priority than "love of fatherland."

At the beginning of the nineteenth century, one of the important factors forming the conscience of Russian intellectuals was a Roman Catholic influence.[8] A few years before, at the beginning of the French Revolution and the Reign of Terror, French political emigrants had poured into Russia. Many of them belonged to the French clergy, who refused to become state functionaries and take an oath of allegiance to the state as a prerequisite for priesthood. The gentry emigrants also brought with them strong spiritual impulses. Most of them earned their keep as tutors, educating the children of the Russian nobility. As a result, Catholic teachings about the autonomy of the spiritual realm were disseminated among members of the new generation of Russian high society. Certainly, these tutors never presumed that they were preparing the conditions for a Russian revolution led by the gentry. Their political attitudes were firmly conservative. But regardless of their intentions, they inculcated in the minds of their pupils the traditions of ecclesiastical independence from secular authority, traditions of resistance to the unjust actions of rulers, and the *general spirit of an individualistic, semi-person-centered orientation in public affairs.* Above all, education in the Catholic boarding school on the Fontanka River in St. Petersburg offered a high quality, purely intellectual training analogous to that offered by the nuns of Port Royal in France. Many future Decembrists learned at this school never to indulge their brains in leisurely idleness; they acquired the habit of doing intensive intellectual work. This combination of analytically minded individuality and Russian reality created a bitter cognitive dissonance and an explosive mixture of radical ideas and aspirations. The way that conservative French Catholicism became a source of a revolutionary movement on Russian soil is thus paradoxical.

The challenge of the Napoleonic wars created the time and opportunity for the emergence in Russia of an intelligentsia based on individualistic principles. This group was the sole bearer of person-centered values and attitudes for several decades. Let us briefly repeat the basic premises that caused the formation of this first generation of person-centered Russian thinkers: (1) the gentry had acquired freedom from compulsory state service and corporal punishment; (2) an infusion of Enlightenment philosophy; (3) an analytical understanding of the core of European civilization and a readiness to use it to reform the Russian social order; (4) an overcoming of uncritical Francophilia; (5) an elaboration of the idea of patriotism as devotion to a society instead of to the state; and, consequently, (6) a love of the homeland shown by a bitter rejection of servile traits in Russian society.

THE MORAL QUALITIES OF THE DECEMBRIST MOVEMENT

Now let us examine the principal moral qualities of those people who made this basic challenge to the dominant Russian system-centered tradition. I assume a familiarity with the major historical events that accompanied the Decembrists' movement and hence focus largely on its conceptual aspects.

First, the orientation of the *Decembrists was a generous wish to help their compatriots improve their conditions of life by somehow using a principle of freedom that served the common good.* They had different opinions about how to pursue their goal, but we are concerned with the spirit of this movement rather than with specific political proposals.

The Decembrists' bedrock was intellectual autonomy. It served as an integrative base for a whole movement, which was rather controversial and eclectic in all other respects. Yakushkin, for example, wrote: "At that time a free expression of mind was an essential feature not only for a decent person, but also for those who wanted to reveal themselves as decent persons."[9] What had been a rare exception beforehand became a standard *conditio sine qua non* for this generation. The Russian authorities failed to understand the changes that had occurred. By their old police habits, they looked for a single conspiratorial source of the "poison" but achieved a discouraging response. When Lunin was asked during interrogation after the failed Decembrist coup d'état "from what time and from where he borrowed his free-thinking manners," he responded: "The free way of thought emerged in me since I began to think; a simple common sense promoted it."[10]

Further, this orientation was not limited to pleasant chats and intentions. It manifested itself in a readiness to act, to devote one's life in service to social ideals. *These incentives had an altruistic, self-sacrificing character,* which occurs only infrequently in history. The egoistic councilors of 1730 had wanted to extend their influence and to occupy some warm seats in government offices as the prize of victory from the new order. But the Decembrists were ready to lose everything—positions in society, serfs, incomes, etc.—for the common good. Vanity was not a significant incentive for them. They never expected to survive until the time when their efforts would bear fruit. They appealed to one another for the "patience of decades and centuries," and later most of them realized that they were doomed when some joined the attempted coup d'etat at the Senate Square beside the Tsar's palace in December, 1825. Without regret, they voluntarily and deliberately sacrificed themselves. When M. Fonvizin, for example, left Siberia after thirty years in prison and exile, just one year before he died, he bowed from the waist in deep respect to I. Yakushkin, who had recruited him to the Union of Salvation almost four decades before and had therefore determined his future course—a life full of deprivations. The Decembrists tried to show mercy, moral improvement, and virtue throughout their personal lives, in whatever circumstance they found themselves.

Their moral commitments played a tragic role during the investigations of the Decembrists' plot. These people, with all their indecisiveness and hesitations, *were incapable of moral compromises,* and this extended even to concealing the truth to achieve some tactical advantages. They supposed that to lie, even to their investigators, for their own or their comrades' salvation was incompatible with their personal integrity. Kukhelbeker, for instance, wrote: "It seems to me dishonest even in a civil sense to manifest yourself like a supporter of a certain doctrine and, at the same time, to be the enemy of it."[11] The investigators, operating by a different moral code, skillfully exploited this trait of the Decembrists as a way to obtain more information and to reveal other participants in the plot. Only a few of the plotters chose a line of behavior more appropriate to the circumstances but contrary to their chivalrous principles.

To judge the morality of the Decembrists correctly, we must consider that most of them belonged to the highest levels of Russian society. They surpassed their fathers and brothers in many respects but still felt themselves to be of the very social structure that they sought to undermine. "We" were not separate from "they." That reason also influenced their behavior during the investigations. Ironically, these officers of the Guards, who would normally have been among the most conservative supporters of the regime, proved to be members of the most liberal part of society. They had a clear person-centered orientation in favor of radical changes in the closed society's status quo. Against the general background of Russian social history, the Decembrist movement seemed like serious discord, but it stirred widespread sympathy.

In the previous centuries, there was only one other case of mass ideological opposition to the dominant state ideology. That was the Old Believers' movement. But that analogy is valid only in a very limited sense because the Old Believers were super-system-centered and anti-Western in their values and style of thought. They were extreme traditionalists compared to the ruling authorities. The split in that case divided two different branches of anti-person-centeredness—ultra-conservatives from and moderate conservatives. But at the beginning of the nineteenth century, the liberal movement challenged all system-centered traditions and principles. For this reason, the Decembrist movement can be considered a *counterculture* in a genuine sense of that term.

Ironically, this counterculture was first associated with Masonic Lodges, surfaced next in officers' meetings, and was then gradually transformed into secret societies. The foundation of the Decembrists' social philosophy was the utopian idea, rather typical during that era, that political arrangements were the key factor in determining the character of social life. From that point of view, political change could be achieved by direct action. The movement presumed that the violent removal of tyrannical rule could alone produce a new and just social order.

It was hard for unaffiliated contemporaries of the December 14 Movement to comprehend its genuine sense, because the core members disguised themselves in Guard uniforms to attempt a coup d'état in favor of a definite successor to the crown. In the history of Russian court life, that was a quasinormal thing to do. But in fact, this coup attempt differed radically from earlier palace revolutions. Its purpose was not merely to enthrone some particular person. The Decembrists motto "For Great

Prince Constantine and his spouse the Constitution" was addressed to soldiers but had been designed to establish a new social order implied by the term *constitution.*

The term *Decembrist* is usually associated with the last phases of this movement—the decision to begin an open revolt; the tragedy at the Senate Square; and the subsequent investigations, executions, and exile (the "Siberian period"). Much less attention is given to the early, constructive stages of the movement, when its members were not yet obsessed with ideas of regicide and immediate revolution. For our purposes, this earlier period is much more important. The early secret societies mainly concentrated on moral, not political, questions. They conceived of themselves as fraternities of free persons who sought to advance enlightenment about the ethical aspects of social relationships.

Mikhail Lunin, one of the most striking personalities of his generation, provides us with testimony from his own experience. In his analysis made about fifteen years after 1825, he wrote:

> The process of enlightenment was stimulated by the new principles which the Secret Society introduced into public thinking. It dissipated the almost universal belief that no other order of things was possible, and brought the mass of the people to an awareness of the need to replace subordination to others with obedience to the law. It sought to demonstrate the advantages of mutual responsibility, i.e., mutual guarantee, which makes the cause of each the cause of all; the importance of trial by jury in civil and criminal cases, and its essential link with civil liberties; the need for unrestricted publicity. . . . The Secret Societies moved from facts to law, pointing to the limitations placed by Providence on any power: morality, intelligence, jurisprudence and the common weal—diverse manifestations of the same truth. . . . To achieve these ends it appealed to all the classes, and they understood the language it spoke. . . . They prepared a new path of improvement for future generations; they directed the people's aspirations to the common benefit. . . . The Secret Society met all these conditions in terms of the basis of its organization, its aims and its methods. The moral stimulus generated by its ideas was so powerful that Emperor Alexander felt it necessary to promise that he would grant the Russians a constitution as soon as they were capable of judging its merits.[12]

That was the original approach of the early Decembrists.

The members of the Secret Societies not only considered and dreamed but also acted. Some army officers, for example, systematically and intensively worked on the education of their soldiers. Some of them organized the collection of food for victims of famine in the Smolensk region in 1818, saving thousands of lives by acting outside the administrative channels of the government. Many future Decembrists worked to improve conditions of life for their serfs and to modernize their economies.

But unfortunately, the violent faction prevailed within the movement. The circumstances, mainly the sudden death of Tsar Alexander, encouraged the radical faction to rebel. This brief impulsive uprising preemptively misrepresented the movement as a whole, and it was easily suppressed.

DESTRUCTION AND SURVIVAL

Unsuccessful revolts usually unleash hands that exercise repressions on behalf of despotic power and, therefore, often reinforce the worst tendencies of autocratic authority. The Bronze Horseman is a monument to Peter in Petersburg that symbolizes the autocratic character of the Russian monarchy. Immortalized in Pushkin's poem, "The Bronze Horseman," the instinct of self-preservation urges the horseman to trample offshoots of the mortally dangerous person-centered plant.

In Pushkin's poem, as in Russia after 1825, those mad enough to challenge the "grim tsar" are pursued by the implacable bronze rider on his terrible bronze horse through the long night, with no place to hide and no one to help them. The bronze horseman becomes a force of nature, the clash and clang of metal hooves sound like thunder, the extended hand of the raging horseman strikes like a lightening bolt. The inept romantic challenge to authority ends in a futile gesture against the reality of autocratic authority.[13]

To criticize these noble, altruistic people is a sensitive and morally difficult task. Above all, they were the first to challenge the Russian autocracy as a system. They bequeathed a patriotic sense of civic spirit to the following generations. But we should not neglect the tragic consequences of the December uprising—the defeat of the entire reform movement and the discrediting of liberal philosophy by a conspiracy to commit regicide. A chivalric drama performed on the St. Petersburg stage during one cold December day became a tragedy for the country.

The opportunity for changing Russian history by choosing a person-centered road had failed again. As on previous occasions, one cannot blame anyone for this, because the necessary preconditions for success did not exist then. Substantial groups were not prepared to champion a person-centered consciousness. But Russia had now developed elements essential for modernization in the form of human capital that could be nurtured for the future. The chief actors in the Decembrists' plot gambled with this capital despite their understanding that the chances to win were minimal, and they lost. It is painful to call them "guilty" of failure; but they bear that historical burden.

The December uprising created a profound social tremor. The society was frightened and paralyzed, its best part was repressed, persecuted, or at least cast under suspicion. As Alexander Herzen wrote much later: "The tone of society changed before one's eyes; and this rapid moral deterioration was a melancholy proof of how little the sense of personal dignity had developed among Russian aristocrats. Except for women, nobody dared to show sympathy or to utter a warm word about friends or relations whose hands they had shaken only the day before police carried them off by night. On the contrary, there were savage fanatics for slavery, some from motives of abjectness, others, still worse, for disinterested reasons."[14]

The Russian poet Fedor Tiutchev expressed exactly the mood that prevailed at the time when he declared that it was "Autocracy that depraved you, / And you have perished on its sword." The law could not save the Decembrists in a land where the people denounced them as "vicious traitors," cursed their names, and consigned their very memory to oblivion. Their reckless effort to overturn Russian autocracy failed and their gesture proved futile, as ineffective as trying to thaw the hard ground during a Russian winter with the steaming blood of martyrs.[15]

As the hands of the historical clock turned back to the eighteenth century, person-centeredness in Russia was utterly destroyed. "Russia seemed to continue to stay where it was, even to move backwards, but in fact everything had assumed a new form, questions became more complex, and decisions less simple. On the surface of official Russia, the 'Empire of Appearances' prevailed while only losses, harsh reaction, inhuman persecution, the intensification of despotism, occurred . . . Barracks and bureaucracy became the mainstays of the political system under Nicholas I. Blind, senseless discipline was combined with soulless official formalism—such were the springs of the famous mechanism of strong power in Russia. . . . In a word, the picture of official Russia inspired only despair."[16]

The impressions of a French traveler through Russia, the Marquis de Custine, are most revealing. Custine's main idea was that Russia essentially is an Asiatic despotism camouflaged in European forms and therefore even more dangerous. His book contains a number of observations and generalizations that should interest anyone who tries to comprehend the meaning of Russian history. Alexander Herzen judged it to be the most entertaining and enlightening study ever written by a foreigner about Russia. This book is available to English readers in several editions. I prefer the earliest one.[17]

I first read Custine's *Russia* several years before the end of the Brezhnev era and felt that I had found a clue to the enigma of Russian history. Since then, I have grown more cautious and moderate in my judgments: I am now more confident that Russia is much more than a "nation of slaves," as Custine supposed. I was also discouraged by the many similarities in the attitudes and patterns of behavior among the people of despotic pre-Communist Russia and the Communist USSR and those among the people in free Western countries.

It is important to reflect on a couple of Custine's key observations: "The movements of the men whom I met were stiff and constrained; every gesture expressed a will which was not their own. The morning is the time for commissions and errands, and not one individual appeared to be walking on his own account . . . everything was dull and regular as in a barrack. Military discipline reigns throughout Russia," he wrote. Later he concluded: "It is to Russia that we must go in order to see the results of this terrible combination of the mind and science of Europe with the genius of Asia—a combination which is so much the more formidable as it is likely to last."[18]

Custine supposed that the main instrument to achieve that "barrack spirit" of everybody's submission was the table of ranks introduced in Russia by Peter. "When Peter the Great established what is here called the *tchinn* [rank], that is to say, when he applied the military system to the general administration of the empire, he changed his nation into a regiment of mutes, of which he declared himself and his successors the hereditary colonels . . . the *tchinn* is the galvanism, the apparent life, of souls and bodies here—the passion which survives all other passions. . . . The *tchinn* is a nation formed into a regiment; it is the military system applied to all classes of society, even to those which never go to war. In short, it is the division of the civil population into ranks, which correspond to ranks in the army. . . Thus it is that Russia has become a regiment of sixty millions strong; and this is the *tchinn*—the mightiest achievement of Peter."[19]

Custine's book was quite popular in the Soviet Union, at least among the intelligentsia in the capital cities. The most important reason was Custine's formulation of the totalitarian conception of society, which prevailed during the reign of Nicholas I. It was true; but only part of the truth.

Custine described Russia as a "country of facades." But he did not observe another Russia that survived behind the facades. Behind this complete and "perfect" despotism marked by humiliated and obedient people, he did not see the antidespotic counterculture, which was a hidden but essential part of the Russian social and political landscape at that time. *The publicly silent, stubborn civic disobedience of the counterculture is what creates the drama of Russian political history.*

Sadly, most Russians were indifferent to the devastation of the Decembrists, the best and brightest part of the nation, who sacrificed for the nation all they had—privileges, careers, fortunes, even the destinies of their families. In Chaadaev's words, Russia responded as the "immense dumb land." According to Herzen: "In Moscow, Chaadaev used to say, every foreigner is taken to look at the great cannon and the great bell—the cannon which could never be fired and the bell which fell down before it was rung. It is a strange town in which the objects of interest are distinguished by their absurdity; or perhaps that great bell without a tongue is a hieroglyph symbolic of that immense dumb land, inhabited by a race calling themselves Slavs as though surprised at their possession of human speech."[20] (The Russian word for Slavs phonetically resembles *slovo,* which means "word.")

These characteristics contain much of the truth but again, fortunately, not all of it. What was viewed as the complete collapse of a moral-intellectual movement for modernization proved to be deceptive. Not all flashes of person-centeredness were crushed by the iron heel of despotic rule. The virus of the counterculture proved surprisingly vigorous, capable of surviving even under the most unfavorable circumstances. This was demonstrated by the destiny of the Decembrists exiled to Siberia. The social background of that vast semiwild area of the country supposedly was completely unprepared for and hostile to liberal ideals. But the Decembrists did not disappear in Siberia. Their tragic circumstances prepared them for new experiences. Most of them continued an intensive spiritual life, and they transplanted seedlings of a person-centered culture to Siberian soil. Elements of such a culture survived in less cultivated and more hardy and vigorous "wild" forms that persisted even through the Soviet era. If we inquire about the sources of the best fruits of Siberian cultural life, we find that most of them, in one way or another, have Decembrist roots.

The Russian autocracy did not manage to extirpate the person-centered spirit. It could not prevent new flashes of resistance but could only try to trample them. Paradoxically, Lunin and Chaadaev, who judged the situation pessimistically, demonstrated by their own existence and actions that person-centeredness could survive even during the gloomy and stuffy 1830s.

N. Eidelman has described Lunin thus: "Mikhail Lunin: one of the most striking personalities of his day. A wealthy landowner, fluent in many languages, a hero of several wars, immensely popular with women and a famous duelist, he was, in addition, a first-class thinker. . . . At first actively involved in conspiracy, he gradually lost faith in such methods of struggle, believing that the people were not yet ready for change, and doubtful of the wisdom of action before millions of people had demanded that things be altered. . . . He began to distance himself from conspiracy but, arrested for old sins after the rebellion, he refused to ease his own lot at the expense of his companions. On the contrary, his attitude was one of defiance, and in Siberia he kept up the fight against the autocracy: he was the only Decembrist to be condemned a second time to hard labor in Siberia, where he died under mysterious circumstances."[21] In this biography, Eidelman showed that Lunin was killed in prison by secret order of the authorities.

Why was this man—who did not take part in the uprising, who had distanced himself from plotters several years before, and who repudiated the very idea of violent rebellion against the Tsar—treated by the authorities as a most dangerous enemy of the system, even long after 1825, when many of his comrades were on the way to pardon? His major transgression lay in letters that he wrote while in prison, addressed nominally to his sister but actually "to whom it may concern." In those letters he discussed, with quiet dignity, a wide range of governmental policies. On some points, he agreed with the actions taken, but more frequently he criticized them. He did no more than openly and quietly discuss public policies. He noted once, not without bitter irony: "My nickname changed during my imprisonment and exile, and with each change it became longer. Now, in official documents, I am referred to as: "A state criminal in exile." A whole sentence accompanying my name. In England they would say: Lunin—a member of the opposition. Such, indeed, is the essence of my political significance. I took no part in the revolts typical of the mob, nor in the conspiracies appropriate to slaves. My sole weapon is my thought, sometimes in agreement and sometimes in disagreement with government policy.[22]

He deliberately suggested that "if from the depths of the Siberian wastes, our exiles were able to raise their voice, they would have the right to say to the leaders of the ruling party: 'What have you done for the good of the people in the course of these fifteen years?'"[23]

According to the standards of the autocracy, Lunin's critique constituted a shattering of the system's basic principles: a "state criminal," while in prison, dared to or pretended to perform the roles of parliament, opposition, and free press, roles that autocracy allowed nobody. The Bronze Horseman had reasons for fury. A tradition of destroying autonomous persons for the expression of their thoughts about public affairs can be traced throughout Russian history. But in the history of spirituality, Lunin's actions represent a bright beacon—evidence that a brave and devoted person can challenge brute force, demonstrating its impotence and his own moral superiority. Lunin and Chaadaev were probably the first Russians to comprehend that the sources of their nation's tragedy lay not in the despotism of Russia's rulers, nor in someone's evil intentions, but in the whole history of the country and the servile culture of its people.

Peter Chaadaev expressed this idea in an almost apocalyptic form in his "Philosophical Letters to Madam N—:

> We belong to none of the great families of mankind; we are neither of the West nor of the East, and we possess the traditions of neither. Somehow divorced from time and space, the universal education of mankind has not touched upon us. . . . That which elsewhere constitutes the foundation of society and life is for us but theory and speculation. . . . We have in our hearts none of these lessons which have preceded our own existence. . . . Our memories go no further back than yesterday; we are, as it were, strangers to ourselves. We walk through time so alone that as we advance the past escapes us forever. This is a natural result of culture based wholly on borrowing and imitation. . . . We grow,

> but we do not mature; we advance, but obliquely, that is, in a direction which does not lead to the goal. . . . We belong to that number of nations which does not seem to make up an integral part of the human race, but which exists only to teach the world some great lesson. The lesson which we are destined to give will, naturally, not be lost; but who knows when we shall find ourselves once again in the midst of humanity and what afflictions we shall experience before we accomplish our destiny? . . . They are the ideas of duty, of justice, of right, of order. They were brought forth by the very events which originated communities; they are the integral elements in the social life of these nations. Such is the atmosphere of the West; this is more than history, more than psychology; it is the physiology of a European. What have we to substitute for this in our country? . . . The whole history of modern society occurs on the level of convictions. There is, thus, a true education to be had there. Originally set up on the basis of conviction, history has gone forward only by means of thought. Convictions have always been the cause of interests, never have interests provoked convictions. All political revolutions were, in reality, moral revolutions. People searched for truth and found liberty and well-being. The phenomenon of modern society and its civilization are to be explained in these terms. Otherwise, they cannot be understood at all.[24]

I do not present these excerpts from Chaadaev's writing because I consider all his thoughts to be the ultimate truth. Some of them now seem at least questionable. I only wish to indicate that the best thinkers in Russia at that time were capable of comprehending the deeper roots of Russia's troubles better than did some of their fellow Decembrists (and better than did the social philosophers in Western Europe, who, with a couple of exceptions, were also inclined to assign the ultimate reason for human misfortunes to the wrong political institutions and despotic rulers).

Fortunately, Chaadaev was too pessimistic in his diagnosis of Russian potential. When the next generation, the people of the 1840s, came onto the historical scene, it became clear that person-centeredness had survived in Russia. These people of the 1840s were followers not of the Decembrists with their Jacobin political radicalism but rather of Chaadaev's philosophy of history.

It is noteworthy that Chaadaev, not some of the other Decembrists with their terrorist intentions, was officially declared by the Tsar to be a madman. Instinctively, the autocratic authorities realized that someone like Chaadaev was more dangerous for an autocracy than were extremists; it is much harder to counteract nonviolent resistance. Violence easily confronts violence. Nonviolent forms of action are much more difficult for state authorities than are political terrorists with bombs and political radicals with their revolutionary obsessions. Political police and the machinery of state compulsion are not designed to struggle effectively against reasonable discourse; they lack tools for that.

NEW HORIZON, OLD BURDEN

The gradual erosion of system-centered values and behavior was not interrupted by the reign of Nicholas I. He was the Decembrists' butcher. But to depict him only as a narrow-minded, one-dimensional reactionary, as many historians do, would be an oversimplification. Nicholas I followed his own conservative, detrimental but certain "code of honor"; he was predictable. He devoted his life to creating a supposedly omnipotent empire, based on strict command-and-control principles; he was Peter's successor in that respect. When his exercise of power failed the test of the Crimean war, he soon died in disgrace. Under his rule, some progress was made regarding serfdom, one of the most troubling features of Russian life. Several important laws were promulgated, but masters—"soul owners"—managed to prevent effective implementation of these. That is part of a general problem concerning the limits of obedience to despotic rulers. They cannot maintain the rule of law. This episode shows again that Russian imperial authority was sometimes more sympathetic to progress than was society as a whole, even trying occasionally to advance reforms. Most often, however, authority and society marched hand in hand.

Another interesting case of reform involves of Michail M. Speransky, who stands out as a man who championed the idea of modernizing Russian life through bureaucratic rationalization of the system. His ideas do not sound very promising today; but for the time and under the conditions of a corrupt Russian administration, his proposals had much merit. During his brief administrative career, in the first half of Alexander I's reign, he introduced a system of examinations and criteria for holding positions in state service on the basis of merit—about half a century earlier than this occurred in England, not to speak of European countries or the United States. Speransky lost the Tsar's support, "and in 1812, almost before the new central institutions . . . had been introduced, [he] was dispatched into retirement at Nizhni Novgorod, with an odor of enmity from court circles and the general public alike."[25] Having been dismissed by the "liberal" Tsar Alexander, Speransky later returned from exile and was assigned new responsibility in the government by the "reactionary" Nicholas. The system of exams for bureaucrats had by then been abolished by the new emperor (it had not worked properly under Alexander either, because under pressure from different ministries he had steadily made exceptions to it). However, a modern rational structure of government was introduced thanks to Speransky; Because of its effectiveness, it remained untouched and worked until 1917. Speransky was a genius of rationality. Thanks to him and some other talented bureaucrats, the system of administration in Russian acquired a functional efficiency and (for better or for worse) was a rather effective instrument in hands of tsars and their confidants. Speransky had a fantastic capacity for work. He managed to systematize all Russian laws promulgated since middle of the seventeenth century, and this code of laws (with additions) was a basic source for justice until 1917.[26] We shall return briefly to the topic of liberal Russian bureaucracy in the next chapter. But to change the essence of system was beyond the powers of people like Speransky. His case merely confirms the conclusion that a true reformer within a traditional structure cannot proceed consistently, even if he manages to enlist support from the very top. This support cannot be stable because it eventually collides with the basic logic of the system, which is not consistent with the rule of law.

The only group in Russia who seriously and consistently opposed the basic logic of the system was the intelligentsia, from its very appearance in the drama of history. It was the only group that championed person-centered ideals. But its spiritual isolation was the source of new tragedies. Public affairs were not openly discussed. A politics of intrigue prevailed.

In other European countries en route to social modernization, the burden of this high mission was shared, in varying proportions, among different social groups and strata, creating common bonds among them, giving them a sense of shared historical responsibility and destiny. As a result, transformations in social values were less dramatic and more successful in those countries. We illustrated this earlier with reference to the nobility in England, who continued to exercise leadership in open deliberation about public affairs. In Russia, the intelligentsia had no partners to share their burden. Times passed, generations changed; but the situation remained the same. The system-centered archetype of intrigue resisted any substantial modernization.

The intelligentsia struggled unaided to achieve the difficult task of person-centered reorientation of society. Even during the most complicated turns of Russian history, the intelligentsia persisted in the effort to treat the common good as a public affair that should be discussed openly. It is difficult to find analogies in history for the lonely heroism of the Russian intelligentsia.

This heroism of a lonely intelligentsia is marked by tragedy. Should the Russian intelligentsia share responsibility for the tragic character of Russian history? Why has it remained so isolated? Was it an unrealistic strategy to try to change Russian society so abruptly? Should the intelligentsia have been less radical and more inclined to compromises and cooperation with other social strata? These questions cannot be easily resolved.

Those who do intellectual work are engaged in critical reflection and the stimulation of innovations. Such efforts inevitably challenge authority. These conditions reach extreme proportions in traditional system-centered societies. Intellectual workers find it difficult to cooperate with despotic regimes if they wish to be honest with themselves and true to their calling. Compromise with despotism leads to the degradation of one's personality and is a form of moral suicide. Examples abound.

On the other hand, the monopolizing of opposition by one social group also contains dangerous potential—the emergence of sectarian psychology with its perverse implications. We should be careful not to reduce the phenomenon of opposition to its political aspects. Most of the Russian intelligentsia kept some formal political loyalty and sought opportunities for cooperation with the authorities in pursuit of social modernization. Their opposition was strongly ethical and psychological in nature, marked by estrangement. Both the authorities and the people sensed this moral estrangement. For this reason, they accepted the assistance of the intelligentsia reluctantly, suspiciously, and only in those spheres where cooperation could not be avoided. When intellectuals tried to extend the scope of their activities in cultural and scientific endeavors, they were sometimes harshly rebuffed. This recurrent limitation of intellectual capabilities by traditional roles of stewardship or tutelage created detrimental patterns of relationships.

If oppositional forces are not listened to and allowed to participate in resolving problems, all sides lose. *Society impoverishes itself because it rejects intellectual potentials and the development of an enlightened community of understanding.* On the other hand, if it is neglected as a partner in dialogue, oppositional thinking itself is harmed. If critical reflections among intellectuals lose contact with others and with reality, there is likely to be a loss of common understanding about many of the practical difficulties of human life. Intellectual schemes can easily become more and more simplistic—black and white—because discussions do not correct errors and stimulate innovations among the discussants. Conditions sharpening opposition can easily come into force when there is a lack of adequate channels for the legal expression of ideas and the conduct of different kinds of pursuits. Such barriers frustrate and alienate people, who become inflexible and uncooperative opponents. Intolerant, narrow-minded people come to prevail as hostile alliances confront one another and opponents become more extreme. We can observe these patterns developing during the reign of Alexander II.

CHAPTER FIVE

A Decisive Junction

The Epoch of Alexander II

■ At the end of the reign of Nicholas I, a complacent imperial mentality took a strong political slap, a humiliating defeat on its own land in the Crimean War. It was a terrible social shock. The myth of the all-powerful empire and invincible Russian army collapsed.

Every cloud has a silver lining, however. Some failures bring societies greater advantages than do victories. Victories reinforce the current state of affairs and patterns of order, but failures raise doubts and create opportunities for change. *If societies need modernization, failure serves as a catalyst for change, stimulates error-correcting capabilities, and offers healing potential.*

This can be seen after the Crimean War in Russia. The failure aroused the country. Society realized the necessity for change; and the death of the Tsar, who incarnated the stability and immutability of the regime, engendered hopes for change. This new public atmosphere stimulated an immediate burst of critical thought and rapid growth of a free, uncensored press and literature. Under conditions of a rigid political regime, I believe these factors are the necessary preconditions for the development of civic consciousness. They can be considered evidence of public receptivity to critical self-analysis. A free literature prepared the moral climate for the changes that were to follow.

THE LIBERAL AGENDA

The liberal intelligentsia stirred the awakening of Russian public life. Unfortunately, that awakening was a prelude that never materialized into a performance. The very word *liberal* became discredited in the Russian political vocabulary, first, by the pre-revolutionary Social Democrats and then by the Bolsheviks, who attached an extremely negative, pejorative meaning to that term. In general, the concept of liberalism and multifaceted discussion of different aspects of it were and still continue to be one of the central subjects of discourse in philosophical, political, historical, and economic thought. It is used in many different variations.[1] I need to make clear that we are considering a concrete phenomenon—Russian liberalism beginning in the middle of the nineteenth century.

Russian liberals were the most mature and politically advanced social group in the country. Their political thinking was characterized by deep social analyses of national life exercised by acute critics of the regime and by an openness to dialogue with any partner who was willing to consider the social modernization of the country.[2] The Russian liberals inherited the person-centered ethic of the best part of the Decembrist generation, while rejecting the negative features of their political radicalism. The liberal program sought to change the very foundations of social life and political power in the country. Let me emphasize this point: *these foundations were the source of the country's troubles*—not the political institutions, which were both perverse and derivative.

To understand this distinction, it is important to examine a classic liberal presentation, *Voices from Russia,* prepared in the country but published in England.[3] The main authors and editors of this edition were Boris Chicherin, who later became a prominent Russian scholar in law and the head of the city of Moscow's self-governing assembly, the Duma, and the historian Constantine Kavelin.

The social analyses of the liberals covered all the basic anomalies in Russian life. These included the almost libertarian position concerning freedom of speech and publication; a pervasive criticism of serfdom from economic, legal, and moral points of view; a clear articulation of the principle that the political order depended on just and free relationships among citizens; an analysis of the destruction and the estrangement of the people caused by the government; and the need for reform to escape further social and political decay beyond military defeat.

In the positive part of their program, the liberals placed their faith in the creative capacities of human individuality, expressed in the release and promotion of private initiative, because only free and interested people are capable of solving their own and their country's problems. The machinery of state bureaucracy is not capable of creativity.

Frequently, Russian liberals were stigmatized for their "flirtations" with power, for their moderate and cautious political speeches. These assertions are true; but liberals preferred to appeal to the common sense of society and, at the same time, to reason with state authorities. Their appeal was to reason expressed through discussion rather than via bombs, confrontation in noisy demonstrations, or revolutionary struggles to seize political authority. They planned to reconstruct the foundations of social and moral orders through quiet persuasion. *They rejected political radicalism and extremism as methods for solving social problems.* They supposed that the confrontation of political power, at least at the beginning of the struggle, could only bring tragedy. If the autocracy won out, a new wave of reaction from the top would inevitably follow, as after 1825. If the radicals managed to unleash a revolution, a wave of reaction would come from the bottom, because the only chance to supplant people's attitude of humility and obedience was to trigger their deep, cruel, and barbarian instincts. Therefore, the so-called liberal "fear of the people" was not caused by lack of personal courage but by a concern for the cruel syndrome of repressed obedience and latent hostile violence manifest in the national culture. Progressive principles of reasoned discussion were not deeply rooted. We know now that their worries were not in vain. The course of Russian history, unfortunately, confirmed the worst apprehensions of the liberals.

TEMPTATION OF RADICAL SOLUTIONS

Clear demarcation between liberals and radicals first occurred in the 1860s. The first accusations against the liberals occurred at that time. The pretext was the appeal of the liberals to moderation with some words of support for some aspects of the government's program. The policies of Alexander II met some of the basic measures in the liberal program, including the liberation of the serfs in 1861, the establishment of an independent judiciary through the Reform of Justice in 1864, and the creation of local self-government through the Reform of Zemstvo (local self-government bodies) in 1867. The move to liberate the serfs was truly epochal in Russian history. The Polish uprising in 1863–64, however, provoked chauvinistic feelings inside Russia. The rise of the radical movement beginning in 1862 provoked a politics of confrontation.

A political leaflet was released by those who identified themselves as "Young Russia." They drew their inspiration from the French Jacobins and proclaimed their commitment to spill more blood to overthrow the Tsar's regime. At the same time, the famous Russian revolutionary Nicholay G. Chernyshevsky proclaimed the slogan to "Call Russia to the Ax"—that is, an appeal to armed peasant riots and promotion of the idea that radicals should make reforms by physical force and should be prepared to sacrifice both constitutional forms and freedom for that purpose. In other words, freedom was only a tool to gain power; it could be used or rejected, depending on the circumstances. I believe that many of the country's future misfortunes originated at this time.

In a theoretical sense, the next step was taken by Michail A. Bakunin, the outstanding champion of anarchism and an active participant in the 1848 revolutions that occurred in several countries in Europe. He proposed to use the "hatred of people" for their "exploiters" as the road to revolution. Such a strategy depended on releasing aggressive instincts, feelings of revenge and envy—manipulating the wrong side of human nature. As a social ferment for "anarchical-social liquidation," he overtly proposed to use thieves, robbers, and the scum of society. The "revolutionary party," according to Bakunin, was determined to perform the role of being the collective organizer of these processes Bakunin's "Robin Hood" program and its seductive influence on the minds of young romantics have been briefly but clearly described and analyzed by prominent Russian thinkers including Georgiy Plekhanov.[4]

In a parallel with anarchism, another branch of radical system-centeredness grew up: socialism. The idea of seizing state power by conspiracy as a decisive step of socialist revolution had been offered by Petr Tkachev, who has been called "the first Bolshevik." As Darrell Hammer writes, "In 1876 Tkachev published a short pamphlet on 'Revolution and the State,' anticipating the book Lenin was to write on the same subject. Tkachev argued that a political revolution must come before the transformation of society: The revolutionaries must seize power before they can carry out their program. The revolution would be a conspiracy undertaken by a small group on behalf of the masses. Once in power, the new government would carry out a 'revolution from above' using the organized power of the state. Thus the immediate aim of the revolution was to seize power and create a revolutionary state. . . . Tkachev emphasized what would later be called the subjective factors in the revolution."[5] Leonard Shapiro remarked that "Tkachev provided an analysis of the art of coup d'etat."[6] The next step in elaborating the concept of the revolutionary state, realized by Lenin's party several decades later, was made by Petr Lavrov, who bridged the gap between Tsarism and the new, socialist order.[7]

It would be wrong to lump all these people and groups together. They differed in certain aspects of their political views and ideals, not to mention in their personal qualities and historic fate. But all were united in one respect: they were a radical minority of conscious revolutionaries who aimed to take command of the system and impose their will on the rest of society. They combined distrust of the masses with the doctrines of classical Marxism. That is why, from my point of view, *the revolutionary movement of the Russian radicals gave expression to traditional Russian system-centeredness, dressed in a new guise but manifest in its most extreme and ruthless form.* In the radical doctrine, the value of an individual practically amounted to nothing. Reliance on principles of destructive violence was ironically declared to be a principle of revolution. It was an overt challenge to the very spirit of European culture and a retreat from the achievements of Russian liberal thought in the nineteenth century.

In some respects, when compared to the more traditional forms of system-centeredness, this was even worse. New radicals became system-centered not by force of tradition or ignorance; they deliberately rejected the historical alternative that they knew about and that was rather well-developed by that time. We even have reasons to consider the Russian radicalism of the 1860s and 1870s a rudimentary form of the totalitarian ideology that appealed to various regions of the world a half century later. This was the main source of the attack on the moderateness of Russian liberals.

In the course of history, the radical movement intensified. The failures and persecutions of the revolutionaries only reinforced their commitment, making them more alert and skillful. Radical ideology looked attractive, especially to the young and semieducated. It contained everything dreams are made of: the romance of conspiracy and mystery, feelings of personal involvement in "making history," opportunities for direct action, hopes for prompt results, and simplicity of the doctrine distinguishing "good" from "evil." The way to do good was made clear, and there was the illusion of a back-to-one's-roots movement intended to purify, to restore healthy principles of life freed from distortions supposedly imposed from the outside. In fact, this possibility presumed to reconstruct the original form of the Golden Age in a system-centered way of life, restored to healthy morality by purification from the distortions of Imperial morality. These fantasies arose not only in Russia but also in many other countries of Europe and in the Americas.

The radicalism was well camouflaged but, in its essence, it was no more than radical conservatism. Yet at that time, the illusion of revolutionary change prevailed. Even liberals, who warned against this danger, could hardly realize the full depth of the abyss into which radicalism sought to push society. The liberals were neglected. Their appeals did not reach the ears of official Russia. The authorities responded to the outbursts of the radicals in the standard way—by police repression. Officials did not realize that final victory over the radicals could be achieved only by removing the social anomalies and injustices that fed and supported radicalism. They perceived that essential changes would undermine their own positions of authority. Position holders of all ranks were not willing to make that sacrifice. Rather than losing their privileges, they preferred to place the social order at risk. At a subconscious level, the established position holders felt that the radicals, with all their bombs and threats to destroy the state, were still less dangerous for the foundations of order than were the liberals. Radicals sought to create some new version of the same system-centered order. Combating bombs and violence was familiar ground for state officials, but they could not cope with reasoned arguments. The liberal program, in spite of its seeming moderation, sought to alter this very foundation of Russian culture and to implant a new person-centered character type and way of life.

Unfortunately, this did not happen. The top officials of the regime did not prove flexible enough; and pressure from liberal circles proved too weak. On occasion, the regime manifested sufficient decisiveness to make a commitment, as in the case of the abolition of serfdom. But in most cases, the actions of Alexander II's government were slack, indecisive, and frequently inconsequential, as in the case of the local self-government reform of 1864 and the following "counter-reforms."

PAN-SLAVIC DREAMS AND AMBITIONS

The other players on the stage of the Russian political drama during the reign of Alexander II were associated with the Slavophile movement.

Emotionally this movement stimulated positive feelings and warmed the hearts of Russians. Analytically, it becomes obvious that in terms of the dynamics of ideas, the Slavophile surge was nothing more than a conservative intellectual reaction to the threat of expansion on the part of the "corrupt" Western way of life—that is, the person-centered way of life. The essence of this reaction is covered by romantic illusions of back-to-nature sentiments, originally peaceful but potentially aggressive.[8] Depending on the circumstances, this potential for nationalism can be activated and directed against both external and domestic enemies. The articulation of nationalism is a way to force confrontation between different types of national entities, to place all of "us" against "them." These strategies were rather typical in nineteenth-century Europe, causing European nations more troubles and tragedies than gains. The best known and most tragic in its consequences, but far from the only example of initially rather peaceful, romantic patriotism evolving into xenophobic nationalism was development of the Sturm und Drang concept toward pan-Germanism and, much later, its transformation to extreme form—Nazism.

In the Russian case, this nationalist attitude manifested itself in the transformation of peaceful, romantic Slavophile sentiment, emphasizing the cultural ties of language communities, into messianic and aggressive Pan-Slavism with its efforts to support Russian imperial claims to the "Byzantine legacy," to Constantinople, to the Bosporus, and to the unification all Slavic peoples under Russian rule. The expression of these aspirations is found in the works of two outstanding Russian thinkers during the reign of Alexander II. One was the philosopher Nikolay Danilevsky (1822–85), and the other was the writer Feodor Dostoevski (1821–81). Danilevsky was the author of the famous *Russia and Europe,* first published in 1869. Some important literary and scientific achievements are expressed in this book. For example, Danilevsky classified all the world civilizations in accordance with a rather well-developed system of cultural and historical criteria and formulated a theory of historical cycles much earlier than Arnold Toynbee, who advanced a similar theory. He also formulated a theory of cultural development from a simple, one-dimensional cultural type to more complicated, multifaceted ones. In some of his systemic considerations, he also anticipated the discoveries of later generations. Moreover, he wrote about the "common treasury" of humankind, a sort of world cultural bank into which the various civilizations deposited their important achievements: artistic accomplishments; scientific laws; and political, economic, and social developments.[9] He placed a high value on universal human achievements.

Paradoxically, he was also strongly inclined to emphasize Pan-Slavic expansionism and messianism. In particular, he was obsessed with the idea of Europe's "hatred" toward Russia and suggested a response to it by means of Pan-Slavic unity under Muscovite leadership. He emphasized that everything wrong in Russia came from the West and that everything good sprang from the indigenous culture, revealing time and again new and different aspects of Russian "uniqueness and multiple talents," in contrast to the less well endowed Western Europeans. For example, "the Russian people had an unusual capacity for the advancement and exercise of political liberty," in contrast to France.[10] Danilevsky combined his original but disputable theory of world dynamics with a strong adoration of indigenous Russian political ideals and values. Without evidence or arguments, he asserted that the Slavic cultural type is the best, most integral, progressive, and many-sided culture. For that reason, the Slavic culture type had a historic mission to supplant the declining Roman-Germanic civilization.

According to Danilevsky, a military solution was appropriate for this great purpose: "We consider . . . the very process of this inevitable war and not only in its desired results . . . as salvational and beneficial. . . . Perhaps we will be blamed for preaching enmity and for glorifying war. But such an accusation would be unjust. . . . We submit that, though war is a great evil, there are much greater evils, for which war can be just the cure, for 'man does not live by bread alone.'"[11] As a political thinker, Danilevsky proved to be far less adequate than his talent as a philosopher suggested. His adoration of indigenous virtues played grim tricks on Russian history.

Dostoevski, another great Russian talent, was captivated by the mirage of Russian exceptionalism and messianism. His *Diary of a Writer* demonstrates that even a genius is not immune to a narrow-minded and cruel nationalism expressed in the guise of a "spiritual" and "patriotic" doctrine:

> The Slavophile doctrine, in addition to that assimilation of the Slavs under the rule of Russia, signifies and comprises a spiritual union of all those who believe that our great Russia, at the head of the united Slavs, will utter to the world, to the whole of

> European mankind and to civilization, her new, sane and as yet unheard-of word. That word will be uttered for the good and genuine unification of mankind as a whole in a new, brotherly, universal union whose conception is derived from the Slavic genius, preeminently from the spirit of the Great Russian people who have suffered so long, who during so many centuries have been doomed to silence, but who have always possessed great powers for clarifying and settling many bitter and fatal misunderstandings of Western European civilization. Now, I belong to this group of the convinced and the believing.[12]

Dostoevski's refrain moves from spiritual to literal ground:

> We, Russia, we are really necessary and unavoidable to Eastern Christianity in toto, to the whole future fate of Orthodoxy on earth, and to its unity. This was always conceived so by our people and their czars. Briefly, this dreadful Eastern question constitutes almost our whole future fate. Therein lie, as it were, all our tasks, and what is most important—our final conflict with Europe and our ultimate communion with her but only upon new, mighty and fertile foundations. Oh, how can Europe at this time grasp the fatal and vital importance to ourselves of the solution to this question?—In a word, no matter what may be the outcome of the present, perhaps quite indispensable diplomatic agreements and negotiations, nevertheless, sooner or later, CONSTANTINOPLE MUST BE OURS, let it be only in the future, in a century. This, we Russians, all of us, must always and undeviatingly bear in mind. This is what I meant to state, particularly at the present European moment.[13]

We who have lived in the twentieth century have the sad knowledge of the terrible experience of modern times. We know the price humanity has paid for the attempts to embody this ideology in practice. The genuine meaning of these high-flown statements is revealed through the writer's overtly militaristic confessions: "We ourselves need this war; not merely because our Slavic brethren have been oppressed by the Turks. We are also rising for our own salvation. The war will clear the air which we breathe and in which we have been suffocating, closeted in spiritual narrowness and stricken with impotent decay."[14]

Dostoevski reveals here what the Pan-Slavic politicians prefer to keep concealed: the liberation of their Slavic brothers is mostly the casus belli for solving their own domestic problems by means of bloodletting. For Dostoevski the bloodletting of warfare was the means of achieving peace:

> Believe me that in certain, if not in all, cases (save in the case of civil wars) war is a process by means of which specifically international peace is achieved with a minimum loss of blood, with minimum sorrow and effort, and at least more or less normal relations between the nations are evolved. Of course, this is a pity, but what can be done if this is so? And it is better to draw the sword once than to suffer interminably. And in what manner is present peace, prevailing among the civilized nations, better than war? The contrary is true: peace, lasting peace, rather than war tends to harden and bestialize man. Lasting peace always generates cruelty, cowardice, and coarse, fat egoism, and, chiefly, intellectual stagnation. It is only the exploiters of the peoples who grow fat in times of long peace.[15]

Scholars who are specially devoted to Dostoevski find different, more or less convincing explanations and excuses for the puzzle of why this writer of a mentality Christian and humanist at its foundations became devoted to narrow-minded nationalism and militarism. Their explanations sometimes help relieve our frustrations when we compare *The Diary of a Writer* with similar passages in Hitler's *Mein Kampf.* Pan-Slavism, Pan-Germanism, and other versions of intolerant nationalism echoed across Europe with the tumult of savage warfare that failed to address either the problems of Europe or the problems of humanity.

The modern Russian philosopher Grigoriy Pomerants gives us a better understanding of the problems of ethnic imperialism. Pomerants advances the thesis that romanticism in contrast to enlightenment has contributed to great artistic achievements expressive of strong emotional attachments but is destructive of social practices needed to face the future. The flights of the imagination that reach beyond common sense have an attraction that is important to spiritual and intellectual life, and literature is an essential part of the life of the imagination.[16] In social practice, a cautious and sober realism needs to prevail unless human beings are prepared for the tragedies of monumental disasters like those that were the products of Marx's, Lenin's, and Hitler's imagination.

Romanticism looks to the past—to an imagined Golden Age—for its idols. The attitude of going back to the soil, to the roots, or to the source may be very productive for talented individuals in giving expression to passionate feelings mixed with flights of the imagination, neglecting the multidimensional facets of life in human societies. These efforts to recapture the spirit of a Golden Age are particularly sensitive to problems associated with an "inferiority complex" mixed with envy and with strong potentials for aggression toward both internal and external enemies.

During the 1870s, the Pan-Slavic nationalistic worldview became rather popular among the educated in Russian society and enjoyed considerable intellectual and moral support. One of the reasons for this appeal was as a counterbalance to the Westernism represented both by the liberal and radical variants of Western thought. *Pan-Slavism was the defensive reaction of a system-centered consciousness that took the form of an emotional appeal to chauvinistic and nationalistic impulses.*

Thus, in my opinion, the diverse approaches to the Russian intelligentsia's response to the epochal character of the reign of Alexander II are necessary features in the analysis of the drama of Russian history. Two different groups were formed during the 1860s and developed during the 1870s. One manifested person-centered values, still strange to Russian society. The other was system-centered and was subdivided into two sections—one revolutionary and the other conservative. The first seemed very radical in terms of formal rhetoric. It chose as its ideal a revolutionary modification of the same system-centered tradition. The second one, smaller in size, but influential, expressed Slavophile ideas; those ideas, owing to their conservative appeal to a Golden Age and their uncritical narcissistic flavor, met with greater response among the less educated strata of society.

THE ROMANCE AND FANATICISM OF REGICIDE

The Narodnaya Volya (People's Will) Party serves as a most remarkable example of intellectual system-centered radicalism.[17] The number of its active members never having exceeded thirty people, it can hardly be considered a political party in the modern sense. But this small handful of people competed rather successfully for several years with the omnipotent government of the empire. Society excitedly watched an unusual pursuit in which the Tsar, master of one sixth of the earth's land, served not as the hunter but as the hunted. This incredible situation became possible only because the *narodovoltsy,* members of the People's Will, enjoyed considerable support in intellectual circles.

Support came in different forms: financial, conspiratorial, moral, and in personnel. It was not by chance that in spite of considerable losses in the party's ranks because of multiple arrests by the police, Narodnaya Volya managed to compensate by recruiting new members. The fantastic energy and purposefulness that the narodovoltsy manifested drew on the "moral mandate" of larger intellectual circles. Thus, purely arithmetical calculation of the party's forces is misleading because it does not take into consideration that the active members were only the tip of the iceberg of this most remarkable manifestation of a rather widespread radical mood among the intelligentsia.

Under conditions of political polarization, the liberal alternative was greatly weakened. The temptation of a radical solution was strong, especially among romantic young people. On the other hand, the rigid reaction of the government against the radicals' terrorist activities, the general swing of governmental politics to the right, and government indecisiveness in pursuing reforms—including stepping back from the reform of local self-government and the judicial system—only encouraged the radicals and, consequently, weakened the liberals. Governmental repression against the revolutionaries only raised sympathies and feelings of solidarity on the part of the victims of police repression, inspiring the radicals to continue their struggle. Young people gathered under the banner of "disorganization"—their substitution for the word *terror* in the narodovoltsy form of double-speak.

The terror of Russian radical nihilists found moral support not only inside Russia itself but among Western intellectuals as well. Among them there were such famous people of different political persuasions as the writer Victor Hugo, the psychiatrist and criminologist Cesare Lombroso, the polar traveler Nils Nordenskiöld, the astronomer Camille Flammarion, the historian of Christianity Ernest Renan, the philosopher Herbert Spencer, the journalist George Kennan, the minister John Morley, the publicist marquise Henri Rousheforte, the poet Charley Swinburne, and many others, who eloquently defended the Russian terrorists. The Russian narodovoltsy became popular and sympathetic heroes in Western literature by the end of the 1870s, as represented in the works of Oscar Wilde, Jules Verne, Émile Zola, Alfons Daudet, Guy de Maupassant, John Galsworthy, Joseph Conrad, Arthur Conan Doyle, Etel Lilian Voinich, Stefane Geromsky, August Strindberg, and many other less famous authors who turned to this image for praise. Even such a moderate liberal and skeptical author as Mark Twain declared publicly in an 1889 appeal: "If such a government, like the current Russian one, cannot be overthrown other than by dynamite, God bless dynamite."[18]

How can all of this be explained? It probably derived from feelings of disgust with the despotic rule and lack of freedom associated at that time with the Russian government, and with suppression of the voice of reason. The Russian autocracy, despite the efforts of its political emissaries in Europe, provoked European suspicions against both its stubborn inclination to expansion and its despotic political regime. Consequently, people who fought against this regime enjoyed goodwill and admiration. Beyond these "rational" considerations, the terrorists were also attractive personally: young men and women burning with a desire to change the world—brave, disinterested, and noble in their strivings, and persecuted by reactionaries, they were the object of widespread sympathy. The terrorists' bombs exploded in a distant country, and Europeans observed these events from boxes in the theater. Blood, conspiracy, daggers, passionate speeches always look romantic and lofty on the stage of a theater, especially if they are directed against injustice. Terror did not discredit itself at that time, nor did it reveal its immorality and senselessness. The talented propaganda of the Russian political émigrés also bore fruit. By all possible means, they presented the Russian radicals as live heroes of Promethean proportions. It is difficult to reproach distant foreign observers when many of Russian intellectuals who lived in the midst of those events were also influenced by euphoria and self-deception.

All circumstances worked to support the system-centered wings of the intelligentsia and worked against the person-centered wing. The radicals, different from the more philosophical liberals, were always people of action. But liberals dominated the situation and events rolled along the road to catastrophe.

To be fair, it needs to be noted that the Narodniks' movement comprised both violent and peaceful appeals to speak on behalf of the people. For several years the two were partially intertwined, partially pursuing parallel courses. When it became apparent that peaceful propaganda among peasants would not achieve quick successes—and, even worse, that peasants did not believe propagandists and sometimes beat them and drove them away or handed them over to the police—the most decisive and passionate wing of the narodniks prevailed in the movement.

The most fanatical among them chose the way of individual terror. Terror from below provoked terror from above. The authorities and terrorists were gripped in a fierce struggle. Any blow from one side was answered with blows from the opposite side. None of the adversaries had wisdom enough to break the vicious escalation of violence.

Late in the struggle, Alexander II made some efforts to find compromises. The work of the so-called Loris-Melikov Commission promised some changes. On the eve of his death, the Tsar signed a document convoking an elected representative assembly to discuss reform plans.[19] This can be considered an analogue to Catherine's commission to create a just code. It was too late.

TRAGEDY

The next day, on March 1, 1881, at about 2:30 P.M., at Catherine's canal embankment, two decades after the liberation of the serfs on March 3, 1861, the Tsar was assassinated with a bomb. The terrorists executed their death-sentence verdict. All hopes for a liberal solution were buried with Alexander's crippled body. The pursuit and assassination of Alexander II became the climax of an epochal scene in the Russian political tragedy.

The people who created that tragedy deserved to be remembered. Most of them were self-sacrificing and individually honest people. Some were talented in different fields. For example, N. Kibalchich, the main manufacturer of explosive materials for the conspirators, while awaiting execution as a prisoner sentenced to death, produced a description and design for a space rocket. All were dazzled by the illusion that an immediate surgical procedure could heal Russian society. As an instrument for that surgery they chose terror—"disorganization." The most bitter paradox of Russian history prevailed: by the hand of its noble people who sacrificed their lives for the weal of the country, the horror of the historic tragedy continues.

The pyrrhic victory of the Narodnaya Volya Party became the failure of the greatest opportunity in Russian history to move along a new course of development. As we have seen this was not the first time that such an opportunity had been lost, but this time the potential for favorable development had been the most encouraging: influential social groups supported reform, the authorities admitted the necessity for change, and many important steps had been taken. The end of serfdom was officially acknowledged. Other reforms were on the agenda. The process of building a free society had begun. But in a moment, everything crashed!

The events of 1881 predetermined, to a certain degree, the inevitable catastrophe of 1917. The prior alliance between those in authority and those who were the bearers of change had been completely broken. As a result, the most stagnant and conservative social groups determined the consciousness of the regime. Those oriented toward reform, including those with professional technical skills, became alienated from political processes.

The intelligentsia had been the only force trying to offer society remedies for its ills. After March 1, 1881, the intelligentsia lost the maneuvering room that it had acquired in the 1850s. Public opinion associated the behavior and fantasies of the radicals with the whole intelligentsia. The purposes and methods of a small minority were imputed to all intellectuals. As a consequence, those in power began to consider the intelligentsia not as partners but as enemies. A large body of public opinion also began to treat intellectuals not as constructive agents of change but as "disorganizers." *Thus, the prevalence among the intelligentsia of a mood and an illusion, traditional in its essence but expressed in new forms, caused the great national tragedy endured by the Russian people.*

There were three and a half decades more—two reigns—between 1881 and the end of the 304-year Romanov dynasty. But those years failed to bring any significant change in the situation. Many new factors emerged; important political events took place; but the main pattern of historical dynamics remained.

Division of the Russian intelligentsia into two hostile camps proved to be the crucial circumstance dominating the reigns of Alexander III and Nicholas II. In a certain sense, the events and portents of March 1, 1881, set the trajectory for much of the Soviet experience.

CHAPTER SIX

After the Catastrophe

The Penultimate Romanov Reign

Recognition of the circumstance that 1881 was a fatal juncture does not presume any simple fatalistic concept directing the course of Russian history for more than a century ahead. The consequent events were not simply the embodiment of a completely "programmed" scenario. Historical regularities, which become more or less clear many decades after the events, were not at all clear to the participants in or the eyewitnesses to those events. Human beings are usually not willing to reconcile themselves to the passive role of being passengers on a ship of state in its course through history. We live and act within the frame of our own individual lives. And even if the course of events in a certain historical situation is determined from a macrohistorical point of view, *the place of individual patterns of behavior may be significant for the course of historical development.* V. G. Korolenko, a famous Russian writer, outstanding liberal publicist, and social actor, very precisely expressed an idea of personal responsibility for the development of social life. Discussing the Marxist neglect of individual responsibility, he wrote: "To acknowledge philosophical determinism does not always mean to be a fatalist. To acknowledge the approach of the capitalist era as a completed fact . . . does not mean to be reconciled with all its consequences.[1]

Our personal choices and actions have consequences. As individuals we are usually not able to change the trajectory of history. But we always have some influence on the manifestations of historical processes, which directly affects the destiny of both individuals and generations. We spend our daily lives in the microcosms of historical processes. And although as individuals we are not able to change macrohistorical patterns, those circumstances should not serve as an excuse for idleness or for a sort of moral self-indulgence. The more knowledge, talents, skills, authority we have, the greater our responsibility.

Periods following historical crossroads are, at the same time, periods leading up to the next crossroads. During these intervals, the direction of a course needs to be recognized and explored by some individuals before the juncture is available to others.

Within any historical period where the course of social development is confined to a single channel, patterns of turbulence may occur. New obstacles may emerge and the flow of events may become more hesitant before accelerating again. Individual persons cannot seriously change the direction of such "secondary" movements; but we can influence their intensity and character. They can be accelerated or smoothed, blocked, or sometimes stifled when they have scarcely begun, but individuals cannot set the basic trajectory. In Russian history, the revolutions of 1905 and especially 1917 were examples of such secondary impulses. Hence analysis of the periods following the critical juncture of 1881 also requires serious attention.

THE INSTRUMENTS OF REACTIONARY POLITICS

Alexander III responded to the "progressive" political radicalism of revolutionaries by strict conservatism in state politics. As in the previous chapters, the moral and psychological aspects of historical processes, represented by the dynamics of two types of social and political consciousness—not the historical events themselves—are the center of our interest.

In the history of Russia, rulers with more or less liberal attitudes mainly proved to be indecisive and weak persons, while the conservatives were consistent, powerful persons convinced of their own rightness. A strong-handed liberal may verge on being a contradiction in terms. Strength in holding to a liberal commitment may be important, as in the case of the current king of Spain refusing to acquiesce in a military coup or of several prime ministers holding to a liberal course in postwar Germany. I had hoped that Boris Yeltsin might hold firmly to a liberal course in Russia, but regrettably I have been proven wrong in that hope.

Alexander III completely corresponded to this tradition of the strong-willed conservative. By some accounts, he originally had a kind heart and other qualities that under favorable circumstances might have compensated for his obvious lack of education and parochial views. But the course of events led in a different direction. He came to the throne under the star of bloody confrontation—the assassination of his father—which transformed his basic orientation. The only thing he was capable of doing was to conduct a fruitless politics of efforts to "freeze" the development of Russian society, particularly by means of prohibitions and restrictions on social activities not sanctioned from above, by means of nationalistic Russification of imperial politics, and through repression against various kinds of dissidents. The autocratic pattern of power developed the darker side of his inclinations. Such measures inevitably tend to escalate from bad to worse.

His government, with one exception—S. Y. Witte, minister of railroads and later of finance—contained individuals of poor intellectual capabilities and low moral qualities. They simply were not capable of offering a reasonable alternative to the formulations of the opposition. Thus, they chose the avenue of appealing to the emotions and instincts of the less enlightened part of population, to the older, more stable attributes of a national system-centered consciousness, playing on the deepest and most reliable form of mass psychological stereotypes.

Crusade for Russification

By Russification, I mean the *exploiting of traditional Russian xenophobia,* directing suspicion and enmity toward "others" and placing on those others responsibility for all their own troubles, real and imaginary. A perpetual scourge of human history is to identify ourselves with virtue and others with evil, declaring them the source of our own troubles. These were the concrete historical circumstances for the great Russian chauvinism that became the focus of politics.

The government unleashed and headed a crusade for Russification of the country. All through the country, the government's emissaries trampled like angry rhinoceroses on any signs of national cultures that drew inspiration from non-Russian nationalities in the empire. The pretext chosen was the "eradication of local separatism." These pressures applied not only to ethnic but also to religious features of life, and not only in the provinces but also in the capital cities. The "true patriots," both in government and among the ordinary people, coordinated their actions almost without words, by slight hints that were unclear to the uninitiated. They began to persecute their main "internal enemy"—Jews.

The government's calculations were precise. Struggles against "strangers"—many of whom lived within their native territories, which had been conquered by Russia—directed public attention away from other problems and gathered very different groups of the Russian population under the banner of a "national front." Chauvinism—enmity toward internal foreigners—became a kind of powerful magnet, drawing together "true patriots" regardless of their social status, which indeed ranged from aristocrat to peasant. The main difference was that mobs simply made pogroms in Jewish neighborhoods, while the authorities and the "noble" or "enlightened" chauvinists expressed hypocritical regrets concerning the more dreadful acts of vandalism—but at the same time made use of the state machinery to persecute the Jewish population, thus promoting new pogroms. (It must be noted here that although pogroms were certainly nothing new in Europe, including Russia, there had not been pogroms in Russia for several centuries up to that time; despite restrictions on settlement and some professional restrictions for heterodox people, national politics until this point was rather tolerant by the standards of the time.)

Unfortunately, this chauvinistic hysteria was not adequately rebuffed either within Russia or from abroad in Europe. This phenomenon can be explained by the rising tide of nationalism in most Western countries. Nationalism manifested itself as a growing and threatening factor across the European continent around 1870 and, with some exceptions, persisted until the middle of the twentieth century. Then its pernicious influence on the fates of people, nations, and cultures declined for several decades; but alas, not forever, as many recent events demonstrate.

One of the greatest European humanists of modern time, Albert Schweitzer (1875–65), treated nationalism as the main culprit provoking crises in European civilization. He indicated in *Culture and Ethics* that the idea of the national state was formed as a tool designed to serve high human values and ideals until the beginning of the nineteenth century; but gradually the significance of national ideologies grew, accompanied by the decline of other cultural institutions, until nationalism came to dominate other values. He wrote: "A national state should seek its greatness struggling for the ideas capable of bringing good to all the nations. . . . Therefore, the national feeling takes guardianship over reason, morality and culture. The cult of patriotism as such is to be considered as a sign of barbarism, because it reveals itself in senseless wars which inevitably accompanied it. In the end, national ideas supplanted the true ideals of culture and complicated a situation with a lack of culture by the ideas and convictions instilled via perverted nationalistic views on life."[2]

Social Corruption

The other leverage that the government of Alexander III used as a means to rule—or perhaps it is better to say to manipulate—was corruption of the social classes through bribery. The authorities began to create financial privileges addressed to different strata. The golden rain poured first on the heads of gentry. A bank for the gentry was established, where loans could be procured under very favorable conditions. By this means, the loyalty of the nobility was bought. But this privilege did not bring them prosperity. Most of the gentry conceived these loans to be Heaven's gift, rewarding them for their lackey-like devotion to the dynasty. The funds mainly were not invested in economic development but merely wasted. As the most serious Russian theorist of the social-democratic movement, Georgiy Plekhanov indicated in his work on the reign of Alexander III, published in 1894: "We have currently the gentry, more faithful and more indebted than ever before. The government of Alexander brought the first estate to an economic crash and to complete demoralization."[3]

Similar programs were made available for the peasantry. A special peasants' bank was established and some other privileges were arranged for peasants. But these measures did not bring peasants much prosperity either, because they were out of touch with other political developments.

A similar but more intricate method was used to buy the allegiance of merchants and entrepreneurs, who gained from "the sale of the gentry's allegiance," as Plekhanov noted. An economic policy of strong protectionism became the main tool for the support of merchants and entrepreneurs. In combination with its chauvinistic, nationalistic program, the economic policies the Russian Empire fostered were unscrupulousness in business, a quest for short-term advantage, and the use of political methods to reduce economic competition. These policies failed to stimulate long-term economic development.

The principal thrust of policy during the reign of Alexander III, the penultimate tsar of the Romanov dynasty, was to restore as far as possible the social order characteristic of the reign of his grandfather, Nicholas I, and to reverse as far as possible the reform policies pursued by his father, Alexander II. The Tsar's closest advisor and the architect of his working policies was Konstantin Pobedonostsev, the Procurator of the Holy Synod—the appointed head of the Orthodox Church. Pobedonostev expressed the basic idea of his political efforts in the sentence: "Russia needs to be frozen." Policies based on such a conception cannot be successful during periods of dynamic change like the phase of technological, scientific, and cultural developments of the last two decades of the nineteenth century. Those policies brought about increasing alienation between governmental policies and patterns of development in Russian society, leading to increasing estrangement between the rulers and the ruled.

GALLERY OF SOCIAL ACTORS

In characterizing the social ethics of different classes during the reign of Alexander III, the obvious place to begin is with the first estate. Up to this point we have been concerned largely with the intelligentsia and have treated the bureaucracy only glancingly, but we now need a clearer assessment of the standpoints of clergy, bourgeoisie, peasantry, and proletarians as well.

Gentry

Many contradictory things have been written about the *dvoriane* (gentry). On the one hand, their extreme conservatism, the cruel tyranny of landlords, and the gentry's cupidity, arrogance, lack of cultural and political sophistication, extreme conformity to power, and other unattractive traits have been noted in the literature. On the other hand, a cumulative image of the gentry also reveals generosity, nobility, disinterestedness, a high degree of integration into progressive world culture, liberalism, and even devotion to revolutionary causes. All this was true. None of these attributes was lacking; all can be confirmed by factual evidence. The problem is that these characteristics depict different groups of gentry in different historical periods. The Russian gentry, especially from the second half of the eighteenth century, was neither homogeneous nor stagnant.

As we have seen, it was the gentry who began the new search for a person-centered way of life in the early nineteenth century and served as the cultural milieu nurturing that way of life across successive generations. But, beyond this innovative wing, *the bulk of gentry remained system-centered in cultural orientation to the very end of the Romanov dynasty.* Boris Chicherin, an outstanding Russian liberal theorist in constitutional law and an acute political writer and analyst during much of the nineteenth century, provides us with an example. He belonged to an old gentry family and served for many years in various unpaid public positions in local self-governing bodies, both provincial and in Russia's "second capital," Moscow. He was head of Moscow's City Council during several years covering the end of Alexander II's reign and beginning of his son's reign. I consider Chicherin one of the best informed experts on Russian political and social life and particularly on the gentry's moods and attitudes. The gentry was his native cultural environment. That is the reason we can trust his critical reflections about his own stratum of society. He remarked, for example, the constitutional tendencies among the Moscow gentry, who were superficially motivated by a short-term offense provoked by the liberation of the serfs, but this offense was completely displaced by later developments.

The government abandoned all reforms of the previous reign in the field of local self-government *(zemstvo)* and seriously restricted the gentry's corporate self-organizing authority. In exchange for this disfranchisement, the government arranged financial recompense through privileged loans, as already noted. The gentry not only accepted this pejorative form of compensation; they also began to compete in their servile expressions of gratitude in hope of gaining a larger share of the imperial bounty. The newspapers were full of group letters—"addresses"—to the government, lyrical with thanks and obsequious devotion to authority. Thus, as Chicherin remarked, even the idea of honor had been lost in the "honorable estate"; the most unpalatable thing, in his opinion, was that gentry was employing language and terminology more appropriate to the servitude of the seventeenth century than to the end of the nineteenth century.[4]

Unfortunately, most of the Russian gentry had not adopted the norms and attitudes of civic life. Without those norms and attitudes of civic virtue, all political reforms were reversible. Political changes could be reversed by commands from the top. This was what happened after 1881. *The gentry, in the aggregate, did not pass the test of civic virtue that history offered.* The ruling elite was recruited from that broader mass of the gentry, not from the best representatives of the first estate. Moreover, during the reign of Alexander III, the ruling oligarchy, with insignificant exceptions, was recruited from the worst representatives of the gentry class. This oligarchy was able to manipulate the destinies of tens of millions of people!

Clergy

The second estate, the Orthodox clergy, was not homogeneous, and the same tendencies prevailed within it as among the gentry. Historically the Orthodox Church, unlike most Western churches, performed the role of a subordinate partner under autocratic authority, not that of an independent source of spiritual authority. It had, and still has, a rather strict hierarchy, like the Roman church; but in contrast to the organization of that body, the Orthodox hierarchy was subordinated to the Holy Synod—a bureaucratic body under the control of the government. In particular, the Procurator or chairman of the Holy Synod was selected by the Tsar. But this formal, institutional side is only a part of the story. All the traditions and customs of the official church, at least since the beginning of the seventeenth century, worked not for its spiritual independence but, on the contrary, in favor of complete submission of the church to the needs of the state.

Personalistic principles of individual responsibility were rejected by Orthodox doctrine. "Aloofness" was a severe sin in contrast to submission to religious authority. Parishioners were not encouraged to read the Bible. A Russian translation of the Bible did not exist until the 1860s. Sermons were not encouraged. Choral arrangements and rituals predominated in religious services. For most of the nineteenth century, the texts of sermons had to be affirmed in advance by the Consistory—regional agencies of the church's administrative structure. Members of the flock were presumed to be obedient to formal ecclesiastical rules, and their first obligation was to fulfill formally prescribed rites and rituals. Services were administered in the ancient Slavonic language, which people were not able to understand. There was thus not much room for the moral and spiritual enlightenment of parishioners within the formal religious life of the Orthodox Church.

In their training for conducting mass, priests were prepared only to perform the true rituals and to act as shepherds in the exercise of rituals rather than as mentors for their parishioners. As a rule, they lacked the skills and had neither the responsibility nor the will to serve as mentors in their communities. They were financially and spiritually dependent, poor, badly educated, conservative, and frightened persons. They can be depicted, by their practical social status in the country's life, as a special branch of state servants, a clerical officialdom, so to speak.

I do not mean to vilify all the members of clergy. There were many good priests of high moral and intellectual achievement, but they were not typical cases; they existed at variance with the prevailing customs, norms, and attitudes. The body of clergy as the organized second estate did not honor individually preeminent priests. On the contrary, it sought to level everything to an average standard of performance. The interests of the clerical corporation and those of the social system as a whole coincided in placing emphasis on obedience. Outstanding spiritual authority, either in church or in civil life, frequently become uncontrollable; a popular preacher, in particular, tends to become a social leader who influences devoted followers. Such a preacher is a challenge to the system. In terms of corporate interests, a preacher of excessive popularity undermines the positions of his less popular clerical colleagues. Both systems—larger and smaller—react in the same negative way to deviations from the normal, routine, order.

The tactic of taking preventive measures against unusual priests gave priority to dull conformity, created disincentives to recruiting able clergymen, and contributed to the degradation of the clergy. Many of the most capable and independent members of the clergy felt bound to abandon it. This tendency developed especially during the last two Romanov reigns. Usually these people joined groups within the intelligentsia. Many of them made significant contributions to the progress of society, including the development of the person-centered system of values; some became radicals and revolutionaries. What they did was not accessible to them through their positions in the Orthodox Church.

As a result, the better educated members of society, stratum by stratum, gradually moved away from the Church. People fulfilled some formal obligations, but nothing more. The moral prestige of the Orthodox Church was low and continued to decline. In the period we are considering, the clergy kept their influence only among the peasantry. Even the peasantry did not conceive of the priests as their spiritual mentors but mostly as a specific kind of "authorities" with their particular demands. We will return to this question later in this chapter, in the discussion of peasant morality. During the last pre-revolutionary decades, the Church, to a considerable degree, also lost the peasantry—its last social base.

Consequently, the moral consciousness of the peasantry was bitterly damaged. A society with a servile state religion and strict formal ecclesiastical rules wins the sarcastic smile of history by becoming mainly atheistic in response to the practical exigencies of life. The gradual and cumulative destruction of a faith and its moral code revealed themselves in the terrible destruction of the revolution, when the myth of deep religiosity and basic Russian adherence to Christianity was dispelled by the actions of people who were presumably "good Christians."

Bourgeoisie

The historical destiny of the Russian class of entrepreneurs was different from Western patterns. It was a class unto itself. We know the conditions of the ethical formation of the European bourgeois: Renaissance in culture, traditions of free cities, the liberty of merchant and craft guilds, protection from arbitrary authority in the economy, polemics concerning the basis of a sovereign's authority, and struggles around religious freedom. Everything was the object of doubt, discussion, and revision. Nevertheless, even under these favorable conditions, the process of person-centered consciousness took ages to crystallize.

We do not find similar conditions in Russia. We should remember the circumstances under which Peter formed a basis for Russian entrepreneurship: enforced despotic rule, lack of freedom, reliance on negative incentives—the flogging, scaffolds, financial punishments, the encouragement of denouncement as a tool of "market competition," brutal pursuit of Old Believers to force obedience to formal orders—the use of serfs to supply labor in quasi-capitalistic manufacturing enterprises, and the extension of monopoly privileges in selective markets, such as textiles, in exchange for supplying uniforms for the ranked services of the state.

As a result, *the Russian bourgeois inherited qualities from a social background that was directly opposed to the very spirit and ideas of Western capitalistic ethics.* In Russian circumstances it more or less "worked." The rules of the game existed, but these rules were not consistent with those operating in Western enterprises, operating beyond the official patronage of mercantile policies. Instead of Western-style principles of labor ethics, other patterns of relationships prevailed. This was clearly expressed in metaphorical form by a Russian proverb, the rough English equivalent of which is: "Honest labor brings no stone chamber." In other words, honest labor brings no rewards.

Nevertheless, the liberal measures of the previous reign had some positive influence on the third estate as well. Under conditions of economic revival and some progress, entrepreneurial independence from governmental authorities began to emerge. Both common sense and practical needs had begun, step by step, to erode the preemptive type of the Russian quasi-bourgeois. These efforts bore fruit in the end: *liberal-minded merchants and entrepreneurs emerged.* As a byproduct of that process, some of these entrepreneurs became patrons of arts, and as a perverted byproduct, some entrepreneurs began to sponsor revolutionaries. This group became remarkable during the next reign, that of Nicholas II, the last of the Romanovs.

Bureaucracy

To turn briefly to Russian officialdom, the bureaucracy was becoming an increasingly important stratum in Russian society during the reign of Alexander II. Its composition and strategic place in Russian society needs to be understood. This rather numerous social group, different from those already considered, was not a class embodied in a corporate estate but a professional stratum; its members were recruited from different social sources. Their number by the end of the nineteenth century reached around half a million, making the bureaucracy twice as large as the gentry. The great influence that officialdom enjoyed in a country as overbureaucratized as Russia is even more important than the number of people involved.

No other social group in the country has been criticized as bitterly and constantly under any ruler or regime as the officialdom. Speaking ill of Russian bureaucrats has always been a sign of good manners. They served as the usual target for writers and publicists of all backgrounds. People from the lower classes hated the bureaucrats as their main oppressors, who distorted the "goodwill of a kindly Tsar." High authorities have not missed opportunities to criticize them publicly either, to demonstrate their "solidarity" with society and to disguise their own responsibility for the unpopular policies of government. The merchants who corrupted officials with bribes and gifts also lamented loudly. Thus, the vices of Russian officialdom became a commonplace. As a whole, this opinion is just; but it also simplifies and ignores the real dynamics of political processes.

In the traditional view of historians, the first attempt to create something similar to a modern bureaucracy occurred in the reign of Peter I. This is true in a limited sense but is greatly exaggerated by the myth of the Great Reformer. Russia already had a well-developed if loosely organized system of centralized administration. What Peter I did was to introduce a table of ranks relying on a universal system of fourteen ranks that applied to nonmilitary affairs. This mania for ordered ranks was to organize society like an army, into something like military detachments differing by functions and tasks, using the same principles of organization in a system of command and control. He failed to understand that the Dutch navy could be supplied by autonomous shipbuilders. As a result, the country acquired a highly stratified, outwardly obedient but extremely corrupt administrative system that was not subject to the patterns of accountability applicable to modern bureaucracies. This system survived without serious change until 1917.

I prefer to consider such a system as a pseudo-bureaucracy that is devoid of any sense of service to the people who comprise the public. In terms of historical perspectives, Peter's reforms were more concerned with building an imperial system of rule over subject peoples. (Much the same conception of ranked order in an imperial system of command and control was reflected in the creation of the Soviet *nomenklatura;* that is, those subject to the instructions and discipline of the Communist Party secretariat over the personnel assigned to exercise command functions over all aspects of military and state administration, industry, agriculture, labor, and other associated aspects of Soviet life.)

In spite of the notorious perverseness of the bureaucracy, Russian officialdom needs both sympathetic and critical consideration. As a matter of fact, Russian officialdom, like other social group, has not been stagnant.[5] In its main features during the nineteenth century, it followed the same patterns as prevailed in Russian society. During the reign of Alexander I, one can find within this milieu some elements of pre-person-centered consciousness. Some of the state servants, as we have noted, were members of secret societies and dreamed about social progress, civil liberties, and a lawful constitution. Under Nicholas I, any such dissident type disappeared: the dense, clinging fog of system-centeredness covered all official Russian life, in spite of a certain increase in its functional efficiency. Certainly officialdom, in accordance with its formal status, was the most servile and obedient social group. As in other fields, defeat in the Crimean War gave members of the Russian bureaucracy incentives for innovation. And it proved capable of change! The new times called new people to governmental service. Some responsible individuals were found.

The author of a solid study of Russian officialdom in the nineteenth century writes that in the process of the preparation and implementation of reforms *many talented representatives of the official bureaucracy held top positions,* both in the two capitals and in the provinces. These new liberal-minded officials tried to enroll persons of similar orientations in positions of influence in effective working relationships. A process of administrative modernization began. The main problem that persisted was an acute lack of appropriate people.[6]

Unfortunately, this "rosy" period of Russian bureaucracy proved too short. The changes were not deeply rooted, political power began to hesitate, and after March of 1881, all processes of modernization were stopped. The assassin's hand pushed Russian officialdom back to the system-centered swamp. As in the other fields of official life, a restoration of system-centeredness took hold.

Peasantry

The peasantry, unfortunately, proved to be estranged from the positive side of these processes of cultural diversification and adopted only the negative—destructive—side. The compulsive character of Russian peasant communes and the whole style of peasant life prevented the emergence in their milieu of any well-developed ideas concerning the high value of human personality. Like other social classes, the peasantry was system-centered from the beginning of history; the original form inherent in peasant consciousness was a communal form of system-centeredness; in the eighteenth century, an imperial form of system-centeredness also began to emerge. Up to the time of Alexander III's reign, the positive, potentially person-centered effect of the liberation of the serfs had not yet developed; but the negative features of change—the decline of traditional communal morality—had already appeared.

Russian authors often wrote about the peasantry with compassion. A simple "people-loving" ideology clearly prevailed among writers and publicists. But among the heroes and heroines in the Russian literature on peasants, one cannot find any noticeable elements of individualistic consciousness. The absence of individualistic consciousness is indicated by socialist-minded authors who argued on behalf of "spontaneous socialist ideals" in the peasant cultural milieu and, consequently, for their preparedness for socialism—a form of system-centeredness.

Processes of economic differentiation gradually undermined the moral base of communal ethics and molded premises for a new, more individualistic type of morality. But the destructive side of this process developed much faster than did the constructive side. Thus, *the erosion of moral authority outdistanced the formation of alternative moral values* and processes of moral interaction. By one means or another, a sort of moral anomie, normlessness, and loss of moral code afflicted different aspects of peasant consciousness, particularly at the core of their morality: Orthodox religious ethics. By the 1890s, the erosion of that core was already considerable. And the worst thing was that *no new core of faith was allowed to exist* to replace the lost ethical norms. A moral vacuum emerged. The results were increasing drunkenness and brutality as people lost the sense of becoming or of being.

One of the most humanistic Russian writers, the outstanding Anton Chekhov (1860–1904), left us a belles-lettres depiction of the life of such "normless" peasants in his short story "The Peasants." Chekhov was usually able to reveal good qualities in every person; more than anyone else, he was sympathetic to any human being's internal, spiritual world. That is why it was especially remarkable and discouraging that he was not able to say anything good about these characters and left us with a bitterly frustrating picture of a universal moral degradation under the umbrella of Russian Orthodoxy:

> They fasted, prayed, and prepared for the sacrament. From those who had failed in this duty during the Great Fast, the priest, when he went round the huts with his crucifix, took a fifteen kopeks fine.
>
> The old man did not believe in God, because he had hardly ever thought of Him; he admitted the supernatural, but held that that was an affair for women; and when others spoke of religion, or of miracles, and asked him questions on the subject, he scratched himself and said reluctantly—Who knows anything about it?
>
> Grandmother believed vaguely; in her mind all things were confused, and when she became confused, and when she began to meditate on death and salvation, hunger and poverty took the upper hand, and she forgot her meditations. She remembered no prayers, but at night before lying down, she stood before the icons and muttered—"Mother of God of Kazan, Mother of God of Smolensk, Three-Handed Mother of God . . ."
>
> Marya and Fekla crossed themselves and fasted, but knew nothing of religion. They neither taught their children to pray nor spoke to them of God; and they taught them no principles save that they must not eat meat during fasts. With the other villagers it was the same; few believed and few understood. . . .

> On Elijah's Day they drank, at Assumption they drank, at Elevation they drank. At Intercession Zhukovo had its parish festival; and this the muzhiks observed by drinking for three days; they drank fifty roubles from the communal funds: and then went round the huts and collected money for more vodka. On the first days the Tchikildeeffs killed a ram, and ate mutton in the morning, at dinner, and for supper; and in the night all the children got out of bed to eat more. Kiriak was drunk all three days; he drank away his cap and boots, and beat Marya so badly the she had to be soused with water. And then all were sick with shame.
>
> Despite this, even this Zhukovo, this Kholuefka, had once a real religious festival. That was in August, when through every village in the district was borne the Life-giving Ikon. . . .
>
> All at once, it seemed, realized that there is no void between earth and heaven, that the great and strong of this world have not seized everything, that there is intercession against injury, against slavish subjection, against heavy, intolerable need, against the terrible vodka.
>
> "Intercessor, Mother!" sobbed Marya. "Mother!"
>
> When the service was said and the icon carried away, all things were as old, and noisy, drunken voices echoed from the inn.[7]

Let me stop with that depressing picture of moral anomie, moral vacuum in the people's souls and in discourse about the Russian peasantry during the penultimate Romanov era.

Proletarians

The workers in manufacturing plants became a rather important social force during this period. However, an increase in the number of workers changed neither the social status of this group nor its social mentality. We should recall the despotic command-and-control principles of Peter's industrialization based on monopolies, the despotic Tsar's power to grant privileges and exert repressions, and the almost slavish treatment of laborers. Unfortunately, this legacy of the Great Reformer survived for ages. That is why Russian proletarians proved to be excellent material for the propaganda of Marxists and other radical manipulators and utopians. Very soon afterward, some radical agitators flattered this group by calling them "the hegemonic force of Revolution." That gave the radicals an opportunity to speculate and manipulate others on behalf of these "hegemons." So, *this group originally, both by its place within the social structure and by the character of its labor, was completely system-centered in ethical orientation.* These circumstances predetermined the specifics of their revolutionary activities.

Plekhanov wrote a special work about proletarian psychology. He indicated there that "the liberating struggle of the proletariat is a mass movement. Therefore a psychology of this movement is also a psychology of mass. . . . A proletarian, first of all, is a 'social animal,' to apply Aristotle's well-known expression in a slightly different sense. This is apparent to every comprehensive observer. Werner Sombart, in his depiction of the modern proletarian soul, refers to the feeling that one has no value, if taken alone, and acquires meaning only in association with many others. . . . It is a fact that the intelligentsia is mostly inclined to rely on the individual and the deliberate worker on the masses."[8]

It would be difficult to give a more definite depiction of the core of the system-centered worldview than is indicated by Plekhanov's formulation. One aspect can be challenged in Plekhanov's typical Marxist imputation that the proletariat was of revolutionary inclinations. Only a few examples of proletarian involvement in revolutionary political activities can be found prior to 1905. Workers, in their mass, like peasants, did not share the radicals' ideology and rejected the actions of its bearers, the intelligentsia. Not long before Alexander III's accession to the throne and after one of the unsuccessful attempts to assassinate his father, groups of workers on the central street of St. Petersburg and in other big Russian cities, especially in Saratov, picked quarrels with people who looked like intellectuals and sometimes beat them. Another noteworthy episode occurred earlier, in 1864, in a process of so-called "civil castigation," when the famous socialist N. G. Chernyshevsky was tied to a scaffold for public ridicule: the intelligentsia threw him flowers, but workers hissed him.

The System-Centered Intelligentsia

Unfortunately, *the Russian radical intelligentsia marched in the same cohort of system-centered forces.* At the time we are considering, there were two different varieties of radicalism among the intelligentsia, the anarchists and the statists.

The anarchists proclaimed the ideology of complete rejection of all governmental institutions and the destruction of state and law. They supposed that all the means were available to achieve this purpose, including the support of criminals, of the "lumpenized," marginal social strata, and the unleashing of aggressive mob instincts. Even such an outstanding thinker and person as Prince Kropotkin paid tribute to this dangerous, destructive ideology in *Speeches of a Rioter*, a collection of editorials published in the anarchist newspaper *La Revolte.*[9] In particular, he sought to gather Parisian crowds, to agitate their emotions, and to stir them up against the "bourgeois" and destabilize urban life. While he appealed to principles of mutual aid, his search for cooperative resolutions was still marked by a demand for the destruction of the state.

The other wing of person-centered intellectuals involved the statists, mostly members of the Narodnaya Volya Party. The theoretical reflections of some of them, who considered not only bombs and direct actions but also what to do afterward, gave the key role to the state. As we saw in the previous chapter, this ideology was more precisely proclaimed in Peter Tkachev's pamphlet *The Revolution and the State.* In some crucial respects, this can be considered a direct theoretical predecessor of Bolshevik doctrine.

Most Russian intellectuals at the time were oriented to one of these two ideological poles, even if they did not subscribe to its programs completely. In so far as any legal forms of political activity not in full agreement with the pro-government line were impossible, people of oppositional mind and mood strongly tended to join the radicals who fought directly against the government. *The Romanticism of an uncompromising struggle became the main ideal for the Russian intellectuals, especially during their younger years.* Their mood was mostly emotional, but the fact was that succeeding generations of young Russian idealists dreamed about improvement of social life on the basis of justice and conscience, and their desire to serve their country disinterestedly was closely intertwined with motives of conspiracy, police persecution, imprisonment, and exile. Thus, the great potential of social altruism, the intellectual and noble intentions, were mobilized and misdirected toward political radicalism. This route proved fatal both for these people and for the society as a whole.

Even now, when we have complete and tragic knowledge of the full depth of the abyss into which revolutionary radicals plunged Russia, it is painful and difficult to condemn these people. Their good and honest intentions were the foundation of their delusions, terrible in their historical consequences. To prevent possible replication of this tragedy and to avoid being thrown into such a position in future, we must say "guilty" at the grave of these radicals of the intelligentsia. And the aggravating circumstance is that not all the Russian intelligentsia chose this wrong way. There were others who chose an alternative road.

The Person-Centered Intelligentsia

The generation of the intelligentsia during the reign of Alexander III divided into three branches—artists, scientists, and the followers of the concept of rendering "quiet service for the people."

The artistic branch of the person-centered intelligentsia was the most noticeable; it comprised writers, poets, artists, theater directors, composers, musicians, etc. Hundreds of books have been written about the Russian artistic culture of that period. I mention only briefly some aspects relevant to our analysis.

In the Russian artistic culture of the 1880s and 1890s, the process of depoliticization developed. The beginning of the 1880s was the key turning point. Before that time, the romance of radical ideology was rather influential in artistic circles; after that, most of artists, despite the heightened emotional sensitivity of such people, were disappointed by the prospects of radical solutions and realized the fruitlessness of these impatient actions in principle. They rejected revolutionary ideals and turned their interests either to pure aesthetics or to the subjective aspects of personality. The main object of artistic reflection was not society but individuals and the everlasting moral and philosophical problems of human personality. The emphasis moved to the subjective side of personality.

Most of their creations were marked by a pessimistic worldview. But this social pessimism was not hopeless, because it was partially balanced by the artists' capacity to laugh even at the most scandalous contingencies of life and the stupidities of power. For instance, A. P. Chekhov, N. S. Leskov, and M. E. Saltykov-Shchedrin possessed this skill of social humor and satire to a high degree. Thanks to their ability to keep a sense of irony about indigenous realities, ordinary people gained important moral support in their efforts to survive in a tragic situation and to hope for a better future.

Another branch of the intelligentsia's person-centeredness was its scientific variation. Using their professional tools, the prominent social scientists—historians V. O. Kliuchevsky and N. I. Kareev, lawyers B. N. Chicherin and M. M. Kovalevsky, sociologist N. K. Mikhailovky, and many other less famous scholars—developed liberal and other corresponding views and values. Naturally, the contributions of the humanities were greater. Scholars in the natural sciences played an important role in helping diffuse a person-centered microclimate in academic life and in broader intellectual circles.

Last, but by no means least, the largest part of the person-centered intelligentsia followed the way that can be conceptualized as rendering quiet service for the people. This group involved those who belonged to the so-called mass intellectual professions—teachers, doctors, especially in rural areas, engineers, librarians, agronomists, foresters—in efforts to improve the quality of the land and the social and physical environment. These people spent their lives in hard, persistent work seeking to give help to the poor, the badly educated, and the illiterate in villages, in the small towns, and in the slums of big cities. They did their day-by-day work without rhetoric or theatrical gestures, frequently under uncomfortable conditions in their own lives, not expecting honor or rewards. They gave their lives in efforts to help rid their compatriots of the persistent companions of system-centeredness—poverty, ignorance, and brutishness. They did not make speeches about their high calling or moral duty. *Their own way of life served as the best example of person-centeredness devoted to the service of others as worthy persons.* They were the core of the person-centered counterculture.

Certainly, there were individuals of different moral qualities within this group. But most of them had great moral integrity. The very specifics of such activities produced a kind of selection by moral qualities. In contrast to some artists and scientists, these people could not expect any compensation, any adequate reward in the form of publicity, honors, or wealth. As a rule, their wages were low, their environment was meager, their personal lives were "unsuccessful" by some standards, and their work was endless and exhausting. Most of these people had behind them the experience of university education and of life in capital cities. They had a clear understanding of their own life values and the uniqueness of their own personalities; but they voluntarily and deliberately sacrificed themselves in their service to others for the future common good and did not expect to win renown.

At best, they could afford themselves a form of psychological compensation—dreams about a better life that might come someday in the future, about a more humane world that might be realized after the end of their lives. As the heroine of Chekhov's play *Uncle Vanya* put it:

> Well, what can you do? Life goes on! (Pause.) We'll keep on living, Uncle Vanya, through a long succession of everlasting nights and days, enduring whatever the fates have in store. We shall work for others now and in our old age, never knowing rest or peace. And when our time comes, we'll die without complaining. And beyond the grave we will say we have suffered, and wept, and that our life was hard and bitter, and God will take pity on us. And then, Uncle Vanya, we shall see a life which is bright and beautiful and fine, and we'll look back on our present misfortunes with a feeling of tenderness, and smile. And we'll be at peace. I believe this, Uncle, I really do, fervently, passionately. (In a tired voice.) We shall find peace! And we shall hear the angels, and see the whole sky shining like diamonds. We shall see all our suffering, all the evils of this life drowned in a mercy that will fill the whole world, and then our life will become quiet and gentle as a caress. I believe this. I believe! Poor Uncle Vanya, you're crying. (Through tears.) You've never had any happiness in your life, but wait, just wait, Uncle Vanya, you will. We shall rest. We shall rest. We shall rest![10]

But we who have come after are familiar with the "brave new world" that would come. We cannot know whether these people realized peace in their afterlives; but we know for sure that those who lived later became the witnesses of new national tragedies.

These anonymous heroes gave a lot to their country. They made a great effort to drag Russia out of its system-centered quagmire. They had understood; but historical destiny would have had to offer more time and good fortune. It did not happen.

EDDIES IN THE MAINSTREAM

I have not of course attempted here to give a broad review of Russian philosophical thought. For instance, important intellectual efforts in Russian Christian philosophy have been beyond the range of our considerations.

However, I ought to touch at least briefly on one intermediate, antielitist tendency of social thought, ironically personified by two aristocrats, Prince Peter Kropotkin and Count Leo Tolstoy. Usually these names are associated with only one side of their activities: Kropotkin with anarchist thought and actions in Russia and Western Europe, and Tolstoy with his great novels. But that are only part of their contributions to world culture. Both were also important contributors to thinking about human affairs. Kropotkin contributed to some aspects of federalist thought. The most original of his offerings was a theory of mutual aid as one of two crucial factors of biological evolution. Darwin had emphasized principles of selection relying on competition in a struggle for survival. Kropotkin emphasized the complementarity of patterns of cooperation within and among species. He viewed human evolution as being built on patterns of mutual aid characteristic of many cooperative efforts. Patterns of cooperation associated with mutual aid need to be seen as fundamental to human cultural evolution. Kropotkin's emphasis on mutual aid is consistent with Adam Smith's emphasis on sympathy as the foundations for jurisprudence.

This is an appropriate place to note that to mark people only by their political views or to divide them only by their party affiliation is not sufficient for purposes of deeper analysis. In their political views, both Kropotkin and Bakunin were anarchists. But on a more substantial moral level, Kropotkin was mostly a person-centered thinker and actor—(his concept of mutual aid and striving with voluntary, nongovernmental human cooperation are completely within the frame of person-centeredness)—while Bakunin was a typical and consistent system-centered man who gave practitioners of anarchism theoretical grounds for antihuman actions.

Tolstoy pondered deeply about the true meaning of the Christian message. He even wrote his own version, "My Gospel," recently edited and translated into English by David Patterson and entitled *The Gospel According to Tolstoy.* "In the language of Tolstoy's religious discourse, love is the definitive element, the very essence of consciousness."[11] The official Orthodox Church treated Tolstoy's teachings as heresy and excommunicated him. Those teachings left us with deep deliberations about the evils of state, government, and nationalism as incompatible with a true notion of Christianity. Tolstoy believed in the moral value of physical labor. Many hardworking peasants were influenced by his religious and moral writings. Some Tolstoyans organized various types of cooperatives and communal ventures before the Revolution and during the first decade of the Soviet era. Kropotkin and Tolstoy had moved from different starting points to a kind of federalist solution emphasizing the covenantal character of human associations freely undertaken.

In terms of the dichotomy between system-centered and person-centered thinking, I believe that these eddies were formally closer to system-centeredness but generally tended to exceed its bounds to find a solution in a kind of commutarianism—that is, a higher and completely voluntary form of human collectivity. Unfortunately, Tolstoy and Kropotkin proved to be ahead of their time. Their approaches came into opposition with the prevailing spirit of the epoch. Moreover, some of Kropotkin's views and actions were a source of influence among the system-centered revolutionary radicals. Both Kropotkin and Tolstoy sometimes failed to adhere to their highest ideals and intellectual achievements. However, I believe, that a new and attentive reassessment of their legacy offers suggestions worthy of consideration in efforts to achieve a constructive equilibrium of person-centered and system-centered perspectives. The teachings of Kropotkin, Tolstoy, and more modern dissenters, such as Andrei Sakharov, provide the intellectual ingredients for constituting a person-centered counterculture appropriate to the emergence of a new evolutionary path in Russian civilization.

Leo Tolstoy, known to much of the world as a great Russian novelist, devoted himself seriously to questions of nationalism, the meaning of patriotism, the nature of government, and the place of Christianity in the development of European civilization, including Russian civilization. These works were the center of hot disputation at the time of their publication until World War I began and made further discussion irrelevant. Unfortunately, not many people are familiar with these ideas, which alas are once again becoming all too timely. Tolstoy's writings about civic consciousness are important for the contemporary world. He explored and criticized nationalist feelings under the name of patriotism, particularly in the essays "Patriotism and Government," "Patriotism or Peace," and "Christianity and Patriotism."

In the first of these, he wrote: "Patriotism as a sentiment of exclusive love for one's nation and as a doctrine about the virtuous sacrifice of one's peace, property, and even life for the defense of the weak against the murderousness and violence of their enemies, was the highest idea of a time when every nation considered it possible and just, for the sake of its own good and greatness, to subject the men of another nation to murder and pillage; but as far back as two thousand years ago, the highest idea of the brotherhood of men, and this idea, entering the consciousness more and more, has in our time received the most varied realization. . . . Men are beginning to understand the deception of patriotism, in which all the governments are trying so zealously to maintain themselves."[12]

Moreover, he considered patriotism an anti-Christian sentiment:

> If patriotism is good, then Christianity, which gives peace, is an idle dream, and the sooner this teaching is eradicated, the better. But if Christianity really gives peace, and we really want peace, patriotism is a survival from barbarous times, which must not only be evoked and educated, as we now do, but which must be eradicated by all means, by means of preaching, persuasion, contempt, and ridicule. If Christianity is the truth, and we wish to live in peace, we must even rejoice in its weakening, and contribute to it. A Russian must rejoice when Poland, the Baltic provinces, Finland, Armenia, are separated from Russia and made free; and an Englishman must similarly rejoice in relation to Ireland, Australia, India, and the other colonies, and cooperate in it, because, the greater the country, the more evil and cruel is its patriotism, and the greater is the amount of the suffering on which its power is based.[13]

He may appear unduly categorical in stigmatizing patriotism in such statements as the following: "Patriotism in its simplest, clearest, and most unquestionable significance is for the rulers nothing but a tool for attaining their ambitious and selfish ends, and for the ruled a renunciation of human dignity, reason, conscience, and a slavish submission to those who are in power. Thus is patriotism actually preached, wherever it is preached. Patriotism is slavery."[14]

He believed, however, that it is not governments, with their immense inclination to be abusive toward freedom of individuals, but rather people themselves who are better able to cope with external evils, mobilizing potential kindness from the core inherent in human beings, from the depths of our souls; he hoped that the simple human quality of honesty might become so powerful that governments with all their mechanisms of coercion would not be needed. Governments "know that the force is not in force, but in thought and in its clear enunciation, and so they are more afraid of the expression of independent thought than of armies, and establish censorship, bribe newspapers, take possession of the management of religion and of schools. But the spiritual force which moves the world slips away from them: it is not even in a book, a newspaper—it is intangible and always free—it is in the depth of men's consciousness."[15]

He underscored his point about honesty: "It is really a shame to think how little is needed for all men to be freed from all those calamities which now oppress them; they need to stop lying. . . . If men only understood that terrible power which is given them in the word which expresses the truth."[16]

Tolstoy was a great man, a great preacher, and also a great idealist. Perhaps he overestimated our potential as human beings. He did not want to acknowledge the darker side of human nature, which sometimes needs to be protected from itself; that is, to be constrained by force. And historically the state has been the primary arrangement providing this force. It runs the risk of becoming a Leviathan, and as a result, people are forced to pay an enormously high price for the supposed protection that states themselves abuse.

The teachings of Kropotkin, Tolstoy, and others associated with quiet service to the people, more recently exemplified by Andrey Sakharov, as noted, constituted the person-centered eddies in the mainstream of Russian system-centered sociopolitical thought. It is these features of a Russian counterculture deeply committed to service others and to enduring hardships in the perverse and tragic circumstances of Russian imperialism that held the promise for a person-centered future.

Summing up, one can emphasize the four major characteristics of the person-centered ideology: (1) *a general orientation to highest value of human individuality;* (2) *a constructive approach to reality*—the aspiration not to destroy the existing world but to create, patiently and gradually, new kinds of human relationships, new kinds of persons; (3) *the prevalence of an enlightening attitude;* and (4) an *effort to build self-reliant patterns of relationships* without being dependent on officialdom, while declining any involvement in imperial politics.

This last peculiarity proved to be impractical. On the one hand, it allowed the person-centered intellectuals to keep their moral purity—to keep their hands clean and maintain their distance from intrigue in the political kitchen. But by so doing, they voluntarily conceded an important arena for the realization of their own ideals. Instead, this arena was dominated by extremists from both poles: radicals and reactionaries. That arena was where, in the end, everything was resolved.

For a long time, a coalition of moderate politicians failed to exist at all. When such a coalition evolved at last, under the pressure of circumstances, the people who joined it proved incapable, by their personal qualities, of resolving the historical tasks facing them. If one could consider the abolition of inhuman system-centeredness and its replacement by person-centered values as a common good, one might conclude that *the political alienation of the liberal intelligentsia brought great misfortune for Russia.* While liberals were conducting their scholarship, creating fine art, and trying to enlighten the nation, radicals continued their tireless underground work to overturn the state's power pyramid. The only social force that was potentially able to prevent the final victory of another version of system-centeredness had abandoned the political arena voluntarily. Using force to destroy the state required a new power pyramid to realize the dreams of the radicals. A new autocracy was necessary to replace the old.

Thus, *Russian society approached the eve of the twentieth century with catastrophic presentiments.* These feelings pervaded various groups at different levels of the social pyramid. People's attitudes and expectations certainly differed considerably depending on their social position. But the fact was that all elements of society—powerful high officials and peasants, proletarians and gentry, radical revolutionaries and their liberal opponents—expected an approaching storm. After the fatal blow in 1881, Russian political life slipped irreversibly backward. An abyss opened in place of the cozy swamp. The country rolled down into this abyss less than a quarter of a century after the end of Alexander III's rule.

CHAPTER SEVEN

The Evening Glow

Every sigh sucks in death's air,
every hour is our hour to die.

—Osip Emilevich Mandelstam

The times preceding social and political cataclysms reveal a strange image. At the moment when the fuse of historical causality is already burning and the whole air is filled with expectations of catastrophe, a splendid blossoming of artistic culture and scientific talents occurs and even economic well-being emerges in some branches of the doomed society. A unique poetical spirit glows among the autumn colors, bringing to social life the feeling of departing summer. Rome glowed just before its fall. Germany glowed just before the turbulence of the Reformation, and one hundred years later, on the eve of the Thirty-Years' War. France glowed before the Revolution of 1789. Russia glowed in the last years of the nineteenth century and the first decade and a half of the twentieth, on the eve of the World War and the Revolution.

The edge of the centuries past and the beginning of the twentieth century are the focus of this chapter. This short period in the history of Russian culture needs to be appreciated. The cultural life of Russian society had never been so bright and intense.

LAST SUPPER WITH THE INTELLECTUALS

Russian fine arts and literary works burst forth not only on the national scene but also receiving worldwide recognition. After the explosion of 1917, the debris and seeds of this blossoming were scattered throughout the continents and became the sources of inspiration for several succeeding generations of young artists in many countries. Thousands of books have been written about this "Silver Age" in Russian culture; but the larger scale of this phenomenon has not been fully appreciated. Too many irrelevant circumstances have affected our judgments about these cultural processes.

This intensity of achievement affected artistic creativity, progress in the sciences, developments in the economy, and improvements in the style of life. Never before or since have the people of Russia thought, spoken, and written so openly, freely, and fearlessly. It seems remarkable that a generation of writers whose early creative years coincided with this period would reflect much later on that time with such feelings of the warmth, integrity, and humanity. It was a time when a free and informal intellectual exchange flourished. In my opinion, it is the most creative, fruitful, and mature form of human experience. Russian society gradually and stubbornly developed the habits for this kind of social and cultural intercourse during the whole nineteenth century.

The broad diffusion of this pattern of free intellectual exchange among those who considered and worried about the destiny of their country and civilization was a new phenomenon in Russian culture. An astonishing form of shared communities of understanding emerged, not only in the capital cities but wherever there were cores of educated people animated by a civic spirit. These people belonged to different social classes and had different material conditions of life and life experiences. Neither property nor leisure, nor professional interests, brought these small groups together. What they had in common were deep attitudes, a way of thinking about and understanding their social role and responsibility—their moral position in society. This was the crucial factor defining the way that individuals belonged to the intelligentsia.

A unique microclimate of shared spiritual freedom and joint intellectual adventure, despite all the differences in personal opinions, was typical for these communities. The main characteristic of their intellectual exchange was disinterested and uncompromising efforts to find the truth. In Russia, such questions always provoked painful reflections about the social and moral orders of the society. Thousands upon thousands of these small circles existed in the country. A kind of gravitational force emerged around each of them as young people joined together and learned the skills of intensive thought, open discussion, and literary expression.

Generally speaking, the Russian intelligentsia of that time had great significance not only within Russian national affairs but also in world affairs. Although in many other respects the country reflected the symbols of conservatism, barbarism, and backwardness, it seemed to concentrate all its potential among the intelligentsia, achieving amazing results among those who participated in the last supper during the evening glow of the nineteenth century. Perhaps no other country in the world has experienced a similar phenomenon. Paradoxically, in the West, with its long-term traditions of positive science and nonconformity, the place of intellectuals was much less remarkable and dramatic than in ultraconservative, despotic Russia.

The deep difference in basic values between the intelligentsia and the bulk of the nation evoked a sense of lonely heroism among Russian intellectuals and sense of dramatic surprise in the larger world. These qualities and a determination to be in social opposition contributed to the Russian intelligentsia's great moral force; but it was also the source of its practical weakness and, in the end, of its tragic fate. Our reference is to an extinct pre-Communist intelligentsia and its Soviet successors and imitators.

Thus, this spiritual development took place against the background of what was still the system-centered and backward mass consciousness of the country's population. The distance between the vanguard and the rest of society became too large. Different parts of the nation simply could not understand each other. This circumstance also contributed to the catastrophe that was approaching. Presentiment of catastrophe, the feeling of doom, and the extreme vulnerability of the social order existed in almost every cell of the social organism.

If this book were focused on political history, we would have to analyze in detail the course of events connected with the Revolution of 1905, so-called quasi-constitutional period from October, 1905, until August, 1914, and a lot of other things.[1] But that would take us far beyond the frame of reference chosen and would be to digress from the matter at hand.

In the framework of our approach, we need to clarify the larger sense of social consciousness prevailing among the diverse strata of society.

Our attention is focused on the dynamics of changes that took place during the reign of Nicholas II, marking the end of the Romanov dynasty.

THE REGAL COUPLE

Our concern begins with the top of the power pyramid. Many books have been written about Nicholas II and his tragic fate. Concerning the personality of Nicholas II and the processes of court life, I shall rely on explanations offered by S. Yu. Witte, one of the most important and long-term political actors of that time—minister of finance, head of the Tsar's Cabinet, and the first prime minister following the October 17 Constitutional Manifesto of 1905. He was probably the most analytical politician of that epoch, he lived for many years at the very center of the country's political life, and had known Nicholas from his childhood. Many scholars consider Count Witte's memoirs the most valuable source on the life of official Russia during the reigns of both Alexander III and Nicholas II. We have reason to trust his observations and judgments.

Beyond Witte's observations and opinion, almost everybody, except extreme monarchists, agreed that in his personal qualities, Nicholas was completely inappropriate for his role as head of state. Some people presumed that he was "too good" for that role; others found him "too bad." His inadequacy for ruling the country in such complicated, troublesome times was indisputable from both points of view.

According to Witte and many other direct observers, the Tsar was not poorly educated by the standards of his time. He was well-bred and visibly kind but a weak-willed, irresponsible, and unprincipled person. He was also highly susceptible to suggestion and psychological influence. This peculiarity was exploited effectively in the second half of his reign, when different manipulators and even rascals managed to prevail within the Tsar's intimate inner circle. Witte wrote, for example, about the "weak and irresolute Emperor, who, despite his analytical mind, was incapable of grasping broad issues. . . . Like most optimists, he recognizes danger only when it stares him in the face, but when danger seems to recede, he regains his confidence and returns to his convictions." His "weak character" was magnified by "his unfortunate marriage to a woman who not only failed to compensate for his shortcomings but in fact enhanced them, whose abnormality was reflected in the abnormality of his actions." The emperor's penchant for "Byzantine" methods was "devoid of the talents of a Metternich or a Talleyrand, his use of such methods leads to bloody or shameful results." Witte described him as "a good man, and . . . by no means stupid, but he has no will. It is from his lack of will that his political sins, i.e., sins that he commits in his capacity as an autocratic and *unlimited* ruler, who feels that he is responsible only to God, derive." He suffered a kind of childish sense of inferiority, resenting "the fact that the German Emperor was considered a more important personage than he . . . He was annoyed, too, that William II was a head taller than he. For that reason, postcards of the two clearly showing their difference in height were confiscated in Russia when they appeared, following the first meeting between the two." Witte notes with patronizing and ironic connotations, unusual for a person belonging to the highest level of state hierarchy, "How petty is the Great, Most Blessed, Most Autocratic Emperor Nicholas II."[2]

This lack of character and determination was combined with cruelty, in the broad sense of the word. His irresponsible policy toward Japan caused a senseless and unanticipated war costing Russia almost half a million soldiers; the events of the so-called Bloody Sunday on January 9, 1905, and punitive military "expeditions" throughout the country after the Revolution of 1905; the conduct of terrorist tactics of nonselective retribution and preventive deterrence; and huge losses of human lives during World War I. Witte also gives many examples of Nicholas's protection of persons responsible for actions marked by excessive and senseless brutality. The Tsar probably considered these actions to be signs of a firm and decisive character, corresponding to the qualities that he personally lacked.

Nicholas's characteristics were marked by his essential trait as a chauvinist. In premodern societies, this trait was based on an instinctive fear, a rejection of the unknown and of those who pose a threat. Under conditions of modern times, in a setting of partially educated people, the main psychological drive of a chauvinist changed from a defensive—frightened—reaction to an aggressive one. The psychological mechanism of an inferiority complex, a feeling of one's own inadequacy, frequently unconscious, *is compensated for by an aggressive self-affirmation* against any potential source of humiliation by those not identified with "us" while attributing aggression to those chosen as a target—"them." Some socially unacceptable shortcoming served as a moral self-justification for persecutions. In Russia, the role of an unacceptable "them" was traditionally identified with Jews.

Nicholas II was an overt anti-Semite. He moved in this direction even further than his father, who at least conducted his nationalistic policy through legislative limitations on settlement, access to universities, and the like. Nicholas not only failed to abolish those medieval laws adopted during the reign of Alexander III but encouraged such chauvinistic terrorist organizations as the Alliance of Russian People and the Black Squadron, and gave direct indulgence to pogroms. And when political circumstances provoked conflict with this or that state, he began to treat all persons associated with the nationality of that state in a scornful manner. Thus, he presumed some temporary exacerbation of relationships with England to be sufficient reason to say that "Englishmen are as good as *Yids.*" To call somebody *Yid* was for Nicholas the highest form of contempt and enmity.

Beyond political and state affairs, Nicholas had redeeming personal qualities. In contacts with people, he was extremely kind, pleasant, and honest. His exchange of private letters with his wife, Empress Alexandra, published in 1923 in Soviet Russia for the purpose of compromising the regal couple, failed to fulfill that task. Those letters were amazing human documents of mutual love and devotion, offering evidence of a devotion to serve the country by all means and a complete lack of understanding of the reality of the situation. We can also remember the Tsar's courage in his mortal hour. The image of Nicholas is deeply tragic. Similar positive personal characteristics also applied to the empress, despite all the dirty gossip about her betrayal of Russia to the Germans. Her German roots notwithstanding, she comprehended her life vocation as a service to the Russian nation and to the Russian Orthodox Church.

But we cannot judge those who occupy the peak of the power pyramid by criteria that apply to ordinary persons. Small shortcomings, narrow-mindedness in understanding the larger world of affairs, and lack of consistency become unacceptable when the destinies of millions of people and the destiny of one's country and the larger world are involved.

THE INNER CIRCLE: WRONG PERSONS, WRONG POLITICS

Those who encircled the regal couple were, with few exceptions, even less appropriate to run the affairs of the country, especially in critical circumstances. The Tsar's incapacity to select and promote the right people for the right positions in his administration is obvious to any serious scholar of imperial policy, regardless of one's political orientations. His constant shifting of key assignments, his stubborn promotion of some favorites who were incapable and frequently dishonest persons, his reasons for assignments and dismissals, and not least the aggregate image of the ruling circle did not create a favorable impression. The main people in that coterie were the emperor's relatives and some mystics and charlatans. Year by year, the influence of mystics on state policy grew. Witte referred to the spirit of the Tsar's inner circle as the Tsar's "Orthodox paganism."[3]

Two people enjoyed the most stable influence. One of them was the Tsar's uncle, Grand Duke Nicholas Nikolaevich. The second most influential person over many years was General Dmitrii Trepov. Most of the general's career was connected with the police and internal security. Then he rose to combine the positions of governor-general, assistant minister of interior, and commander of the garrison at St. Petersburg. He was in actuality a dictator. After the Tsar was compelled to take steps toward constitutional rule in October, 1905, and made Witte prime minister, Trepov abandoned most of his official posts but was made the Tsar's palace commandant. In an autocratic hierarchy, this position, especially under such a weak-willed and inconsistent ruler, was more significant than any other position, including even that of prime minister.

Of the handful of people in this mix whose activities as statesmen deserve respect and high appraisal, Witte was the most prominent. Practically all the main achievements of Nicholas's reign were closely connected with Witte's efforts. These include the establishment of a stable and reliable financial system; considerable development of the railroad system; industrial development; skillful diplomatic efforts to minimize the negative consequences of the war with Japan through the Portsmouth Peace Treaty; formulation and promulgation of the so-called October Manifesto of 1905, which actually created the institutional prerequisites for constitutional government; and the principal formulations for agrarian reform, which were usually associated with the name of Stolypin. Many times the Tsar's courtesans resorted to Witte's assistance to resolve political deadlock, but when dangers abated thanks to Witte's efforts, they reclaimed their roles and tried to make him responsible for their own failures. A craftsmanship of political intrigues has always been at the core of Russian political traditions.

The peak of Witte's political career occurred during the last decade of the nineteenth century and the first five and a half years of the twentieth. But within this relatively long period, he went through several ups and downs. His place in Russia can be compared with that of Jean Baptiste Colbert, minister of Louis XIV, who for a quarter of a century ran French finances, economic policy, and transportation, oversaw the French colonies, and provided for the normal work of state administration in spite of the adventurous and arbitrary policies of the Sun King. Colbert's name was associated with the basic concept of economic mercantilism.

Witte came too late. By that time, the regime was already so ossified that it was not capable of self-improvement, even under threat of its downfall. All Witte was capable of doing was postponing its fall. Everything would otherwise have crashed earlier, probably in 1905. Witte did for Russia less than he wished to do. These circumstances were not only his personal tragedy but also a chapter in the drama of Russian political history. His destiny has certain similarities with that of Speransky, three reigns earlier, and is one more illustration of the limits to bureaucratic power, even for top-level bureaucrats.

Currently, P. A. Stolypin is a popular figure in numerous discussions of Russian history. At least two different kinds of myths have arisen around him. On the one hand, extreme chauvinists enlisted him early as a champion of Russian nationalism; a book published in 1928 was titled *The First Russian Fascist: Petr Arkad'evich Stolypin.* On the opposite side, some moderate liberals have tried to attribute him a consistent liberal agenda; this originated with a book by a certain Zenkovsky, who published a memoir in 1938 in New York including the draft of a liberal project of administrative and political reform in Russia, supposedly dictated to him by Stolypin shortly before his death. This memoir was later exposed as a fake.[4] Without subscribing to any of these myths, we must recognize that there are better grounds for consigning Stolypin to the nationalist camp than for liberal claims. Leonard Shapiro called Stolypin a "most controversial Russian statesman," which is fair enough if we neglect to tally the proportion of his progressive and reactionary steps.[5]

A judgment of Stolypin as progressive gains some justification if one considers the implementation of an agrarian policy involving the promotion of freehold farming, resettlement of peasants on the virgin soils of southern Siberia, and thus some undermining of the conservative character of Russian agricultural estates. One must concede that his efforts to conduct agrarian reform seemed rather promising.[6] However, they contained destructive moral and psychological potential because they marginalized peasants whose whole world had previously been confined by village communal mores and customs.[7] And there was clear conflict between Stolypin's semiliberal agrarian politics and other anti-liberal measures of his government. He maintained a rigid conservative and autocratic line in such matters as his policy toward the Russian parliament, the Duma; in massive and brutal reprisals long after the end of uprisings against people who supposedly took part in revolutionary disturbances in 1905; and in support of chauvinist organizations. He had a certain charisma, was a good speaker, and played skillfully on appearances. That was one reason for his popularity. People went to hear his speeches in the Duma as if going to the theater. But his political line had an organic defect. As an authoritative historian of this period concludes, "he wished to conduct reforms beyond democracy and in opposition to democracy," to transform the economy while keeping the autocratic regime, centralized bureaucracy, and landlords' estates intact.[8] This course was doomed to fail. It was not by chance that reactionary, anti-Semitic forces in the Duma perceived his assignment in 1906, first as a minister of interior and then seventy-two days later as prime minister, with great enthusiasm.[9] Compared with Witte, Stolypin looked both less consistent and less comprehensive as a political actor. Beyond these two persons, others in the inner circle of the imperial court scarcely deserve mention.

What is remarkable is that both Witte and Stolypin eventually fell into disgrace with the emperor. Witte resigned after complete disappointment with the Tsar's failure to conduct an honestly pro-constitutional policy and after half a year of unsuccessful efforts to urge Nicholas to fulfill his constitutional obligations under the October Manifesto. Stolypin did not have the opportunity to resign. On the eve of his resignation, he was assassinated by a terrorist—a former agent of the secret police.

In general, the political course followed by Nicholas II was inconsistent, inadequate both in terms of broader political prospects and short-term political gains, with senseless hesitation and a gradual retreat toward mysticism. *The alienation of competence from power,* which reached threatening proportions under Alexander III, *continued to grow* under his son Nicholas II.

THE DYNAMICS OF SOCIAL-CLASS CONSCIOUSNESS

I turn now to the characteristics of consciousness and positions held by the major social strata of Russian society, as we did in the previous chapter but more briefly, emphasizing the dynamics of interactive processes. Unfortunately, these dynamics were mainly unfavorable for the future of the country. One could see either stagnation or deterioration in the tendencies formed during the previous reign and a lack of new or positive trends and ideas for responding to the challenge of worsening circumstances. *Moral and psychological stagnation blocked or perverted the potentials for those modest positive institutional developments that were initiated in 1905.*[10]

The nobility as such did not function as an important factor in the social, political, or economical life of the country. Many members of this class continued to perform active social roles, but what they did, sometimes very successfully, was in the context of other, more modern forces. The historical role of the nobility had already been exhausted. The Romanovs did not realize this until the very end. They tried to lean on these rotten but habitual timbers instead of looking for working alliances with the more productive forces in the society.

An alliance with the bourgeoisie offered the most promising coalition. Such an alliance was never attempted. A major portion of historical responsibility for that lay with the monarchy, which was timid and inconsistent in achieving a peaceful transformation of society. In all of Russian history, the monarchy had little experience in buttressing its own authority with new independent social forces.

The Russian bourgeoisie, however, was in any event not prepared to assume a full-scale partnership in the exercise of authority relationships. We have already noted the social inferiority of this class in Russia. Bourgeois constitutional-democratic political opposition to the regime emerged only in the first years of the twentieth century. Substantial shifts in this group's consciousness took place in a kind of alliance between the bourgeoisie and the intelligentsia. But the classic formula of "too little, too late" depicts those efforts. Instead, the Russian third estate, as a whole, remained system-centered in its orientation until its destruction in the revolutionary holocaust.

The consciousness of the Orthodox clergy also remained system-centered and completely loyal to the regime. Moreover, most of the changes that took place pushed the clergy to the reactionary end of the social and political spectrum. Russia experienced intensive spiritual and religious searching and fruitful theological inquiries at the time, as is reflected in the works of Leo Tolstoy, Vladimir Soloviev, Nicholay Berdyaev, and others. However, most of that deliberate and innovative religious thought developed outside the official church and with opposition from it. The clerical hierarchy ossified even more than the state bureaucracy. It failed to take note of basic changes that were occurring in its immediate social milieu.

The price of a head-in-the-sand ostrich stance in a dynamic epoch could be rapid degradation and even destruction of a particular institution, shaking and damaging the whole social system insofar as that institution had an important role to play in society. Witte, who was not an atheist, wrote: "Our church has turned into a dead, bureaucratic institution, and its services are conducted to celebrate not God in heaven but the earthly gods. Orthodoxy has turned into a kind of paganism. Herein lies our greatest danger. We have gradually become less Christian than adherents of other Christian religions."[11] This thought corresponds closely to Tocqueville's assessment of religious decline in France before the Revolution as the most important factor predetermining its bestial character: "There is no question that the nation-wide discredit of all forms of religious belief which prevailed at the end of the eighteenth century had a preponderant influence on the course of the French Revolution. This was, in fact, its most salient characteristic, and nothing did more to shock contemporary observers."[12]

Formally, the Orthodox Church enjoyed an doctrinal monopoly, but a deeply indifferent attitude toward the Church and religion prevailed among all classes. The Church performed traditional rituals with a lack of ties to real life. Thus, the Orthodox Church, which was presumably intended to nurture souls as internal regulators of human behavior, was transformed into a purely external regulator satisfied with an ostentatious display of piety.

A spirit of superficial conformity accompanied by internal indifference was precisely expressed by the behavior of a key character in Fedor Sologub's novel *The Little Demon:* "Volodin, however, conducted himself sedately and crossed himself, preserving an expression of profound contemplation upon his face. The church ceremonies meant nothing to him except that they were custom and ought to be carried out. The fulfillment of these ceremonies gave him a certain internal satisfaction: he went to church on holidays and prayed—and was forgiven, then he sinned, repented—and was again forgiven. It was nice and convenient—all the more so because outside of church it was not necessary to think about all this church business, and consequently he guided himself by completely different worldly rules."[13]

The growing moral and spiritual vacuum in the national consciousness was reflected in the decline of legitimacy in the social order. Such circumstances are always dangerous and potentially explosive. They were doubly dangerous in Russia because of the lack of other mechanisms designed to restrain base instincts and alleviate aggressive biological reflexes inherent, unfortunately, in all human beings. In more successful societies, moral considerations, complementary to religious institutions, permeate attitudes of respect for others' personalities and a psychological softening of otherwise aggressive traits making up the national character. But in Russia an unfavorable combination of many moral and psychological factors accompanied unfortunate historical circumstances. The failure of the Orthodox Church to modernize itself was accompanied by increasing moral anomie and by the considerable decline of the Church's moral prestige. These patterns were reflected in Chekhov's sketches of peasants' mores; but it goes without saying that such processes spread among all strata of society. In a more or less educated environment, the negative influence of these processes was compensated for, at least in part, by other cultural mechanisms; but among the lower classes, there was no compensation.

During the reign of Nicholas II the working class increasingly realized the force of its antlike organization. This dawning recognition was accompanied by the inability of the authorities and entrepreneurs to oppose the "collective potential energy" of the working class, as Karl Marx expressed it, even in its most destructive and antisocial forms of action. This historical "recruit" to a system-centered army was already sufficiently adjusted to the historical scene to demonstrate its intentions and power. But the most tremendous movement of the proletarian forces still lay ahead.

We can complement this analysis of processes taking place among peasants with one further observation. Under Stolypin's premiership, the process of gradual destruction of the peasant community *(obshchina)* continued: his reforms accelerated this process. In principle, this could have brought mostly positive changes: first, it undermined the logic of state stewardship by autocratic authorities, who manipulated communal traditions as a convenient way to govern because it is easier to shepherd a flock than to deal with separate persons; and second, the erosion of obshchina promoted the development of individualistic ethics. Unfortunately, this process took a severely perverted form: the economic ties of community were destroyed, but a communal morality persisted, in spite of its inadequacy for the new conditions of life. Therefore, peasants became marginal persons in a normless situation: old modes of regulation proved inappropriate but new modes of regulation had not yet matured.

This general background was highly appropriate for different versions of tempting, promising, and deceptive socialist ideas. "Socialism, which rejects the principle of private property as found in Roman law, spread from the West to Russia, where it found a favorable soil in the last fifty years, partly because of the lack of respect shown by the powers-that-be for law in general and for property laws in particular, partly because of the cultural backwardness of the masses. The influence of socialism has been reinforced by the simple belief in the right of 'expropriation' and pillage. Thus, when revolutionaries promised factories to the workers, the workers engaged in savage strikes. And when revolutionaries promised peasants the land of the landlords, the peasants naturally took to what some call the 'Red Cockerel' and others call 'illuminations' [torchings] . . . , called for in a seditious speech largely plagiarized from one made during the French Revolution."[14]

Taken together, these factors created the atmosphere for the development of one of the worst kinds of social neurosis. The idea is that people try to compensate for the imperfections and uncertainties of their own way of life by means of aggressive impulses directed against individuals or things, through the cultivation of an irrational hatred of the world, while striving to humiliate, soil, dirty, or, in the extreme, to kill all who remind them of their own incompleteness. Erich Fromm observed this syndrome several decades later in Nazi Germany, where it became the base for a wild outburst of Fascist immorality; he described it as "social necrophilism"—a term borrowed from psychopathology. As early as 1902, Russian literature presented with merciless precision and emotional intensity the symptoms of this social necrophilism:

> On the following day, Peredonov went to see District Attorney Avinovitsky. The weather was again gloomy. The wind was coming in gusts and stirring up whirlwinds of dust in the streets.

> Evening was approaching, and everything was permeated with a cloudy, sorrowful mist as if there were no sunlight. A depressive silence reigned in the streets, and it seemed as if all these pitiful houses had sprung up to no purpose, as if their hopelessly decrepit shapes hinted at the poor, tedious, and boring life within their walls. A few people were out, and they walked slowly and with no purpose, as if they had barely escaped submission to restful slumber. Only the children, tireless and eternal representatives of God's happiness on earth, were lively and ran and played. But sluggishness descended even upon them, and some sort of faceless and invisible monster nestling behind their shoulders looked out now and then with its menacing eyes on their suddenly dulled faces.
>
> In the midst of this weariness in streets and in homes, on an earth alienated from the heavens, an unclean and impotent earth, walked Peredonov, tormented with vague fears—there was no consolation for him in the heavens, no joy on earth, because now, as always, he looked on the world with the eyes of the dead, like some demon tormented in gloomy solitude by fear and sadness.
>
> His senses were dull, and his consciousness was a corrupt and deadening mechanism. Everything that penetrated into it was transformed into vileness and filth. His eyes found the imperfection in everything, and he found pleasure in them. When he walked past an erect and clean column, he had a desire to make it lopsided or to spatter it with dirt, and he laughed joyously when something was being dirtied in his presence. He detested and persecuted his cleanly scrubbed students and called them "the sweet little scrubbers." He could understand the slovenly ones more easily. For him there were neither beloved objects nor beloved people, and, therefore, nature could only act in a one-sided fashion upon his feelings and was able only to oppress them. The same was true of his contacts with people, especially with strangers and new acquaintances to whom he could not say rude things.[15]

The spirit of those days in official Russia was conducive to peredonovism—the word itself coined from Sologub's character Peredonov. It sounds incredible, but the peredonovs became one of the buttresses of the regime. The Soviet system also resorted to the services of the peredonovs, both during the Revolution and later, when they gained enormous room for their activities, especially in the punitive network of the Gulag Archipelago.

The regime of the last Tsar was unconscious in the sense of being driven by blind tradition, but it had a strong bias toward the selection of the kind of people with which it preferred to associate. *Its social base became increasingly narrow and precarious.* Alexander III's fatal decision to rely on reactionaries and to reject the party of modernization continued to play its sinister role. Moreover, the dynamics of this process adversely affected the quality of the regime's chosen "partners by alliance." Several decades earlier, the imperial authority of the Tsar had been able to draw upon more or less enlightened conservative circles. But by the time of Nicholas II, enlightened conservatism had virtually disappeared in Russia. *The very logic of events brought the regime into alliance with the most backward social forces* and consequently left it exploiting people's darkest and basest instincts.

EXPLOITING CHAUVINISM

This circumstance manifested itself in the most remarkable way in the field of national politics. *The regime's alliance with what it called the "true Russian people"*—in fact, the intellectually and morally deficient rabble of society—*made inevitable a certain degree of support for chauvinistic "patriotic" mobs* who conducted pogroms in the Jewish neighborhoods of Russian cities.

A terrible pogrom began in Kishinev, for example, on the first day of Easter in 1903 (revealing the "true Christian character" of the nationalists). That pogrom continued for several grim days. Hundreds of Jews were tortured and killed; tens of thousands were traumatized for the rest of their lives; properties were pillaged and ruined. Police and soldiers were silent and passive observers, supposedly expecting "special orders" from above. Orders came only when somebody at the top decided that was enough for now. At that point, order was restored promptly without a single shot being fired. Those who engaged in the pogrom, its victims, and the passive majority of the population all presumed that noninterference was a sign of the moral sanction of pogroms by the regime. This assumption was later confirmed: the imperial minister of the interior was in charge.

Witte has given direct evidence of the government's secret activities in provoking pogroms in his description of the Captain Komissarov case: "The captain was chief of a special section of the Department of Police engaged in the printing of inflammatory literature, largely of an anti-Semitic character, that had been organized under the aegis of Rachkovskii while Trepov was assistant minister of interior . . . , These inflammatory leaflets were being distributed in large quantities in various places, most recently in Kursk, Vilna, and Moscow."[16] This was the same Mr. Trepov who enjoyed a close personal relationship with Tsar Nicholas.

It was not an isolated episode. In December of 1905, after a brutal pogrom in Gomel, Witte as prime minister initiated investigations. "The investigation, conducted by the Ministry of Interior, at my request, revealed that the police, acting under the direction of Count Podgorichani, the local gendarme chief, had organized the pogrom. I asked Durnovo [Minister of Interior, successor to Pleve] to inform the cabinet of what the investigation had uncovered. The cabinet was shocked. When the Emperor read the minutes of this cabinet meeting, minutes that understated the facts, he wrote this comment: 'How does this concern me? Responsibility for the disposition of the case of Count Podgorichani rests with the minister of interior.' A few months later I learned that the count had been appointed chief of police in some Black Sea city."[17]

These two stories provide a general understanding of the position of high authorities and the personal position of the emperor on the "Jewish question." This same policy was directed not only against Jews but against other national minorities of the empire in efforts to "Russify" them through the eradication of manifestations of national culture, particularly indigenous languages. The policy was completely unsuccessful, only serving to provoke other forms of defensive reaction.

Moreover, the persecution of non-Russian subjects of the empire stimulated the development of revolutionary extremism among them. The revolutionary mood was thus heated not only by social conflicts but also by nationalistic discrimination. It was no accident that during Nicholas's reign members of different national minorities took more and more important roles in antigovernment conspiratorial organizations. This circumstance, in turn, opened opportunities for theories concerning the "anti-Russian bias" of the Revolution.

For example, Jewish people were extremely active in the revolutionary movement. The share taken in revolutionary movements by members of other oppressed nationalities—Poles, Latvians, Georgians, Armenians—

was also considerable. Yet ethnic Russians drawing on earlier radical traditions formed a solid core of conspiratorial revolutionaries. Nevertheless, the philistine interpretation of the Revolution as a "Jewish affair" reflected, in a primitive and perverted form, some real historical circumstances.

The anti-Semitism and other forms of nationalism of the last Russian emperors and their chauvinistic state policies created a generation of avengers, a generation of extremists who belonged to different national minorities. The largest percentage of Jews were not among the members of the terrorist faction of the Social Revolutionary Party (SRs) but among the Mensheviks—that is, the section of Social Democratic Party more inclined to peaceful forms of gaining power. When the infernal machine of a revolutionary explosion detonated, these "moderate revolutionaries" were wiped away in the blast. All that would happen later, beyond the period covered in this chapter. For the present discussion we need note only that the system of autocratic authority, by its inhuman, narrow-minded policies, created its own future butchers.

THE LAST OPPORTUNITY TO AVOID CATASTROPHE

The tragic consequences of the intransigent course adopted by the contending parties were anticipated by several intellectuals. People like Witte, members of the Vekhi group, and other writers and poets warned about the threat of coming cataclysm.[18] Some appealed to public authorities; others appealed to the common sense of the radicals. Both sides ignored these warnings. The moderate and flexible arguments of liberals confronted the logic of terrorists on the one hand and the policemen's logic of power on the other. The country inevitably slipped into the abyss.

Historical destiny, however, displayed at that time a sort of "courtesy" expression of honor to the country. A rehearsal of catastrophe occurred in 1905. It offered an extra chance—not for salvation of the regime but to preview a future that might have been avoided with appropriate leadership and fundamental reforms. The Tsarist regime failed to take advantage of this final opportunity. Its actions ironically worked to fan the flames of the Revolution, first by recourse to an unprecedentedly stupid and senseless war with Japan. Second, in light of growing opposition, the regime's recourse to repressive measures escalated. Third, it continued to pursue hypocritical policies even after October of 1905, when it assumed obligations to pursue the path of reform.

Under the pressure of the revolutionary movement, the Tsar signed the October Manifesto, unprecedented in the history of the country. *The main principles of civil liberty were proclaimed* in this manifesto: habeas corpus; freedoms of speech, conscience, meetings, and associations; revision of electoral laws toward universal suffrage; transforming of the state Duma from a consultative into a lawmaking body; establishing executive power with administrative jurisdiction based on law independent of the emperor. In short, the legal basis for a constitutional monarchy was formulated in this document.

Unfortunately, this democratic potential was not realized. The manifesto was proclaimed too late to satisfy the demands and expectations not only of the radicals but of other elements in society. Basic trust had been undermined, and it became clear that the authorities had no intention of adhering to the conditions of this covenant with the nation but sought merely to gain time to regroup and to deceive society by expedient half measures. The regime could not even reconcile itself with the existence of an independent legislature. Tocqueville's idea that "political freedom is no less indispensable to the ruling classes to enable them to realize their perils than to the rank and file to enable them to safeguard their rights," he formulated half a century earlier, proved to be too difficult for the rulers of Russia to understand as late as in the beginning of the twentieth century.[19]

Despite the obligations in the October Manifesto, the regime renewed the main directions of its reactionary and repressive policies. Witte and other people with a liberal, reformist orientation were supplanted within months after the October Manifesto. The Duma was dismissed twice for insufficient reasons. The electoral laws were changed in favor of the upper classes. Suffrage became mostly symbolic. Cruel repressive measures were taken against supposed participants in the revolutionary uprisings; thousands of people were executed by verdicts of courts-martial and by raids conducted as military "expeditions" in different parts of the country. Universities and other educational institutions were subjected to punitive actions. Freedom of the press was constantly violated. The persecution of Jews and other ethnic minorities was aided and abetted.

All these actions were counterproductive even in the purely pragmatic sense with regard to the short-term prospects of the regime. It was as though the authorities had no concern about their own immediate future. The Tsar held a completely erroneous notion about the people's attitudes toward his person, his power, and consequently its limits and possibilities.

Progressive forces ultimately turned away from the government and took a position either of unfriendly indifference or of overt hostility. The autocracy isolated itself from society and incited public opinion against itself both inside and outside the country.

An antipathy to the Russian government became a dominant attitude in the West, even in conservative social circles and governments. Sometimes moral disgust at the aggressive, reactionary system-centeredness of the Russian rulers even overcame the imperatives of financial profit and other economic gains. For instance, in 1911 the United States denounced the Russian-American Trade Treaty, which had been in operation for approximately eighty years. The cause was the stubborn unwillingness of the Russian government to abandon restrictions on entry visas for American Jews. The events of 1905 and the following years demonstrated once again the incapacity of the Russian autocracy to learn from the lessons of history, to anticipate the emergence of new problems, and to influence their development. The Romanov dynasty dug its own grave.

THE INTELLIGENTSIA DIVIDES

One more crucial question needs consideration in our discussion of these years—the social position and turn of mind of the Russian intelligentsia. For better or for worse, this portion of the population held the key to the destiny of Russia.

The autocratic authorities tried to treat the intelligentsia as "learned stewards," but in spite of that attitude, most of the intelligentsia emphasized its own autonomy and accentuated its estrangement. The Russian intelligentsia had its roots in opposition to the regime and it continued this tradition through four generations to the end of the dynasty.[20] But autocratic power was completely incapable of reconciling itself with independent sources of thought. The learned stewards were expected to serve as obedient lackeys. Instead of seeking to understand and cooperate in a search for resolving intellectual differences through dialogue and constructive joint work, the autocrats took the stance of furious tyrannical bosses who could not tolerate objections and either ignored or fired anyone who was disobedient. This absurd position is revealed in a story that almost reads like fable about the Tsar's level of enlightenment:

"In the past when I used the term 'public opinion' in reports, he [the Tsar] would ask in anger: 'How does public opinion concern me?' He believed that what was called public opinion was really the opinion of the *intelligentsia.* And what he thought of them was related to me by Mirskii, who as governor-general of Vilna had accompanied the Emperor through the provinces under his jurisdiction. At one stop, when someone uttered the word *intelligentsia,* the Emperor said: 'How I dislike that word' and added, undoubtedly in jest, that the Academy of Sciences should be directed to expunge the word from the language."[21] Anecdote this may be, but unfortunately a great portion of Russian history has been shaped under the influence of such bad jokes.

Without regard to the emotions and wishes of the regal persons, the opinions of the intelligentsia provoked a vacuum at the center of power during the reign of the last of the Romanovs. The intelligentsia also verbalized the moral isolation of authority from society. Both wings of the intelligentsia—system-centered radicals and moderate person-centered thinkers—contributed to this isolation, each in its own way.

Discussions about the Russian intelligentsia and its significance in the course of Russian history and in the present pivot upon a few key perennial points for every generation of scholars and essayists considering these problematics. However, we often fail to pay sufficient attention to the principal differences in the social role and position of the two camps within the intelligentsia. Even an analyst as effective as Witte neglected this circumstance and wrote about the position of the "educated classes" as a whole: "Had they been sensible, the educated classes would have realized that unless the political system is altered step by step, chaos will result. Instead, they used the occasion of the manifesto to present extreme demands while the left-wing revolutionaries engaged in violence. Such actions led to the creation of right-wing revolutionary parties [meaning Russian nationalists and other ultraconservatives], which soon found support at court, and ultimately from the Emperor himself, support that remained covert as long as I was in power, but not thereafter."[22]

However, the different types of intelligentsia and their respective shares of social responsibility need to be examined much more carefully.

The succession of power from the iron-fisted Alexander III to the spineless Nicholas II gave extremists an excellent opportunity for putting their schemes into action. What is important for us is that the radical intelligentsia undermined the basis for the whole social order, rocking the boat of Russian society ever more sharply. The danger that boats might be overturned with inevitable destruction of people's lives and cultural values did not frighten the radicals but only inspired them.

The idea of the decline of European civilization and the opportunity of revitalizing it by an "injection of barbarian blood" was not original among Russian radicals. Different versions of this idea had been articulated in different times and places in the writings of F. Nietzsche, J. Ortega y Gasset, N. Danilevsky, and O. Spengler.

The Nietzschean outlook and romantic pathos about the destruction of the old world to create space for new "supermen" and to establish a completely new, "just," antibourgeois pattern of order became a rather influential form of intellectual reflection among the European leaders of public opinion by the end of the nineteenth century. A famous Russian writer, Andrew Bely (1880–1934), described that turn of mind in 1910 in his article "The Crisis of Consciousness and Henrik Ibsen": "To place dynamite under history itself in the name of absolute values, which consciousness has not yet revealed—this is the terrible conclusion to be drawn from the logic of Nietzsche and the drama of Ibsen. To explode, along with one's age, in order to strive toward genuine reality—that is the only way of not perishing."[23]

It needs to be emphasized that Bely did not share those revolutionary ideals at all; but he expressed them very precisely. For Bely, both Nietzsche and Ibsen were the great revolutionaries. This radical presentiment was exacerbated in the Russian case by the feeling of marginality about the Russian cultural background, which Bely depicted particularly in his novel *Petersburg:* "From that fecund time when the metallic Horseman had galloped hither . . . Russia was divided in two. Divided in two as well were the destinies of the fatherland. Suffering and weeping, Russia was divided in two, until the final hour. . . . Russia, you are like a steed! Your front hooves have leaped far of into the darkness, into the void, while your two rear hooves are firmly in the granite soil."[24]

Beyond the European source of threat, expectations of a new wave of Asian invasions and a great clash of civilizations were important aspects of this apocalyptic mood. Bely expressed the portents by alluding to well-known military events. Tsutsima is the name of strait near Japan where a huge Russian fleet, while racing from the Baltic around Africa and Asia to support the Russian army at the war with Japan, was badly destroyed by the Japanese fleet; it was the final Russian defeat in that war. Kalka was a battlefield where Tartar-Mongolian squadrons defeated the troops of the Russian princes in 1220—the prelude for two and a half centuries of Tartar domination. Kulikovo Field was the site of the Russian army's first victory over the Tartars in 1380. Bely invoked all three in quick succession:

> In those days all the people of the earth will rush forth from their dwelling places. Great will be the strife, strife the like of which has never been seen in this world. The yellow hordes of Asians will set forth from their age-old abodes and will encrimson the fields of Europe in oceans of blood. There will be, oh yes, there will—Tsutsima! There will be a new Kalka!
>
> Kulikovo Field, I await you!
>
> And on that day the final Sun will rise in radiance over my native land. Or, Sun, if you do not rise, the shores of Europe will sink beneath the healthy Mongol heel, and foam will curl over those shores. Earth-born creatures once more will sink to the depths of the oceans, into a chaos, primordial and long-forgotten. Arise, oh Sun.[25]

The Russian radicals reassessed this warning in their own way: a tragic anxiety about the possible destruction of human civilization's highest achievements yielded to an almost pleasurable anticipation of that possibility as a desirable and progressive event. The possibility of "life after death" was discussed in both uncertain and declarative ways. None of the revolutionaries had any serious designs for this brave new world. This is normal in terms of the psychology and sociology of myth creation: the outline of a utopia is supposed to be very unclear, leaving some room for everyone's fantasies.

On the other hand, the pathos of destruction is much more vivid. That vision could be corroborated by careful plans for a campaign against the bourgeois institutions and by ideological instructions for their future destroyers. These principles of destruction predominated in radical ideas. *Destruction became their self-sufficient goal.* Thus, one of the main heroes of *Petersburg*, the revolutionary Dudkin, developed a theory about the necessity to destroy culture: "The period of humanism had outlived its time and was over. History was a wood-eroded marl. A period of healthy barbarism was at hand, pushing up out of the lower strata of the people, out of the upper strata [the revolt of the arts form, the interest in the exotic], out of bourgeoisie too [ladies' fashions]. Oh, yes: Alexandr Ivanovich had preached burning the libraries, universities, museums, and summoning the Mongols."[26]

As in previous periods, radicals were directed by system-centered ethics. They considered society not as an aggregate of unique individuals, each of whom is a sovereign human being of high value capable of serving other human beings of comparable value, but as a crawling, crying myriapod, a mass susceptible to manipulation. Moreover, the new generation made further "progress" in this direction. Previous generations of revolutionaries had treated the problem of peoples' lives being worthy of sacrifice on behalf of victory for abstract ideas as a sensitive moral dilemma: a dramatic act of self-abnegation from universal humanistic values in the name of "supreme justice" and the "ultimate truth." The more practical revolutionaries of the twentieth century had abandoned this kind of moral reflection. They presupposed their own right to manipulate people on behalf of supreme social interests, to conduct social vivisection in order to realize human liberation. The foci of discussion shifted from moral questions to pragmatic calculations about "gains" versus "expenditures."

The revolutionaries of the 1870s and 1880s were fanatical heroes, prepared to sacrifice themselves in public while exclaiming "Death to the tyrant!" They belonged to a romantic *Carbonari* type of radicals. The twentieth-century revolutionaries shifted to the less spectacular but more consistently planned work of destruction envisioned by the Bolsheviks. Notorious acts of terror remained in their arsenal of tools; but now these instruments became auxiliary remedies either to provoke tension between authorities and people or to serve the even more practical task of expropriating money for revolutionary needs. That was the difference between fathers and sons in the successive generations of Russian radicals.

The circumstance that the Russian intelligentsia was estranged from legal policy making until near the end of the Tsar's regime (the first legal political parties emerged only after 1905) did not allow them to acquire much political experience and thus to learn revise their political theories. The radicals thought and acted in the context of various speculative schemes, and all their intellectual energy was reduced to a total rejection of the regime and its destruction, or to embittered factional disputes between different branches among the revolutionaries. *This situation promoted the development of dogmatism, partisan narrow-mindedness, and social irresponsibility.*

To some extent, one can draw parallels between the Russian radical intelligentsia and French men of letters in the eighteenth century. Both groups followed their best and relatively enlightened intentions, but each opened the Pandora's box of a cruel and bloody revolution.

The Marxists—Social Democrats—proved to be the winners at the finishing line in the pre-revolutionary race to gain power. They were viewed as the "baby brother" in this radical family. The authorities supposed that the major danger existed among the Narodniks—especially the Narodnaya Volya Party—and later the Social Revolutionary Party, the SRs. The terrorist actions of these groups of radicals and their uncompromising propaganda provoked, in response, terror by police and the other repressive instruments of the state. Marxism developed for some time without state interference because the authorities did not pay much attention to the Marxists and were too preoccupied with fighting other foes. When the Marxists were eventually noticed, they looked like the least aggressive group among the radicals and carried on bitter polemics with other radical parties. Therefore, from the police point of view, the Marxists seemed to be a sort of "fifth column," which they could use for their purposes in the radical movement, and temptations developed to use them in that way. The theoretical concepts of the Marxists looked too abstract to be threatening, and nobody cared to prevent their publication. Karl Marx's *Capital* was published during the nineteenth century in three different Russian editions. At the beginning of the twentieth century, the amount of Marxist literature published in Russia continued to grow.

The punitive measures taken against the Social Democrats, including the Bolsheviks, were minimal. Diverging explanations for this police indulgence to Bolsheviks exist: the "wise tactics" of the latter; or the stupidity or miscalculations of the police. There is even some documentary evidence indicating that on the eve of the 1917 Revolution, the majority of members of Bolshevik faction were listed in the files of Police Department as its secret agents. But regardless of all these details, *Bolsheviks undoubtedly outwitted and outmaneuvered both the authorities and their partners in the radical movement.*

While the Narodniks and, later, the SRs fought against power on the front line, the Social Democrats, thanks to their complicated double game, stayed in the shadows and accumulated their forces. Setting themselves against their "older brothers" in the radical movement, they bought with that price an indulgent tolerance on the part of the Tsarist regime.

This was one of the first links in a long chain of Machiavellian intrigues among the Russian Social Democrats. The next was their unexpected move to the political front line accompanied with shameless usurpation of the representation of the whole radical movement. This fantastic, cunning, and dishonest metamorphosis became possible because they kept their cadres intact while the forces of the SRs were undermined by many years of police persecution.

I am not inclined to sympathize much with the SRs over the fact that the main prize they sought was stolen from them at the last moment. I do not want to speculate on whether it would have been better for the country if the SRs and not the Bolsheviks had won the citadel of power. What is important for our analysis is to note that both the SRs and the other radical predecessors of the Bolsheviks share historical responsibility for the tragic course of events that followed after October, 1917.

We have already mentioned the sense of calm before the storm prevailing in the last two reigns of the Romanov dynasty. The 1905 crisis enhanced this presentiment of catastrophe to eschatological proportions. Russian poet Alexander Block expressed this tragic feeling with a metaphor of a bomb mentioned once that the history took and put on the desk in front of us a real bomb, and not a standard, but an improved model of bomb. This idea of history placing a bomb under society dominated Bely's novel *Petersburg*.

The same motif of death looming, but in completely different literary form, was expressed in 1910 by the young poet O. Mandelstam, who saw "no way to come together, no way to compromise," and no escape as blow after blow fell and "poisoned darts" flew from "savage hands."[27]

Unlike Bely's multiple heroes of the radical prototypes, Mandelstam, as we will see later, considered this change lethal and voiced his presentiment of the demise of his culture.

That same dramatic calm before the storm is the context for the great creative thrust of Russian artistic culture. *The creations and the very spirit of the so-called Silver Age of Russian culture, beyond bringing great literary and aesthetic achievements, were the strong source of person-centered "radiation"* because they elaborated and spread an important scale of values in Russian society. In a certain sense, the culture of the Silver Age can be interpreted as the person-centered "creed."

Beyond purely aesthetic and ethical cultural achievements, the artistic intelligentsia also worked intensively on a critical reconsideration of Russian and world history: new approaches to judgments about past and current events. One of the important components of this process was a denial of the heroic romanticism of the Russian past—a "deheroization" of the traditional national symbols of glory. Chaadaev's worldview was resurrected two generations later in poetical images by Innokentiy Annensky, who searched in vain for a heroic reality in the yellow mist of a Petersburg winter. Unsure whether Russians were the intention of a tsar's fiat or the unlucky survivors of a Swedish onslaught, on the grim squares of Petersburg where bodies hung above the dirty snow, Annensky found stones in place of fable, and "terrible facts" in place of history. She found neither shrine nor miracle nor Kremlin. She encountered no images or smiles or tears—just cold stones from "empty spaces." And in the moist white nights of May, Annensky found not the magic of spring, but the "poison of each fruitless dream."[28]

How far Russian literature had moved away from the unthinking pathos of military-patriotic glory that had reached its climax during the Crimean War, half a century earlier! This debunking of traditional symbols was not only a negative process of total denial. Some new, alternative criteria to judge history and current events were also being elaborated and offered to the public. By the last decade of Romanov rule, the kind of people who adopted person-centered values as a kind of practical code of behavior for everyday life had become widespread, extending far beyond the circles of intellectual elite. To underscore this, let us turn to the small poem of an unknown nun from the Novo-Devichii (New Virgin) Monastery located on the outskirts of Moscow. The verse is childishly simple and poetically weak but nevertheless contains the core ideas of a person-centered worldview. We know these lines only by accident: the great Russian poet Marina Tsvetaeva acquired them after the nun had died, and Tsvetaeva reproduced them in her book *Art in the Light of Conscience.*

Cautioning her "dear children" that life would bring "much sorrow" and "years of suffering," temptation and contrition, "hopeless desires" and "cheerless unending toil," the good nun encouraged her readers not to let their spirit weaken. We survive the tribulations of life, she reminded them, through our own goodness, by listening to our hears and heeding our souls, by helping each other without expectation of reward in a "round robin of good."

Tsvetaeva, usually a very severe judge of others' poetry, wrote of the nun's verse: "Take the rhymes—they are obviously commonplace . . . obviously weak. . . . Take the metre—again nothing to make you prick up your ears. But [by] what means was this obviously great deed done?—By no means at all. By the bare soul. This unknown nun of an irretrievable nunnery gave the fullest definition of goodness that has ever existed: 'goodness as a round robin,' and flung the most unmalicious challenge to evil that has ever been heard. . . . To say that these lines have 'genius' would be blasphemy, and to judge them as a literary work would be mean-minded, so far is all that beyond the threshold of this great (as earthly love) trifle of art."[29]

It appears that Russian society at the time was not far from the point at which the diffusion of person-centered values and such a way of life would have become a mass social phenomenon. Certainly it is difficult to prove this empirically. But as indirect evidence, we have plenty of literary and verbal testimony by people who lived then; most of these judgments expressed ideas about how human, how attentive to one another, and how good people were.

These "good people" managed to forward their principles of the round robin of good to the next generation, and as a result the elements of pure, high-style human relationships survived in Russian society for some time after the catastrophe of 1917, in spite of the dominant antihuman spirit of the next epoch.

But we also need to recognize that only a relatively small part of the country's population was seriously influenced by these aesthetic impulses. The importance of this influence was reduced because it was quite different from the processes that affected mass consciousness in relation to two other crucial variables of social development—the ethical and the socio-psychological. The growing immorality—the erosion of the traditional system of moral values and psychological restraints, without any adequate substitution—prevailed in the society. It was not possible to fill this dangerous vacuum of normlessness solely by means of productive efforts created in the fields of art and literature. In that respect, we can say in summary that the person-centered intelligentsia (not just in the arts but in all other aspects) achieved its constructive tasks of moral reorientation much less successfully than the radical system-centered intelligentsia achieved destruction. The tasks of construction are always more difficult than the tasks of destruction.

The serious mistake of the person-centered intelligentsia was their underestimation and neglect of opportunities for cooperation with the entrepreneurial class, which was potentially closer to them than was any other stratum of Russian society. During the last decades before 1917,

Russian entrepreneurs became a small but active part of the society who had cured themselves from the influence of system-centered attitudes. Their activities took the form of many public enterprises, including charities, hospitals, schools, museums, canteens, and inexpensive housing as well as private enterprises. They participated actively in local self-government and in promoting the sciences and the arts. For example, the merchant brothers Tretyakovs established the largest Moscow gallery of Russian art, the famous Tretyakovka. The Russian intelligentsia, although they strove by all means to find contact with the "Russian people," failed to discern that capitalists were the most energetic, active representatives of those same people, capable of self-reliant initiative in advancing human welfare. The old nobility's habit of fastidious treatment of commerce and entrepreneurship as not respectable matters for decent people had a perverse effect. The most the intelligentsia were prepared to do was graciously receive the help of the bourgeoisie. This promising alliance among truly creative social forces, each pursuing its goals of social progress alone and in its own way, was never realized. The split of the intelligentsia into two intransigent camps, which had occurred during the reign of Alexander II, widened. The destructive tendencies accelerated and destructive processes outstripped constructive ones.

These tragic results, clear to us as observers of the past, were also apparent to some who lived through the events: the presentiment of catastrophe was the essential component of the epoch's spirit. "In the pall of the daytime's departing," Blok wrote, the destiny of his generation was becoming clear as the sun smoldered and set. Defenseless, he and his cohort were being engulfed by the waves of time. "We were," he concluded, "fated to last but a moment."[30]

CHAPTER EIGHT

The Inverted Pyramid

■ Alexis de Tocqueville, who studied the French revolution about six decades after it began, wrote: "Today we are in a position to see this memorable event in its true perspective and pass judgment on it. For we now are far enough from the Revolution to be relatively unaffected by the frenzied enthusiasm of those who saw it through; yet near enough to be able to enter into the feelings of its promoters and to see what they were aiming at. Soon it will be difficult to do this."[1]

According to the logic of our conception, the years of the Russian Revolution as well as the following period were the time for reaping the fruits from the seeds sown and cultivated earlier. Those were the years when the crisis disclosed in extremely sharpened form general socio-ethical and psychological patterns of behavior that had been forming and developing for decades and even centuries. In other words, during the revolution the traditional system-centeredness had cunningly changed most of its social masks and, as a result, managed to become firmer and stronger. As in previous chapters, I shall not describe the events. The following pages are devoted mainly to a middle level of analysis—the analytical assessment of ethical and psychological factors and mechanisms as well as their derivative political ones, which directed the course of events.

MORAL AND PSYCHOLOGICAL GROUNDS OF THE REVOLUTION

Let us look first at the social-ethical framework of the events. The first factor of this kind that pushed the course of events in a fatal direction is *anomie;* that is, loss of moral meaning, resulting in potentially aggressive normlessness.[2] We should keep in mind that the moral vacuum so characteristic of anomie emerges when one system of moral standards ceases to play its role as the regulator of people's real behavior before a new system has replaced it.

Among ordinary people, anomie spread widely. The character of revolution is the best demonstration of this. It took two forms—first, destroying the norms of communal ethics and, second, removing the Christian spirit from Orthodox morality. Only its ritualistic structure remained intact, but even this was ready to collapse with the first gust of social turbulence. Precisely this happened during the Revolution, and the vast majority of the population proved to be in a spiritual vacuum. The fatal circumstance was that the Orthodox Church, for all its outward piety and seemingly paramount influence over its parishioners, did not fulfill its most important role of being the collective conscience of society.[3]

Among the more or less educated and influential people, anomie manifested itself in another way—the loss of the feeling of moral responsibility for the destiny of the country. This loss became apparent in many respects: in the alienation of the most competent people from political power, in the inconsistency of political strategies, in the impulsiveness of important decisions, in chauvinistic national policies, in the putting off of solutions to social and political problems, in a predominant tendency to obtain immediate benefits at the cost of the country's long-term interests, and in the unprecedented irrationality of the top holders of power.

With regard to the intelligentsia, anomie was manifest in different ways in both of its system-centered and person-centered wings. System-centered intellectuals who snatched power out of the weakened hands of its previous holders in 1917 revealed their anomie with the triumph of an everything-is-allowed "ethic." This kind of ethic permits actions that are incompatible with the usual moral regulators in human relations when a speculative utopian ideal appears to be at stake. Among person-centered intellectuals, anomie expressed itself in an eschatological social pessimism or, as Albert Schweitzer put it, an "ethics of life-negation."

Such solemn pessimistic feelings during the hour of approaching darkness proved very fruitful for the artistic life of the epoch; but at the more general level they did not serve well. Among the intelligentsia such pessimism cultivated a fastidious ethic of keeping oneself aloof from "dirty politics." As a result, no worthy person was seen on the political horizon of Russia at that time or at other critical periods of our history. By "worthy" I mean a strong liberal who could combine democratic convictions with a practical grasp of public affairs. Alexander F. Kerensky, the head of Provisional Government until the coup of October, 1917, tried this role but proved incapable of it. Thus liberal weaklings at the top accelerated the tragedy. They provided an advantageous political background for the Bolsheviks because "a country which was accustomed to vacillation in policy and inefficiency in administration found itself under the rule of men who seemed to know what they wanted and how to get it."[4]

The second socio-ethical factor in the situation was the activation of a *pseudo-collectivist ethics* as an inherent feature of the Russian genotype. It was Berdyaev who called it "irresponsible collectivism" and described it in the following way:

> I see the illness of Russian moral consciousness first of all in the denial of personal moral responsibility and personal moral discipline, in the weak development of a feeling of obligation and a feeling of honor, and in the absence of a realization of the moral value in the choice of personal qualities. The Russian man does not feel himself morally responsible in sufficient degree, and he has too little respect for these qualities in the individual. This is related to the fact that the individual feels himself immersed in the collective, the individual is not yet sufficiently open and conscious. Such a condition of moral consciousness gives birth to a whole series of claims directed at fate, at history, at authority, and at cultural values which are inaccessible for the given individual. The moral attitude of the Russian man is characterized, not by healthy responsibilities, but by sick pretensions. The Russian man does not feel the indissoluble link between rights and responsibilities, in him both the consciousness of rights and responsibilities are obscured. He is buried in irresponsible collectivism, in claims on behalf of everybody.[5]

This type of morality recoils at times into the background but recovers itself at the moment of a revolutionary outburst in the form of a horrible inhuman force.

The third socio-ethical factor was a *militant moral relativism,* which developed parallel to anomie and became allied to it. Its main principle was that revolutionary expediency prevails over common moral rules. Under the name of revolutionary morality, this principle had been proclaimed earlier in Europe during the French Revolution.

There exist two different justifications of revolutionary amorality: the first is the magnitude of the purpose, and the second is the sublime, integral, uncompromising character of a revolutionary. The first justification is countered by the very simple evangelical idea that a great purpose cannot be achieved with the help of improper means. The second one, in the practice of the Russian Revolution, was expressed by the pretensions of unselfish Bolshevik fanatics. However, in reality, this ideological "consecration" proved highly opportune for people with a criminal psychology who easily adjusted their asocial attitudes to the phraseology of revolutionary morality.

This kind of morality was first clearly formulated in revolutionary France. The Lyons "Convent Instruction"—the most radical document composed to rouse class hatred—was directed against property, against clergy, and against laws, summoning mass terror. It began with the words: "Everything is allowed to those who act in the spirit of revolution. There is no danger for a republican except the danger to be dragged behind republic laws." These words were written not by the fanatical Marat or the incorruptible Robespierre but by Joseph Fouché, a man whose name has been a symbol of political unscrupulousness, and who served in top positions through four succeeding political regimes. The very personality of the manifesto's author conveys the corrupt meaning of revolutionary morality.[6]

However, Russia is not lacking in its own grounds for justifying amorality. It was not by chance that Berdyaev, following Dostoevski, revealed the rejection of honor and dignity as one of the fundamental principles of the Russian revolution, and a result was recognition of 'the honor to dishonor' as the source of the traditional disrespect for human personality.

Summarizing these socio-ethical characteristics of the forces involved in revolutionary events, we must establish the victory of the old ethics of system-centeredness, but in a more modern and dynamic form. In accordance with the spirit of the age, it was rejuvenated at the surface, exchanging its conservative garments for radical ones, but its nature remained the same. The political system had changed but not the social ethics.

To look at the socio-psychological factors that determined the course of events, we need to remember that natural regularities are not the same at different stages of historical development, such as during crisis and postcrisis periods. Let us begin with the socio-psychological mechanisms that determine human behavior in crisis situations.

First, destructive intergroup antagonism increased drastically in the pre-revolutionary years, attaining its peak by 1917. In common consciousness, this intergroup antagonism was the *projection of the everlasting "we" versus "they" opposition in a Marxist social-class variant.* Besides agitation by radicals whose aim was to arouse class hatred, some objective circumstances favored this development. The Socialists' slogan of uncompromising class struggle had an obvious destructive character. In the most unambiguous manner, these agitators stirred up peasants against landowners, proletarians against bourgeoisie, and both poorer groups against the institutions and persons in power. In this way, the ties providing the integrity and stability within the society grew weaker. Stirring up the masses against those in power and the poor against the rich destroys stereotypes of obedience and arouses brute barbaric instincts. "The materialistic interpretation of history" was transformed into the crudest materialistic interpretation of life. All higher manifestations of the human spirit—conscience, honor, the need for truth, justice—disappeared under pressure from the most elementary lusts of the human animal. "The economics of the theory was transformed, in practice, into a nightmarish debauch of totally unrestrained animal instincts, into an orgy of murder, mockery and robbery."[7]

Second, the war, which served as the powerful catalyst to revolutionary rumblings, *stimulated the psychological syndrome of revolutionary social neurosis* in the midst of the people. The mass behavior in this case is characterized by heightened excitability, unbalanced character, aggressiveness, irresponsibility, and even irrationality. The usual social relations are destroyed, the common regulators of behavior—law, morals, and other stabilizing factors—do not function in such periods. People begin to obey occasional impulses and savage instincts. Revolutionary neurosis appears in different forms of mass behavior—in meetings with a prevailing irrational or criminal character, in almost complete cessation of normal working relationships, in increasing susceptibility to rumor, in bloody skirmishes, robberies, and violence against innocent victims. The spirit of militant ruthlessness at both group and individual levels of behavior began to dominate social life.

Freudians hold that in some periods of history, cultural communities and whole civilizations sink into social pathology. Revolutionary neurosis is just one such social pathological state. Erik Fromm described such patterns in the context of fascist regimes as a sadomasochistic complex and a social necrophile syndrome, the two in close parallel.[8] In such circumstances, there were no idealists or even fanatics devoted to ideas but rather a different kind of people, who were intoxicated with a feeling of complete impunity and devoted to human destruction, who propelled the revolution. The psychological type of peredonovism outlined in the previous chapter became manifest in social life.

A relatively bloodless variant of such necrophilic attitudes of the revolutionary masses appeared in Peredonov's desire to mess up, to destroy, to demolish everything beautiful and especially to destroy the attributes of the old culture.[9] It was sometimes realized quite literally by making the landowner's manor house into a pigsty. Russian sans-culottes seemed to find such expression of social contempt simple and obvious. My late father, Valentin Nikolaevich Obolonsky, described in his memoirs, not meant for full publication, the condition of his home in Kiev after the visit of revolutionary soldiers in March, 1918 (the occupants were lucky to be absent). He was only thirteen then, but the impressions haunted him for life: "The flat was completely demolished. Wardrobes were emptied, sofas were ripped open, pictures were torn down, mirrors and dishes were broken. Ten to fifteen bottles of Madeira had been drunk and the bottles left broken. But I was most impressed not so much by that picture of devastation as by the quite unbelievably strong odor in the flat. It was a mixture of strong perfumes from the broken bottles lying next to the broken mirror in my sister's room, tobacco, Madeira, and human excrement. Feces were not left somewhere in the corner, but were lying proudly on the top of our beautiful grand piano. It was an obvious expression of contempt for bourgeois culture, the bourgeois way of life."

One can find many other similar kinds of evidence of a "contaminating syndrome" of behavior in the press and literature of that time, including an essay by "the first proletarian writer" M. Gorky entitled "V. I. Lenin," in the series of his newspaper articles later collected and published as *Inopportune Thoughts.*

This spirit of neurotic demoralization of society grew stronger and spread like wildfire, turning into the predominant force in the development of the revolution. A. A. Minin, who made one of the first attempts to describe the behavior of revolutionary masses from the socio-psychological point of view, retraces this process and divides it into periods.[10] He explains the peaceful character of the first period of the Revolution up to May, 1917, on the basis of the psychological inertia of the masses, who did not realize what was happening. Mass psychology was being agitated and it gradually became aroused. At the same time, the basis of the social integrity that had existed for centuries fell apart. The second period began during the summer of 1917. It was characterized by passionate impatience, the desire to do everything, even to try for the impossible.[11] Demystification, demythologizing of power took place at the same time because the mass either took part in or at least witnessed the overthrow of one power and the formation of another—one that demonstrated its dependence on the people in every possible way. The combination of these two factors resulted in elemental raging: mass seizure of property, the destruction of material values, and other antisocial actions began. Those in power and responsible for maintaining order tried in vain to prevent this destructive process. However, not obtaining any social support they found themselves isolated and collapsed. The third period (in early autumn of 1917) is characterized by the triumph of the asocial element of destruction. Destruction prevailed over mass psychology and behavior.

Third, *a very particular human type, different from the preceding ones, came forth onto the historical stage.* The triumph of this Jacobin type—a fanatical doctrinaire without moral taboos who is able to manipulate the mob or to "saddle" it—is to be accepted by existing and potential leaders. Among the masses, riots and low instincts triumphed. Almost all the authors represented in the *Vekhi* blame the socialist intelligentsia for unbridling mass instincts: The intelligentsia "was able to cast slogans out into the dark and ignorant masses that could destroy whatever remained there, roused the basest instincts, and led toward the destruction of the most ultimate and elementary bases of society. And it did it. . . . They injected it [the people] with ever new doses of poison. First individuals, and then whole categories, were declared 'enemies of the people' and 'outside the law,' which naturally meant a direct invitation to new murder and mob rule."[12]

On this problem only Berdyaev offers a perspective beyond groundless political charges against a whole social group: "That inhuman boorishness . . . is not an offspring of the old order, it is not conditioned by social and political factors; on the contrary, boorishness gave birth to all that was nasty in the old order, it was imprinted onto political and social forms" and multiplied increasingly as it appeared in the Revolution.[13]

Our conception of cause and effect relationships coincides to a certain degree with Berdyaev's view of the problem. It is my belief that most of the cruelties and crimes in the Russian Revolution, and at any rate their scale, were determined not so much by the social situation and political motives as by the wrong side of the system-centered genotype, characteristically revealed under favorable conditions. It was this that defined the very destructive character of the Revolution. Even those leftist-minded Russian intellectuals who initially accepted the Revolution could not shake off the feeling of horror and enmity with regard to the main subject of Russian revolution—the Russian people. "It was painful and terrifying to look at those . . . on whose behalf the revolution was made."[14] M. Gorky depicts in the gloomiest colors the spirit of dull vindictiveness reigning in the streets of revolutionary Petrograd: "The offended person when he has recognized his right to revenge and has an opportunity to is frightening. It is about him that social reformers and political leaders should have thought first of all."[15]

Certainly, such atrocities are not characteristic only of the Russian Revolution. There were any amount of such atrocities in France and Spain—it is enough to mention Ernest Hemingway's *For Whom the Bell Tolls*—to say nothing of the revolutions in Latin America and Asia. The governing motives of social psychology and morals seem to have more or less universal characteristics at crucial points of human history. But neither can we neglect local specifics—mass participation of Red Army soldiers in robbery and pillage.

Returning to my father's memoirs, we can read about the technicalities of the mass shooting of officers and intelligentsia in Kiev during the spring of 1918: "Who was an executioner and how was it carried out? There were no professional executioners. Any soldier could be the one among those who were ever present in front of the palace. This mob—several hundred soldiers—camped in front of the main entrance. They were sitting or lying on the grass, smoking and chattering. When the next victim appeared in the doorway, there were always two or three volunteers among them who joined the escort leading an officer to execution. Victims were to take off their high boots and clothes before the shooting in order that the executioners got them unspoiled afterward. I remember the appearance of one of them that struck me then. A tall peasant fellow. His face was covered with a beard and mustache and without any expression on it. He had a smashed papakha on his head and was dressed in belted overcoat. He wore good officer boots and two other pairs of boots were tucked under his belt on the right and on the left of his belly. There was a tightly packed sack on his back. One look at him was enough to be sure that he had shot at least two or three officers. He appeared equipped in this manner before his commanders and commissars, took his place in a line. . . . To tell the truth, not all of them looked the same. There were more modest ones, with only one pair of boots under the belt."

Note that there were no professional executioners. Any soldier took such a profitable charge upon himself. This was one component of the psychological "cement" of the new regime—a round robin of bloodshed.

Bolsheviks were keen to value and exploit people's worst traits. They blessed the raging "irrational element full of impatience and discontent, ready for destruction and seizure."[16] They directed it ably, then governed it and used it for their aims. All the aforementioned circumstances brought forth suitable psychological types and defined the rule of perverse socio-psychological mechanisms.

Other kinds of socio-psychological factors and behavioral stereotypes emerged at the end of the Revolution when mass exultation calmed down and the sense of crisis began to exhaust itself.

The attitude of obedience based on Russian authoritarian tradition, which had not been lost or even badly shaken, came forth. The short period of revolutionary neurosis that brought a powerful outburst of anarchy and nihilism as a response to accumulated ages of social tension ended in a search for a new yoke, which was at hand. We know that the key task of the Bolsheviks was not to destroy the center of power but to seize it. That is why, with the calming of destructive tendencies, they quickly managed to enslave the people. Bolshevik cruelties recalled to people's minds the strong hand of previous rulers and the old psychological inertia of obeying the force that exercised the ruling hand. The system-centered genotype remained the same. After the Revolution, the destructive revolutionary turned into its seeming opposite (its own alter ego)—a completely obedient lackey. We must not forget that *unprecedented mechanisms of suppressing any opposition and brainwashing now pushed the people into absolute submission.*

Second, *psychological weariness dominated the postcrisis* period. As is known from history, people cannot tolerate endless revolutionary agitation—a crisis situation accompanied by instability. The signs of weariness and tendencies to calm down and stabilize the situation appear rather quickly. The generation who went through the vortex of revolution were ready to pay a high price to regain peace. Only recently people would not have recognized any limits to their freedom imposed from "above"; but now they were prepared to accept even the most despotic rule if this rule promised to restore order and saved at least a minimal sense of change from the preceding regime. We can recall, as an example, political apathy in post-Revolution French society, where Napoleon easily gained unlimited power and enjoyed it for almost two decades. Such radical shifts from general agitation to social apathy can also be noted after the victorious ending of national liberation movements. Unfortunately, we can see signs of a similar social mood in the Russia of the present.

Third, *the psychological mechanisms of suggestion and countersuggestion* (psychological suppression of any opposition to suggestion) began to work intensively. Here, we must again admit the Bolsheviks' ability to manipulate the masses, their grasp of the importance of propaganda. We turn now to considering the specific forms of this mass psychological manipulation in the context of examining the problem of political levers of Revolution.

I assume that socio-ethical and socio-psychological factors determined the regeneration of the Russian army. The armed man who had stopped obeying orders became a semiprofessional political extremist, a kind of fermenting fungus of the Revolution. Such men were also decisive for the development of the social tumult and the extremely rapid concentration of state power with its further radicalization.

In line with the style of analysis of preceding historical periods, we have not discussed the concrete events of the Revolution. As an exception, I would like to draw attention to a point that has been continually repeated in Russian political history: I refer to the unbelievable weakness of Russian liberal politicians.

Many members of the Provisional Government cannot be reproached for their lack of either progressive political ideas or noble determination to bring these to life. History can accuse them of other failings—their political incompetence, indecisiveness, lack of fighting spirit, unwillingness to struggle for their ideas, or readiness to escape from the political arena at the most decisive moments, which I believe looks much like political irresponsibility. These liberals wasted their limited time in endless disputes, sitting on the heating powder keg of the Bolshevik plot. Kerensky, seemingly stronger than the others, was not able to play out to the full his adopted role as an idol and a tribune of the early periods of the Revolution; he proved absolutely helpless facing the hurricane of the Revolutionists. It can be said in his favor that only completely unscrupulous people were able first to make use of the revolutionary tumult for their own aims and later to subdue it.

Was there any other possibility? We must remember that political careers attracted neither the best nor the most talented intellectuals with person-centered notions and attitudes. The best of them preferred other, cleaner fields of activity. This overfastidiousness of the Russian intelligentsia could be justified by the fact that under the autocratic regime, politics was really a dirty business. A politician had to learn early the lessons of servility, intrigues, and unscrupulousness, features not included in the intelligentsia's morality code. As a result, there were no politicians among the liberals able to prevent the catastrophe or at least to diminish its scale at the crucial moment.

POLITICAL MECHANICS OF UPHEAVAL

We turn now to the concrete political mechanisms derived from the system-centered ground of Russian society and providing for the success of the Bolshevik coup. Once more our task is not to describe historical events but to explain them on the basis of historical-philosophical concepts. For those interested in the empirical details of Bolshevik methods of rule or still supposing that the revolutionaries' crimes against their own compatriots were unwarranted, I would recommend, for example, works by Dmitriy A. Volkogonov, Alexandr N. Yakovlev, and Stefan Curtua. All three had maximum access to previously top secret archives and data, and their assessments are well documented and include many statistics.[17]

1. *The demagogic ways that radicals profit from real difficulties and problems.* As we have seen, social problems in Russia had not been solved for decades but had been pushed aside or simply disregarded. As the whole situation grew worse, the necessity of changes and the unwillingness of those in power to bring them about became obvious to most people. As a result, criticism of the regime became an effective and unfailing tool for propagandistic speculations.

The propaganda success was made easy by the political inexperience of the population—the underdevelopment of social consciousness and responsibility. The mass psychology had reached the stage of a primitive group selfishness expressed as a right to pillage and plunder. "The idea of redistribution of material welfare promoted by the Bolsheviks was interpreted by the masses as direct division of property, as immediate access to better life standards. The slogan 'bread and peace' had also a natural and direct meaning for them. The most backward social elements came forth onto the proscenium."[18]

The unsuccessful war situation contributed to growing social irresponsibility. Along with a rise of revolutionary tension, any attempt to attain a compromise or peaceful agreement was proclaimed opportunistic and condemned. On the eve of the October Revolution, political juggling of irresponsible slogans and unrealizable promises reached its peak.

2. *Use of new faith symbols.* For almost 250 years before the Revolution, ideology had been used in Russia as a subsidiary tool by those in political power. Beginning with the Ecclesiastic Council of 1666, which had obediently cursed ultraconservative Old Believers, efforts were made to eliminate every kind of opposition to innovations advanced by the Tsar. Ironically, the Bolshevik program corresponded closely to the Russian tradition of political gamesmanship. The only innovation was the substitution of ideological weapons—a new doctrine. Like a new religion, Marxism in its Bolshevik variant supplanted the Orthodox faith, which had discredited itself by means of its complete submission to crown. Communism had become the new symbol of faith. Purely scientific abstract notions introduced by Marx, in the form of a speculative class psychology, took hold of the minds and feelings of the illiterate or, even worse, the half-literate masses. Quite ironically these abstractions, which were intended to serve as a new secular social science, became cornerstones for the new faith—became new religious symbols. N. A. Berdyaev considered socialism to be a kind of pseudoreligion:

> Revolutionary socialism is not an economic and political teaching, it is not a system of social reform—it pretends to be a religion, it is a faith, a faith antithetical to Christianity. . . . The religion of socialism partakes of the temptation of turning stones into bread, the temptation of the social miracle, and the temptation of the kingdom of this world. . . . In Russia, a special cult of revolutionary holiness arose. This cult had its saints, its holy legends, its dogmas. And for a long time any doubt about these holy legends, any kind of criticism of these dogmas, any kind of disrespectful attitude toward these saints, led to excommunication.[19]

One of the atrocious proofs of the religious character of Soviet official Marxism was the ever-burning flame of inquisition in this new religion during the revolution and long afterward.

3. *Moral relativism became a common principle of political life.* The theory and the practice of Bolshevism—as reflected in a great number of statements by Lenin and other ideologists on this subject, making up the real policy of the Bolshevik party—reveal clearly that there were not any moral taboos for the Bolsheviks. Everything promoting the revolutionary cause was proclaimed moral. Since the Bolsheviks identified themselves with the Revolution, everything useful for them became moral too.

For example, when necessary they could easily appropriate the key positions of their opponents' programs, as happened in the case of socialist-revolutionary propositions on communalizing land or renouncing their own slogans. "The Whole Power to the Soviets!" was placed on the agenda one moment and removed from it the next moment. The Bolsheviks loudly proclaimed the sovereign authority of the nation and its sacred will expressed in just (that is, universal), direct, and equal suffrage by secret ballot. But as soon as the poll results proved to be against the Bolsheviks, they at once forgot these proclamations. The story of the blockading and dispersal of the elected Constituent Assembly in January, 1918, is the classic example of the unlimited hypocrisy of the Bolsheviks.

The principal purpose of the Bolshevik radicals was seizure of power and its further monopolization. Lenin's work *State and Revolution,* so highly esteemed by romantics, indicates that political theory was merely an instrument for the Bolsheviks in striving for power. The main idea expressed there is that the state, being an obviously reactionary social institution, should be abolished, and this could be done only by the Bolsheviks. "Only we, when seizing the power, can make the state wither away"—this is the essence of the work. Now, after more than seventy years of experience with Bolshevik power, it is apparent that such a claim was obviously false. It was clearly a political trick to snatch power from the Provisional Government.

On the contrary, when the doctrine was used to maintain and strengthen the power of the state, it was firmly held in spite of the evidence against it, common sense, and the suffering imposed on millions of people. This can be seen in the Bolsheviks' criminal persistence with the economically absurd and politically irresponsible doctrine of "war communism," even when the result became obvious—production and distribution of food and other necessities were completely stopped and the whole country was starving.

In 1921, the peak year of famine, when the situation was worsened by drought in the Volga area and tens of thousands starved to death, it was a group of non-Bolsheviks who founded the All-Russian Committee of Help to the Victims of Starvation, or Komgolod (Starvationcom)—a completely nonpolitical organization. The committee went energetically to work and managed to draw the world's attention to the tragedy. Large stocks of food and other material supplies began to come from abroad. Many thousands of Soviet citizens held a lifetime of gratitude for the American Relief Administration and other organizations whose activity had saved their lives.

What was the reaction of the Bolsheviks? They did not reject the help. But they were worried that the leaders of the committee might gain people's sympathies and in this endanger the Bolsheviks' hold on power. The campaign against the Komgolod began under Lenin's personal supervision. The Extraordinary Commission for Struggle with Counterrevolution and Sabotage (Cheka) proclaimed the Komgolod a counter-revolutionary organization. Why? The Cheka report to the chairman of the Council of People's Commissars or Predsovnarkom offers the following explanation: "The campaign for help to the hungry will be accompanied in Great Britain with vivid pictures of the Russian people's sufferings. . . . The emigration expects the Soviet power, cooperating with right organizations, will become more and more rightist itself... Owing to their anti-starvation activity anti-Bolsheviks will gain access to power. . . . This activity gives ground to the organization of public forces."[20] The committee was prohibited and arrests, imprisonment, and deportations followed.

What other evidence is necessary to testify to the absolute amorality of the regime? When the good of the people came into conflict with the principle of unlimited control over the life and death of their subjects, it was abandoned.

4. *Stirring up the "revolutionary people," the mob, against "social enemies," the bourgeoisie and the intelligentsia.* This tactic was based on the socio-psychological phenomenon of releasing vicious instincts and passions in a crisis situation. Violence was openly proclaimed a basic principle of revolutionary power directed against those who were not on the Bolsheviks' side of the barricade. "The whole historical period is

characterized by capitalist resistance, hence the persistent *violence* against the whole class (the bourgeoisie) and its accomplices," said Lenin (italics his).[21] The idea of the bourgeoisie as the image of the enemy was introduced. M. Voloshin described this process in his poem "Bourgeoisie." "There was no bourgeoisie," he wrote, but the revolution needed capitalists, and so they pieced together a bourgeoisie from shopkeepers and merchants, landowners, midwives, and cadets, then mixed in "the blood of officers," and melted it all in the torture chambers of the Checka. The Civil War created not only the dictatorship of the proletariat, it created the bourgeoisie that justified it.[22]

One revolutionary practice to stir up social groups against each other was direct incitement to seize another's property. It was persistent and took different forms, including making plunder and pillage legal and absolving people from responsibility for future predation. For example, the Red Army in Kiev was urged to supply or "dress itself at the expense of the bourgeois" before going into action.

This process readily went on in Russia because the Russian people had traditionally had little respect for the property of others, compared to circumstances in the Western tradition, where respect for property was one of the foundations of society. This destructive tendency worried authors beyond those representing the bourgeoisie. Even Gorky, who had earned the trust of the Bolsheviks as a "storming petrel" of Revolution, was distressed in the 1920s: "We live in the period of a bold experiment to abolish private ownership of land and workers' tools and witness this dark, cursed instinct [to capture the property of others] which ironically grows, strengthens, [and] makes criminals out of honest people."[23]

We cannot blame the Bolsheviks alone for the destruction of property rights. The previous regime in Russia also demonstrated a constant neglect of its subjects' rights. As noted, Witte considered this problem with regard to land reform in 1861 and the Tsar decreed the compulsory alienation of landowners' estates in favor of peasants. We can also compare this with the situation in China, where imperial authority was exercised against land holders over the possession of land and prevented the development of the private property principle in its Western meaning. Even in France, in the eighteenth century under the reign of the last two monarchs before the revolution, "the administration was persistent in demonstrating to the people, in the most practical and understandable manner, what scorn should be shown to private property."[24] One of the negative consequences of the policy of "robbing the robbers" was to ruin the incentives for work, for a people's work ethic. The more efficient and successful your work, the greater the probability you would be being listed as a person whose property was to be confiscated.

5. *Monopolizing channels for propaganda.* The Bolsheviks understood very well the advantages of a strategy of monopolizing propaganda channels for convincing the population of their own rightness and infallibility.

One of the first decrees of the Provisional Government after the February Revolution was an announcement of unlimited freedom of the press. Bolsheviks adopted their own decree on the press forty-eight hours after their coup d'état. They declared the situation to be an emergency and asserted the authority to close down all opposing editions. "During four months of the Bolshevik rule from the moment of the upheaval to the 22nd of February they closed down 168 newspapers. There were sixty-nine socialist ones (including thirty-six socialist-revolutionary, half of their whole number) among them. The Bolsheviks confiscated twenty-six printing-houses, prosecuted according to the revolutionary law nineteen newspapers, arrested and deported eighteen editors in chief and reporters, the sum of fines on newspapers amounted to 142 thousand rubles."[25]

This was only the beginning.

The task of bringing the press to submission was assigned to the Cheka, the most brutal and direct agency of the dictatorship. The Bolsheviks presumed that the press was the most dangerous threat to their regime. In late January, 1918, the "revolutionary Tribunal on the press was organized as a branch of the Revolutionary Tribunal. Crimes and deeds committed against the people by the press were put under its authority."[26] Among sanctions for violation of the decree were "confiscation, imprisonment, deportation from the capital, to other places of the Russian Republic or beyond its boundaries, and deprivation for the guilty of all or some civil rights."[27]

After the end of the Civil War, when any reason to refer to extraordinary circumstances disappeared, the Bolsheviks' fear of the press did not diminish. Lenin personally supervised the press restrictions and controlled their fulfillment up to the end of his active life. In particular, he issued orders to close down magazines and to repress their publishers.

Censorship was regulated and institutionalized at the same time. On the June 6, 1922, the Council of People's Commissars or SNK adopted a statute creating a Central Board for Press Affairs (Glavlit). Remarkably, this statute was even tougher than the censorship statute of 1826, nicknamed at the time "the cast-iron one."

All these repressive measures against the press were but one aspect of the Bolsheviks' struggle against all opposition ideas. A month after the seizure of power, they found an opportunity to proclaim one of their main opponents—constitutional democrats—the party of the nation's enemies. The whole party was declared to be the enemy of the people! There were no exceptions; their recent allies the Social Revolutionaries and the Mensheviks were included. The latter also were system-centered but not to such an extent as the Bolsheviks.

This monopolization of access to public opinion looks even more perverse if we recall Bolshevik tactics during the period between February and October under the Provisional Government. They used and abused press freedom to the utmost in their opposition to the regime. For demagogic propaganda against the government, they sought to discredit it in every possible way, including the organization of antigovernmental forces in direct preparations for armed resistance.

6. *"Two-layered" ideology.* The ideological hypocrisy of the Bolsheviks can be explained in part by the phenomenon of "principled amorality" already considered. I introduce the term *two-layered ideology* in order to explain an immanent coexistence of two opposite principles in the doctrine and practice of the Bolsheviks. One of them was for the external use, addressed to the masses; the other was for internal use within the party core, for the insiders. George Orwell dubbed the divide the "inner" and "outer" party. This dichotomy began as early as 1903 when the Bolsheviks, despite their pretensions of being both democratic and egalitarian, chose the conspiratorial type of command organization in which members were carefully selected and committed to strict secrecy and strict obedience. The genuine purpose of this organization was to establish its exclusive control over society. Everything else was merely the means for achieving absolute control. For understandable reasons, such totalitarian intentions were always deeply concealed. They were constructed so as to create a facade behind which iron discipline was maintained by strict secrecy.

Such an organization can work successfully only if it maintains two quite separate levels of politics—one for show and one for real action, the legal and the conspiratorial. This tactic followed the tradition of an unscrupulous political two-facedness—a cynical opposition between words and deeds.

The first posture was a hypocrisy as regards peasants: they were publicly promised freedom of land tenure and guarantees of support for their personal labor. Actually they were destroyed through a system of "appropriating the surplus," through terrorizing of the peasants by food-confiscating armed detachments; through placing unbearable taxes on them; and in the end, through completely subjugating the peasant population to work the "collective" farms (so-called *kolhozy*).

The second pretense was an ostentatious propagandistic move to deprive the Cheka and revolutionary tribunals of the right to sentence people to execution, which was adopted at the beginning of 1920 in connection with the end of Civil War. This was followed by a number of decrees applying to different categories of citizens, removing the "laws" of the period of revolutionary war—that is, prohibiting arbitrary shootings at the sole decision of Checka officials. The word *shooting* was removed from circulation for several months, obviously for propaganda purposes, but it was soon put into practice again.

The third pretense was a national policy that publicly proclaimed the right of nations or nationalities to self-determination. It was not by chance that Stalin became the People's Commissar for National Affairs from the very beginning. The essence of Stalin's nationality policy is all too well known: we deal still with its terrible consequences in Chechnya and other places in the territory of the former USSR. This method of publicly proclaiming one principle but actually carrying out the opposite was brought to perfection through the decades of the Soviet system.

7. *The use of marginalized elements in social support of the regime.* This mechanism included criminals, soldiers who disobeyed orders, and other marginals. The first years of the Soviet regime were characterized by a raging of organized crime. The criminal atmosphere prevailing in the country was well described in early Soviet literature, so close to them in time that it was impossible to conceal the details. Later the same events were cloaked in myth as heroic deeds. The victorious regime did not consider offenses committed for the purposes of the Revolution to be crimes or moral misdemeanors.

If we take a close look at the classic novels of early Soviet literature, such as *Iron Flood* by Alexander Serafimovich, *Defeat* by Alexander Fadeev, *The Quiet Don* and short stories by Michail Sholochov, and poems by Demian Bedny, we see on practically every page that the deeds of the revolutionary heroes were literally scenes from the criminal world, where the merciless laws of criminal predators prevailed. We can take as an example the situation portrayed through the eyes of the poet Maximilian Voloshin. He always tried to remain above the situation since he believed that in the heart of every villain hid a "confined angel."

And who were the Red Guard? Voloshin answers that they were those who loved "to gallop in grand review with a cocade on the head" through Petrograd in the spring and through Moscow in revolution. Delirious and drunk, they surrendered to a game of defending the Motherland one season and Bolshevism the next. They crowded the corridors of the Winter Palace, they addressed meetings, and they twirled their mustaches as they cursed and cocked their hats. They probed locks with bayonets, smashed doors with rifle butts, broke into homes, broke open wine barrels, seized grain, smashed windows, and burned the whole lot. They lectured the peasants on liberty, then searched for horses and canon in drawers and boxes. They played with machine guns and became hateful to their own kind, ending up in a ditch, shot for simple theft.[28] Such were the supporters of those who claimed to be the vanguard of progressive mankind!

8. *The use of terror as a power principle.* It became obvious during the first weeks after the October coup that organized violence was one of the main methods of the new regime to rule over society. It would not be an exaggeration to say that terror became one of the basic principles of the regime. The regime consciously and calculatedly conducted this policy of terror against those strata of society—organizations and individuals—that at that time or later could be a possible or imagined source of danger. Any form of enmity, disloyalty, or even getting beyond control was considered a direct threat to the regime. From the standpoint of self-preservation, this judgment was correct because such rigid systems can be viable and stable only within very narrow limits of deviation. This was confirmed by how fast the system disintegrated as a result of Gorbachev's attempt to make it "more human."

The first appeal of the new regime to terror occurred only ten days after the coup, on November 5, 1917.[29] The mechanism of control by terror began to be created at once. It acquired complete organizational form in the Cheka and its regional branches in December, 1917. At the same time, executions became widespread as a normal measure put into common use in SNK decrees and other official documents. Terror was directed not only against enemies of the regime; it came to be used every time something went wrong with the policies of the regime. It was also used as a preventive measure by being deliberately unpredictable as a way of frightening and subjugating the population.

The decision to exterminate, "as a class," officers and other "non-Bolshevist elements" of the former Tsarist army was taken even before the beginning of the Civil War. In late January, 1918, Kiev was placed under the control of the Bolsheviks for the first time. Let me turn again to my father's memoirs:

> The massacre of the officers continued for several days. We watched it through the windows of our flat which looked on Mariinsky palace facade. These memories remained lifelong for me. Officers captured in the city were brought to the palace from early morning till late at night. They were brought in groups, sometimes only one at a time, sometimes a great number of them together. They stayed inside the palace where their fate was being decided for several minutes. Then they were shot in the square in front of Mariinsky park. Before execution they were ordered to take off boots and clothes. . . . The first group was very big—200–300 officers taken in the Hotel Prague, the largest one in Kiev. They were brought under escort and crowded with their heads lowered in front of the palace. Some still had shoulder-straps, but most were without them, and there were also people in civilian clothes. Two of them, seemingly of higher rank, were kept in the palace for 5–10 minutes. When they returned, the whole group was led into the square and machine-gunned; the wounded were shot with rifles. Later the groups executed became smaller; sometimes there was only one at a time.

This record is striking in its minute detail, bringing us to the conclusion that the terror was well organized, especially by the standards of that anarchic times. In my opinion, these measures not only demonstrate the orgy of a vandal mob but also reveal *the inherently criminal character of the Bolshevik regime itself, which made genocide one of its main methods of control from the first days of its existence.* Whole categories of people were exterminated. A little later, during the Civil War, this policy of terror was also pursued within the Red Army to keep it under control.

The food-confiscating detachments used the policy of terror against peasants. When peasant resistance occurred against this form of armed robbery, the regime sanctioned it in the name of the system for appropriating the surplus while cruelly suppressing the peasants in the name of Cheka and special elitist detachments (one of them—ChON consisted of some 40,000 armed men in 1919).[30] The early years of "worker-peasant" power are marked by the growing scale of peasant unrest and uprisings—and by reprisals against them. There were 245 peasant disturbances in 1918 and about 100 during the first half of 1919, for example. By 1921, peasant resistance to the regime included most rural areas. In response, the Bosheviks officially declared a campaign against them that amounted to war. Reprisals were beyond all conceivable limits in brutality, including, for example, lethal gas attacks against villages and forests where insurgents were supposedly concealed. After this "victory" over their own people, the regime, effectively an army of occupation, introduced a chain of concentration camps and mass executions in the "conquered" territories.[31]

Terror against employees was conducted in various ways. According to the SNK Decree of June 28, 1918, "On nationalization of the most important enterprises," and a series of earlier decrees on confiscation of specific plants, factories, and joint-stock companies, not only was their property confiscated but even the personal bank accounts of employees were seized, and employees themselves were transformed into serfs by means of threats of severe consequences for leaving their new master.[32] The June decree was formulated as follows: "All employees and technical workers must stay and fulfill their duties; for unauthorized leaving of the work and sabotage the guilty will be prosecuted according to the revolutionary law."[33] This policy of terror was especially severe as regards basic services of vital importance to the regime itself. such as transport. The RKO Council Decree of October 10, 1919, "On responsibility for deliberate demolition of railway constructions," reads: "Persons caught in flagrante delicto must be executed at once [and] those suspected in the same crimes must be tried within 24 hours according to wartime laws."[34] Terror also was used against the population in general, including local Soviet authorities and even teenagers. Mass taking of hostages and executions of people suspected of disloyalty took place in the Ukraine, for example.

The taking of hostages was applied broadly and in various situations. Its principle was to hold completely innocent people under arrest and threat of extermination. Lenin and other higher authorities gave direct instructions to this effect. Another tactic favored by the leader was the advisability of preventive arrests and even executions of representatives of groups held to be disloyal to the regime, simply in order to keep them frightened.

An imputation of counterrevolution could always be alleged, and then the threat to human life became imminent. Hence later punishments, like a twenty-five-year prison sentence decreed by a Stalinist court for a diary containing political reflections and a ten-year sentence for putting a hat on Stalin's bust at a school graduation party, were the consequences of policies identified with counterrevolutionary measures.

By the end of 1917, quite unprecedented measures of total control over subjects had been adopted. On December 7, Lenin sent Dzerzhinsky a note on measures against counterrevolutionaries and saboteurs. All wealthy people and their employees were obliged to denounce themselves as potentially disloyal to the regime under the threat of severe punishment and then to keep an appropriate document about themselves constantly available.[35] I believe these efforts would have done credit to the Spanish Inquisition at its most repressive.

The terror was almost banal, a routine that would become familiar, a bureaucratic procedure. M. Voloshin gives an emotional rendering of events in his poem, "Terror." "In the night," he writes, the officials would gather to read through the certificates, judge the cases, assess the reports, and sign their decisions "with a hasty hand," stifling yawns and drinking wine. Mornings they distributed vodka to the soldiers; evenings they read out the lists of those to be eliminated. Both men and women would then be herded into a dark yard, and the soldiers would take from them their clothing and shoes, their watches and rings, and drive them "barefoot and hungry over the icy ground," through the cold wind, into the fields outside the town. The victims would be prodded with rifle butts toward a ravine where they were machine-gunned and bayonetted. Those still alive were simply dumped into the ravine, which the soldiers filled with earth before hurrying home.[36]

Commentary would be superfluous. What can one say of such casual savagery?

The Bolsheviks were known to be adherents to the idea of the strong ruling hand—strict discipline—in spite of their short period of flirting with anarchists and exploiting destructive anarchists in their tactical use of antistate phraseology. In accordance with this, they considered a state-directed system of terror one of the main instruments of their rule. In the period under discussion, there existed two bodies—special commissions and tribunals—charged with the task of fulfilling punitive terrorist duties. Initially the Bolshevik authorities did not even conceal their terrorist strategies. A couple of years later, they realized that to be candid in such matters is not always useful. A glance at Lenin's state documents of 1921–22 shows many notations of "confidential," "top secret," "return to me personally," "not to be copied," or "read and return without copying." These were not characteristic of the earlier period following the October coup. The terrorist nature of things began to be concealed under decent forms of law and legal procedures. There were two reasons for this change: the rulers wanted, on the one hand, to acquire a more decent appearance, and on the other hand, to bring under control the terrorist machinery that showed some Frankensteinian tendencies to disobey its creators and to gain the upper hand.

These special bodies, called "organs," became especially attractive for criminals of every kind. Even the authorities who always tried to cover for the Cheka and "Chekists" were sometimes obliged to acknowledge their systematic lawlessness and arbitrariness. The crimes committed by Chekists under the umbrella of secrecy and their official standing as organs of the state began to worry even their political masters—the Bolsheviks themselves.

Terror was introduced in earnest and for the long haul. Top ideologists for the Bolsheviks had no illusions concerning the necessity of quickly suppressing resistance to their regime. That is why beginning in January, 1918, signs of concern for "a greater number of penitentiary establishments" and enlargement of the existing ones appeared.[37] This concern became constant and persistent, and in due course it received added motivation from seemingly remote concerns about problems in the national economy. The unique "worker-peasant state" managed to combine two state functions that had never been combined before in classical theory of organization. Criminal law and economic development were brought together by the use of compulsory prison labor in the operation of economic enterprises on a large scale.[38]

It is interesting to quote here Marx's opinion on terror psychology in his letter to Friedrich Engels dated September 4, 1870: "We believe it [terror] to be the domination of terrifying people; the actual situation is quite opposite—it is a domination of terrified people. Terror consists mostly of useless cruelties committed by frightened people to calm themselves."[39] Marx's opinion seems to supplement our considerations with one more important aspect.

9. *The use of privileged military detachments.* Besides marginalized and criminal groups, the regime was supported by organized forces of janizaries—teams of armed people tied to it by material and other group interests. Such detachments occupied an exceptional, elitist position in the structural base of the regime. They had substantial material privileges. They were trusted to guard top leaders of the regime and to fulfill the most important and ticklish tasks. These detachments had little connection to local populations and interests. Their fate and well-being depended completely on their unconditional support of the regime and its top leaders. Therefore, the more hostile the population's attitude was toward them, the more devoted these detachments were to serving their masters. They realized that the defeat of their masters would mean their own destruction.

Any dictator having reason to feel his life endangered cannot manage without such personal bodyguards. Roman emperors had praetorians; Turkish sultans, janizaries; Nazi leaders, SS detachments. In Russia these functions had been performed by the Oprichniks under Ivan the Terrible, the Preobrazhensky regiment under Peter I, and the Guards regiments under the following emperors and empresses up to the beginning of the nineteenth century. Revolutionary regimes need such support no less than do conservative ones. They were the "ironsides" under Cromwell and the Marseillaise under the Jacobin dictatorship. The latter serve as the best prototype for the mercenaries of the Russian Revolution.

The Bolsheviks, concerned first with the preservation of their power, improved this system by simultaneously using several detachments of this kind. These corps were in conflict or, at least, in a kind of rivalry with each other. During the first revolutionary years these roles were performed by sailors who had left their ships, by Red Guard detachments mostly reinforced by deserters from the front, by Lettish riflemen, Chinese battalions, special-mission detachments (ChON), or Kremlin riflemen. Here again, Chekists gradually occupied the leading positions. All these socialist janizaries' differed clearly from armed robbers in only one respect—they were controllable from the top and became organs of the state.

On the other hand, the Bolsheviks were not overfastidious. They also cooperated with genuinely uncontrollable bandits, such as bat'ka Makhno in the Ukraine, because they were sure of their ability to take anybody in. As a matter of fact, the Bolsheviks turned out to be the most shrewd and unprincipled of all. Makhno detachments, by agreements with the Soviet government, took active and effective part in the battles for Crimea against the White Guards in 1920. Immediately after the end of this campaign, the high command of Red Army (Frunze personally) ordered them to relocate to the Caucasus, to leave their native Ukraine for another shore of Black Sea, for another kind of war. Naturally they refused. Then all their commanders were suddenly arrested and shot. Their detachments, mixed with Red Army troops and deprived of their own leadership, were easily destroyed. This little-known episode of the Civil War characterizes the Bolshevik way.[40]

10. *Subduing system-centered mob elements and their manipulation by means of the bureaucratic machinery of government.* We have already seen that the Bolsheviks, by their fundamental nature and deep attitudes, were further from anarchism than anybody else. Thus when the "untamed" elements had performed their role, the task of subduing them arose. Here, the Bolsheviks revealed again their utmost skill in solving political problems for their own benefit. They also used the natural phenomenon of psychological fatigue.

This fact did not diminish their art of manipulation. They mastered the skill of staying on top of objective political tendencies and using these for their own purposes. The Bolsheviks closed out the "people's rage" element or, more precisely, its low instincts and passions, and allowed it expression only by targeted impulses against the next set of enemies—the bourgeoisie, kulaks, opposition within the party, nobility, intelligentsia, "enemies of the nation" in general, and against Germans, Jews, Imperialists, Chinese, Poles, Americans, etc.

This constantly repeated trick of creating scapegoats never failed because of its psychological infallibility: every time the people confronted a concrete enemy in the flesh, they found a target for their troubles and sorrows, the impersonation of the ever-present "they" as a hostile force. The intermediate groups of the population who recognized their proximity to those hostile forces in any particular case either kept silent or zealously sought to persecute the "enemy" to gain the favor of those in power. It never helped them to avoid their own doom. Sooner or later, their turn came.

The major political instrument for these efforts was the bureaucratic machinery of the central administration. Terrorist methods were ever present as ready means for deterrence and reprisals. So the regime put the people's rage under bureaucratic control as one of its tools.

The politics of "war Communism" included as its essential component ruthless persecution of the economically active population, which brought the country to economic catastrophe. The victims lost all incentives to work. By 1920, the real threat of complete collapse of all economic activity in the country made the Bolsheviks attempt to correct their line toward small producers and tradesmen. They had to turn to the New Economic Policy (NEP), which Lenin called "a temporary retreat."[41] It was forced expedient and tactical step. The main idea of this retreat was to admit some freedom of economic enterprise but without any liberalization in the fields of politics and ideology. Moreover, in spite of some minor differences in views among party leaders, it was confirmed and mutually reconfirmed that under conditions of limited economic freedom, political control must be even fiercer to prevent dangerous side effects for unlimited Bolshevik power. It seems rather remarkable that the same Party Congress that passed the NEP (the tenth congress), had also prohibited "factions" in its own party and had ordered that the so-called Kronshtadt revolt be drowned in blood. (That revolt was rather a moderate action by the navy, involving a resolution appealing for a stop to full Bolshevik dominance in society, for democratic elections in the Soviets, and for release of political prisoners.) The Bolsheviks feared to the point of irrational panic even the specter of opposition. Any potential opponents or even independent-minded people, either inside party ranks or outside, were perceived as a mortal threat. Endless political repressions running all through Soviet history demonstrate this clearly. The entrepreneurs themselves were under growing pressure of taxes, forced "donations" for purposes of industrialization, direct contributions of money, and extortion by means of temporary arrests. Later they faced confiscation of property and trials. Even under these conditions, NEP provided a certain economic growth and actually saved country from starvation. But the Bolsheviks were not able to coexist with any independent forces in society. NEP was gradually abandoned. In 1929—called the year of "great change" (or the "big leap," to use Maoist phraseology)—the NEP policy was completely broken at the cost of new millions of human lives. We return to this theme in the next chapter.

One more universal mechanism to hold the subjects in obedience was created and brought to perfection in its practical application by the Bolsheviks. This was the *mechanism of a mass political party* founded on the base of the so-called principle of democratic centralism. It was used very effectively to command the entire social structure from top to bottom. Its possibilities of corrupting any society were widely discussed and its monstrous dehumanizing capacities were obvious enough.

11. *Taking advantage of the deep depression of a bitter hangover.* When revolutionary passions had calmed down and the excitement in mass consciousness changed to depression, the feeling became that of a joyless, bitter hangover. Revolutionary criminal types found themselves unclaimed, at least until the beginning of mass collectivization of agriculture. The doctrinaire revolutionary fanatic type also felt deceived when the fervent revolutionary activity failed to achieve paradise on earth and in the end proved to be an illusion. Average people whose reaction to the Revolution was rather passive, but who were misled to some degree by the rhetorical slogans of radical ideologists and by some of the new authorities' measures to eliminate obvious evils of the prior regime, fell into even deeper depression.

This depressed spirit of the 1920s was noted by many observers at that time. In particular, it found expression in an increased suicide rate. In 1925, Leningrad occupied seventh place in the world among big cities in its suicide rate per million inhabitants—344. "Only 5 cities in Germany, plunged at that period into the most disastrous crisis period of hyperinflation, and Budapest were ahead of it. Moscow was in the 14th place but far ahead of such 'diseased breeders of capitalistic evil' as Chicago, New York, London, Amsterdam. . . . The peculiarity of the USSR with respect to suicide was age. In other countries, the older people suffered a higher suicide rate. In the USSR, both in cities and in the countryside, suicide occurred most often at the young age of 20–24 and in the adjoining groups of 16–19 and 25–29."[42]

The young people whose worldview was just being developed at that period of peak revolutionary passions became the "lost generation" who adopted the "radical solution" to end their disoriented lives. It is also noteworthy that a considerable wave of suicides occurred within the ranks of Bolshevik party activists. This tragic referendum of people voting with their lives is an important indication of the spirit of the time.

Another serious consequence as evidence of the deformation in the psychology and ethics of the nation as a result of the Revolution was revealed in the crime rate dynamics. If we compare the data for April, 1917 (the peak criminal period of the preceding era), with the first quarter of 1923, we observe a considerable rise in serious crime. "The number of recorded murders had doubled," a gigantic rise for a six-year interval.[43] Organized gangsterism became widespread—was it a result of the Revolution sanctifying the right to seizure, its rob-the-robbers ideology, and its support of "a man with a rifle"? Cities were terrorized by gangs of armed robbers rivaling one another. Human life, never highly valued in Russia, cheapened considerably.

Former moral taboos had been destroyed, and new ones were not created in the course of the Revolution. As a result, the character of post-revolutionary crimes became more vicious. M. Gernet refers to the number of crimes that were incomparable in their calm "businesslike character" and their cold-blooded mockery of human life and death. This was one more side effect of the anomie and demolition of previous norms of human behavior, of barbarism under revolutionary slogans.

One of the most popular revolutionary proclamations was the idea of equality. It was this idea that attracted a number of people to revolutionary banners, because it promised not material gain but the elimination of all formerly existing social barriers. Generally, this myth of equality sounds tempting for many people, including honest, noble, and altruistic people. But it especially attracts those who consider themselves unfairly passed-over in life, deserving of a better lot. Their number is always rather high. The peculiarity of this characteristic is that psychologically it is subconsciously driven not by a striving for equality but by the desire to acquire higher social status, better corresponding to one's imagined merits. Sometimes such aspirations are justified; sometimes they are not. But such people are always ready to support a radical social movement.

The myth of equality was one of the first to be dismissed in post-revolutionary Russia. New privileged groups representing the new elite soon appeared. It is important to note that *gaining access to this elite was accomplished according to criteria that were far from the ideals of social justice and human merits than had existed under the previous regime.* Berdyaev's sad predictions came true. To his "foes in social philosophy" he wrote: "Inequality . . . justifies the existence of a human being and is a source of any creative movement in the world. Any birth of light in the darkness is an emergence of inequality. Any creative act is also an emergence of inequality, elevation, appearance of characteristics out of characterless mass."[44] Another letter was "On aristocracy": "There exist only two possible powers—aristocracy and ochlocracy, the rule of the best and the rule of the worst. . . . If the real hierarchy is distorted and the real aristocracy is extirpated there come false hierarchies and false aristocratic forms."[45] This was more or less Russia's way. I do not completely share

Berdyaev's arrogant aristocratic attitudes, but I concur that a denial of the individuality characteristic of a person-centered approach to life is a denial of creative potentials.

12. *Creating a new religion, repressing the old.* The Russian Orthodox Church had been the chief source of belief in Russian society for centuries, at least formally. The Bolsheviks, whose aim was to convert people to the new faith, could not tolerate the old one. That is why as soon as they seized the instruments of state power, they began their persistent repressions against the Church. Their aim was to deprive it of any influence over society. Some deviations from that general line can be explained by expedient accommodation to the political situation of the moment. According data from clerical sources, in 1918 alone, 3,000 members of the clergy were executed, some suffering medieval atrocities.[46] But it was only the beginning.

A general assault against the Church was waged after the end of the Civil War. The starvation of the Volga region was chosen as an official ground for the struggle against the Church. The Church had designated some of its wealth for the relief the starving population. The Patriarch agreed to that commitment. But such peaceful resolution was unacceptable to the Bolsheviks, and a decree on the compulsory requisitioning of Church property was issued. The Church tried to protest but under growing pressure was obliged again to seek compromise, despite substantial provocations and humiliations. But for the Bolsheviks, no compromise was feasible; only a complete victory would serve. Church properties were confiscated everywhere in the most ruthless way, aimed at offending the sensibilities of the priesthood and the believers. The inevitable demonstrations provided the grounds for armed suppression. Processions of monks were machine-gunned and court prosecutions against the priesthood resulted in severe prison sentences and in some cases the death penalty. A top secret letter by Lenin to Molotov for members of the Political Bureau, dated March 19, 1922, became known first in *samizdat* and was published only at the end of perestroika.[47] Lenin suggested that the confiscation of Church property be used as an opportunity to provoke the clergy to resist and to serve as the occasion for severe repressions against the clergy as a whole. A cynical inquisition-like plan for a campaign against the clergy was proposed. Some extracts from that document follow:

> Now and only now . . . we are able (and, therefore, must) confiscate the Church treasures with the most pitiless and drastic

> energy, suppressing any possible resistance. . . . I came to the definite conclusion that right now it is high time to attack decisively and mercilessly the reactionary priesthood and to suppress their resistance with a cruelty that they will remember for decades to come. The campaign should be waged according to the following plan:
>
> The official measures should be suggested by com. Kalinin—in no case can it come from com. Trotzky. . . .
>
> One of the most energetic and efficient members of the VTSiK [All-Russian Central Executive Committee] should be sent to Shuya [middle-sized town not far from Moscow] . . . with verbal instructions . . . to arrest there as many representatives as possible (not less than several score) of the local priesthood, petty bourgeoisie and bourgeoisie on suspicion of their direct or indirect resistance to the VTSIK decree on the confiscation of Church treasures. . . . [He is] to report personally at the meeting of all Politburo members. . . . On the ground of this report the Politburo will give a detailed directive to judges: also a verbal one, in order to conduct this process against Shuya rebels who oppose help to starvation victims as fast as possible and definitely finished by shooting a great number of the most influential and dangerous reactionaries in Shuya and, if possible, also in Moscow and several other spiritual centers. . . . The more representatives of the reactionary priesthood and bourgeoisie who are executed on this occasion, the better. They should get such a lesson now in order that they forget about any possibility for resistance for decades.[48]

Thus it is obvious that the anticlerical campaign was planned and directed at the top from the very beginning of 1920s. The mention of "help to starvation victims" was purely a demagogic trick: Lenin wrote in this same letter about the probable use of confiscated treasures; there is no word about victims of starvation in his proposition. Later in the campaign thousands of churches and most monasteries were closed; their buildings were confiscated, deliberately desecrated, and either demolished or used as factories, cinemas, or for storage. The number of parishes during the first ten years of Bolshevik rule diminished from 48,000 to 26,000. Even this was only the beginning. There were several peaks of persecution. Brutal repression against clergy of all faiths during almost every year of regime destroyed tens of thousands priests, mullahs, and rabbis.[49]

The new rulers decided to introduce a new state religion of their own. It was necessary to substitute an ideological component in the traditional triad "Orthodoxy, Autocracy, Nationality" (formulated in 1826 by one of Nicholas I's ministers). They succeeded in this transplantation because it did not challenge the basic stereotypes of national consciousness. Despite the fact that Orthodox faith appeared to permeate the flesh and blood of the people of the Russian Empire, it turned out to be a source of serious error. We have already seen the gradual departure from the moral foundations of Orthodox faith in various population strata and the change to formal or ritualized performance. When the situation changed and the new ruling power introduced atheistic symbols instead of Orthodox Christian symbols, the switch was not as dramatic for national consciousness and history as had been the case in other nations in similar circumstances. Part of the nation demonstrated a certain commitment and even heroism in defense of traditional sacred objects of Orthodox faith and of their right to profess it. But another portion of the nation, not less in quantity, revealed readiness and even a desire to blaspheme and to demolish religious symbols once these were no longer under the state's protection. The majority was quite indifferent to the fate of the Church and repressions of the Church. And the Church was doomed in such a situation. Through centuries of its history, the official Orthodoxy had not been prepared to stand up for its dogmas when the internal situation was not favorable (in contrast to the Russian ability to defend their faith against external enemies).

Obedience to the central power proved to be stronger than religious belief and feelings. Orthodox stereotypes appeared not to be the basis of national consciousness but a secondary feature easily removed. Unfortunately for Russia, this trajectory was quite different from the events in the other countries that came under Soviet domination. There people found the Church and their faith a source of strength to resist Communist rule despite repressive measures.

THE TRAGEDY OF THE INTELLIGENTSIA

The fate of the Russian intelligentsia became a fatal tragedy during the course of the revolutionary years.[50] We have emphasized two principal orientations within this social group, but in spite of these differences, most members of the intelligentsia professed unselfish idealistic service for the sake of the people. However, the fruit of these aspirations proved quite different from that ideal. The enduring selfless activity of the radical part of the intelligentsia was one of the basic reasons for the catastrophe in 1917. They themselves became victims in due course. That is one of the bitterest paradoxes of Russian history.

The authors of the *Vekhi* and their followers were sure that all of the intelligentsia bore the main responsibility for what had happened. They were themselves part of the Russian intelligentsia, representing its religion-reviving group, but they would not be associated with it as a whole, as they occupied quite different positions. Even those within the intelligentsia who opposed the revolutionary way of solving Russia's problems shared a sense of guilt for the course of events and accepted their fate without self-pity.

What can be said about these opinions? I share both a tragic understanding of the events and the opinion that the role of the intelligentsia was crucial at that moment in Russia history. But I cannot agree with the vekhovtsy on some points. First, I cannot accept their opinion that the Revolution in 1917 meant the complete demolition of the old Russia. The march of time was not interrupted. Only a comparatively new branch of historical development in Russia had perished. This branch united the best that existed in Russia at the time, and there were hopes that it would lead the country in a more progressive direction. But the old way survived the catastrophe of the Revolution. The changes were only partial: the participants merely exchanged positions. The country acquired new rulers according to the principle that those who had been nothing should acquire everything. New masters and new slogans appeared; the order of the marching columns and the color of banners changed; but—contrary to what the vekhovtsy claimed—the basic principles of social organization and self-organization remained the same.

Second, their judgment as regards the intelligentsia seemed to be both too general and partially unfair. Their accusations applied mostly against the radicals. The liberals can be reproached for underestimating the danger and for their weak response to it. The moral and other support given by the politically neutral intelligentsia to the persecuted radicals appeared to be noble and ethically irreproachable but, ironically, yielded the wrong historic consequences. A compromise between two polar forces—the authorities and the radicals—seemed impossible. The regressive power of the autocratic elite even lost its instinct for self-preservation. Possibly some chance for dialogue and for bridge building still existed; that is difficult to judge now. The point is that the mutual hostility of the parties appeared irreconcilable because the very idea of tolerance, of compromise with the opposition, was totally unknown in the Russian political tradition. One way or another, it is incorrect to blame the intelligentsia as a whole and especially to identify it with socialist orientations.

Radicals constituted a very small part of the intelligentsia—that is why it is unfair to condemn the whole estate. Within several months following the October upheaval, the number of intellectuals sympathizing with the radicals dropped substantially. And the feeling of reciprocal hostility between the ruling radicals and the majority of the intelligentsia prevailed. The verdict of guilt by the vekhovtsy against the intelligentsia also seemed to contradict the fact that from the very beginning the Bolsheviks considered the intelligentsia neither a former (or at least potential) ally nor a neutral force but a hostile one, incompatible with the "new society."

It was natural for the Bolsheviks—whose fundamental principles were monopolistic control over the functioning of society, with strict ideological unity, implying monopolistic control—to take advantage of the underdeveloped and conservative consciousness of society. These principles were completely incompatible with the very spirit of the intelligentsia's moral code and social modus vivendi, which could be realized only in a pluralism of ideas and organizations, with freedom and independence of thought, and the possibility of discussion as a way of resolving problems. Therefore, despite the fact that the Bolshevik movement owed a great intellectual debt to the intelligentsia and was a child of those intellectuals, *the conflict between the Bolsheviks and the major part of intellectuals was both deep and pervasive.*

In December of 1917, Lenin considered it a vital matter to register all intellectuals and to introduce police control over them. His attitude toward the intelligentsia is well-known. He acknowledged the necessity of using their intellectual abilities but denied them the possibility of autonomy in the exercise of their abilities. He worked out a policy of how "to draw the cooperation of bourgeois experts." It was a combination of bribery, strict control, "moral enslavement" (Lenin's own words), and intimidation by selective arrests—"frighten them to death." This undisguised policy of exploitation and manipulation of intellectuals was combined quite naturally with hostility, suspiciousness, and contempt on his part. We can recall some of his expressions about "petty intellectuals," "intellectual spongers of the bourgeoisie," "their hypocritical cries for 'freedom,'" the "screaming of 'philister intelligentsia,'" and his judgment that "as a matter of fact, they are not the brain of the nation, but shit."[51]

A secret letter from Lenin to Minister of Justice Kursky, with a copy to Supreme Procurator Krylenko, on March 31, 1922, is significant in this respect:

> On my instruction the former Moscow ChK [Cheka] has begun an investigation of criminal negligence, procrastination and inactivity in the scientific-technical department and the Committee for Inventions. The investigation results were sent to Mosrevtribunal, which instead of a thorough inquest, identification and punishment of the guilty (there are a lot of learned loafers, idlers and similar kinds of riffraff in these offices as has more than once been mentioned in press, in articles by com. Sosnovsky and others) showed criminal indulgence to the prosecuted, tried them without a prosecutor and in the end declared the evidence insufficient and acquitted all the accused. I have just been informed that Mosgubotdel has appealed against this verdict of the Mosrevtribunal to the Court control department of NKJust [People's Commissariat of Justice]. I recommend you acquaint yourself with the case thoroughly and try to find additional evidence on these office activities with the help of the RKI [Worker-Peasant Inspection]. If it is necessary you must appoint an inspection working in agreement with com. Avanesov. It should consist not of functionaries and ditherers but of persons who are able to inspect everything in detail, to find out the proper evidence and the guilty. Retribunal should organize a political trial (with com. Sosnovsky as press representative) that would overturn this "scientific slough."
>
> I suggest also severely reprimanding Mosrevtribunal for its indulgence and bureaucratic attitude to this case.
>
> Chairman of Sovnarkom
> V. Ulyanov [Lenin][52]

The document speaks for itself. One can hardly believe that this letter was written by a former intellectual; its consequence is clearly the complete denial of intellectual values and of an appropriate self-conscious sense of modesty in presuming that error is possible.

Even loyalty to the regime could not guarantee security from reprisals. However, occasional and curious circumstances saved some people. Tragedy and comedy sometimes coincide in everyday life. A witness to a house round-up waged in Petrograd in 1918 according to a "list" (Lenin favored lists) told me the following: "A writer, Tatiana L. Shchepkina-Kupernik, was saved from arrest and probable execution not due to her pro-Bolshevik views but the 'erudition' of a Chekist who took her for a relative to . . . the astronomer Kopernik."

The statement of the Republican Supreme Procurator at the trial of so-called Tactical Center in August, 1920, underscores that the Bolsheviks had declared a true war on the intelligentsia: "Besides landowners and capitalists there existed and continues to exist a social stratum whose social being makes the revolutionary socialism representatives ponder over. . . . It is the stratum of so-called intelligentsia. . . . At this trial we will have to do both with History's verdict on Russian intelligentsia activity and revolution trial of them."[53]

However, one cannot accuse the people involved of being a "so-called" intelligentsia—witness their quick apprehension of the real danger of the Bolshevik regime, the noble protest of thousands of intellectuals against Bolshevik crimes and general methods of arbitrary rule, and their courage in trying to struggle against the regime. They realized that their chances of succeeding or even surviving in this struggle were minimal. But these people who viewed their role in life as being of service to society could not behave in any other way.

We can suggest several reasons why the intelligentsia was doomed in this struggle. First, its aspirations and aims were unclear to the rest of population. Second, the revolutionary spirit that it bred did not need the intelligentsia any longer and turned against it. Third, its adversaries were not the lazy old watchdogs of the old regime but young, alert, and pitiless wolves of the new regime. And finally, their main weapons in this struggle were words, which were not highly valued at the time.

Moreover, even words lost positive meaning and became imbued with intolerance and hatred. This is true not only of the language of political meetings, decrees, circulars, and the press. The language of the arts also became involved in political passions. If we turn to revolutionary poetry, we can get an idea of the public sentiments that formed the prevailing atmosphere of the epoch.

In 1917, Vladimir Kirillov wrote a paean to the "uncountable dread legions of Labor," who had conquered the seas and ocean, and then set the cities afire "with the light of artificial suns." Their souls aflame with insurrection, Kirillov wrote, they prided themselves on being the mutinous, passionate, "executioners of beauty" and the destroyers of museums and art in order to user in Tomorrow. They had thrown off the weight of the past and rejected its sterile wisdom, trading the Venuse de Milo for a simple working girl. Calloused and hard, they were in love with the machine, enchanted by dynamite, intoxicated by power, not by sylvan streams and spring flowers. They were the vulgar against the poets, free and bold, their muscles seeking a "gargantuan labor" that would transform the entire planet. In love with love, intoxicated and possessed of a spirit hardened by struggle and suffering, they were everybody and everything, their "own Deity and Judge and Law."[54]

In the poem "Left March," Vladimir Mayakovsky urged the legions of labor, the vast proletariat, to step forward, to "march out to the fore" and clear the floor for Comrade Mauser to speak. To reject the "laws of Adam and Eve," to take the world by the throat, to march into the future with head hight and chest thrust out.[55] As Mayakovsky expresses in "Ode to Revolution," this was the destiny of workers and soldiers and sailors who, shouting wildly and drunk with power, their mustachios "twisted in bravado," had driven out the "grey-haired admirals" with rifle butts.[56] As the proletariat surged forward, Mayakovsky caught the chaotic and romantic excitement of its revolution in his verse.

In such emphatic and romantic poems, there was no place for whiners, as the revolutionary poets proclaimed, or for normal human feelings of ordinary kindness or respect for other human beings. The poems are permeated with a belief in the adoration of evil, in the omnipotence and impunity of the organized mob that is bonded by a common crime against humanity and where every individual can be easily replaced like a simple cog.

While millions of her contemporaries ran wild, in her poems Anna Akhmatova mourned the tragic fates of individuals trapped in the charnel house Russia had become. In a poem to a new man, her son, and everybody's son, now no longer alive, lying pierced by "twenty-eight bayonet and five rifle holes," she recalls the happiness in his eyes, his songs, the Madeira toasts, and floating by torpedo-boat to and from far distant Anatolia. But she wonders if she bore him in her arms only to offer him as a sacrifice, if he grew strong and brave only to be slaughtered, if he grew tall and slender only to be cut down before his "bright blue eyes" could take in God's ancient world for twenty years. A quarter of a century later, she would return to these themes in her poem "Requiem."[57]

How did poetry oppose that roar of tribe? Was it the philosophical fatalism of Osip Mandelstam who felt the spirit of "the century wolfhound" and had realized the profundity of the tragedy happening to his contemporaries?

In "The Twilight of Freedom," Mandelstam bitterly calls his brothers to "praise the twilight of freedom," the "momentous burden" assumed by the people's leader, "the twilight burden of power." In a world in which all seemed marked for death and in which time bears down inexorably, those with a heart will hear the ship slipping beneath the cold dark waves.[58]

In a poem to Petropolis (1918), Mandelstam contemplates a "wandering fire at a terrible height"—perhaps a star shining?—and announces that Petropolis, the star's brother lies dying: As "dreams of earth blaze" and "a green star" burns, his brother lies dying. As a massive ship rises and spreads its sails, as "transparent spring" rises over the "black Neva," its brother lies dying, immorality ebbing, as Petropolis watches.[59]

But who would dare to look Time in the eyes and apply his own blood to heal the shattered backbone of two centuries? In his 1923 poem, "My Time," Mandelstam describes how blood, gushing from the earth's gullet, might create new worlds. Waxing hopeful, he writes that buds will swell again and green shoots push their way up through the carnage. He likens his "beautiful, pitiful century" to a crippled beast, pondering its tracks in the sand.[60]

Was it the regal contempt of Tzvetaeva, who ignored the topic of the day in silence that spoke more clearly than any words? Was it the choking Muse or unfortunate Block who mistook the first flashes of the robber's arson for the dawn of a new day? Was it the lofty and exotic pathos of Gumilev, who was made silent (like many the others) not by literary means but by bullets?

Here we stop our enumeration. Its continuation cannot add anything to our analysis. We should not forget that not only marginalized dilettantish rhymesters but also some true poets—like Bryusov and Mayakovsy, partially Esenin and Pasternak—shared a perception of the events in a heroic-romantic light and actually played into the very hands of the Bolsheviks. As a result, the triumph of fighting, the irony of "civil" war, and the slaughter of brothers and sisters was inevitable.

October of 1917 marked the beginning of the decline of the intelligentsia's social significance in Russian life. This process developed quickly and accelerated—within fifteen to twenty years the intelligentsia lost the main functions that it had maintained during the hardest years of the Romanov reaction: to be the social conscience and to stimulate individual self-consciousness of the human condition. *The intelligentsia as an independent social force had been practically destroyed under the new regime.* This should not be misinterpreted to mean that it was extirpated totally or that its members were forced to emigrate, although both methods were widely used during the war the new regime pursued against intellectuals. A large segment of them survived physically. A few of them even preserved their former material well-being to some extent, and some continued to work in their professions and were able to educate students. But there were three repressive mechanisms that oppressed them all: (1) the suspicious, hostile attitude both of those in power and of the common people (the respect formerly accorded to an educated person was demolished by fierce "antibourgeois" propaganda); (2) the complete absence of the possibility of expressing and freely discussing their ideas as a vital component of the spiritual life of any intelligent person; and (3) the loss of even partial material independence, so that they suffered humiliating and morally destructive total economic dependence on the power structure, which monopolized all sources of material support—took charge of all life-support systems in the country. Intellectuals were allotted the place of educated clerks and technicians, who were distrusted but tolerated by those in power.

Under these circumstances, it was natural that the intelligentsia was soon deprived of its position. Other constellations arose in the Russian political sky. Some misappropriated the name *intelligentsia* but actually had little to do with it; they were of one flesh and one bone with the new social forces. The rest of the true intelligentsia were able to perform only two missions: to preserve in the sphere of social reflection the remnants of their own culture in order that it could survive the darkest period of our history and be handed down to the next generations, and to realize in the sphere of social action a modicum of activity aimed at preventing irreversible moral and mental degradation.

These two modest but important missions were more or less fulfilled. But the losses in the intelligentsia proved to be atrocious and irreplaceable. The price cannot be expressed solely in human lives. The post-revolutionary tragedy of the Russian intelligentsia includes two more crucial elements.

First, there was considerable weakening of continuity, if not its complete rupture. Nobody knows the exact number of families in which the passing on of an intellectual spirit from one generation to another was cut short after the revolution. Persecuted and oppressed morally and physically, intellectuals instinctively—and sometimes consciously—stopped reproducing themselves among their descendants. As a result, their children did not become their spiritual successors. The spiritual and moral values gathered across generations were buried together with their last bearers. And this spirit of continuity is especially important for the intelligentsia. It goes without saying that affiliation with the intelligentsia is not handed down genetically: it is difficult to acquire, particularly within one generation, but very easy to lose.

Besides this, it is evident that in the process of turning into a Soviet intelligentsia, the Russian intelligentsia was degraded morally. The purely pragmatic and sometimes cynical operators came forth. This decline of genuine spiritual bearers of the Russian intellectual heritage became only one of the components of the general moral regression in the USSR following the Revolution. The defeat of the intelligentsia in its conflict with the new regime was both its own tragedy and the tragedy of the whole nation.

CONCLUSION

It is time now to review the whole. What were the actual results of this cataclysm unprecedented in the scale of its turbulence and in its deluded social aspirations and human tragedies? Let us first consider the most essential parameters. *On the socio-ethical level, system-centeredness thrived.* We observe its renaissance and strengthening on a new, more dynamic and durable basis. On the socio-psychological level, some derivative stereotypes of national consciousness were demolished and exchanged for others that were formally more modern but effectively the same. *The traditional psychological genotype was strengthened.*

Aspects usually reviewed as the most important in standard political or sociological analysis—religious and political beliefs—are derivative from the point of view of socio-ethical and social psychological considerations. *As regards beliefs, a new official religion had taken the place of state Orthodoxy.* It was quite different in phraseology but similar in its dominant methods of thought, in the social formation of personality, and therefore very successful in exploiting the most conservative traditional stereotypes.

As for the political regime, the changes were much less substantial than is usually supposed; they were mostly external and formal. They concerned the structure of social groups that had ascended to power, but the political purposes and the means of their achievement remained the same. This succession is most obvious in the domain of political spirit, which reveals itself through categories of political consciousness and the political culture of the society. The cornerstone structures of the Russian political system not only survived the revolutionary "time of troubles" but became more durable, once more confirming the acuity of Voloshin's insight.

History, Voloshin wrote, is faceless and deaf and ingnores the puny wills of individual men. It acts on its own, as it sees fit. It directed Peter's ax and prodded the peasant Rus to cover three centuries in a single, aching stride, leaving imperial Russia astraddle the earth from the frigid beaches of the Baltic to the fozen shores of Alaska. History also drove the Bolsheviks along paths familiar to every Russian, through the bottomless, oozing whirlpools of Time. As the new belched out the old, the sons found themselves—despite their intentions and their ideologies—stuck in the deep, ancient ruts furrowed by pervious generations. Not parties, nor programs, nor men with their puny wills mattered—but History mattered, and it was History's will that determined the outcome of the Revolution, not Lenin, not Trotsky, not Kerensky, not Wrangl, but History.[61]

The only real change was in the structure of the political elite—the traditional Russian pseudo-aristocracy had been replaced by true ochlocracy, steered by those who manipulated the mobs.

We have not considered the economic aspect in the field of our analysis. But it should be noted that the evident economic failure of the new system speaks for itself. The system proved to be able to satisfy only the elementary material needs of its citizens. In light of the world's unprecedented technical and technological progress, the Soviet quest for progress could only be regarded as a failure. Hence the Russian revolutionary tragedy confirmed the illusions of materialistic philosophers and radical politicians. In their terms, human misfortunes derived from the wrong sociopolitical structure and could be eliminated if the structures were remade according to some speculative ideal.

The truth of Tolstoy's belief that improvement of external forms of human relations—that is, in the social sphere alone—could not be fruitful was proven by the revolution. World evil can be vanquished mainly through the internal—that is, spiritual—perfection, the revealing of the good that is entrusted to every human soul, as optimists had assumed. Social institutions can only facilitate or prevent the realization of those goods that are latent in the human spirit.

CHAPTER NINE

Stalinism

High Noon of System-Centeredness

In terms of the approach offered in this book, one cannot discover any new principle at work in the unfolding of events in the USSR during the period of Stalin's rule. It was the time of a bloody harvest: tendencies formed during previous periods reached their extreme. If our purpose were to write a political history of Russia in the standard meaning of history, this cannibalistic era should be described in all its terrible details. But for understanding the general logic of historical processes, such descriptions hardly add much. The process was already predetermined, the last crossroads was far behind, the next crossroads lay far ahead and was invisible. No alternatives were in sight. As under the rule of Peter I, it was the high noon of system-centered authoritarianism in its worst variation.

That is why in this chapter I restrict myself to an exploration of the rather sophisticated mechanics of system-centeredness in its higher, terrorist stage and at its practical level—that is, the moral and psychological factors and leverages that drove behavior during the climax of this tragedy. Fortunately for mankind, the criminal substance of Stalinism and its genocide against Russians and a number of other nations are much better recognized than are the crimes perpetrated under Lenin's regime. Everyone who has a minimal interest in the story of the twentieth century, I assume, is familiar to some degree with the factual side of historic events. Many documents and well-documented books were published about this in 1990s, both in Russia and West. Some of the relevant authors are mentioned in preface; others are referred to in the course of this book. In addition, but with no claim to comprehensiveness, I would recommend studies by Martin Malia, Richard Pipes, Sergey P. Melgunov, and Robert Conquest in the abundant literature on Stalinism.[1] There remain people, both in the West and in Russia, who are inclined to underestimate or even deny the massive losses of human lives under Stalinism, demanding "more evidence." No amount of evidence can convince this category of people, apparently. To my mind, this is a problem of another kind, definitely beyond the scope of this book. We follow the same structure of analysis as in preceding chapters, discussing the questions as applied to major segments of the Russian people.

STALIN'S FALCONS, A MARGINAL ELITE

Servile propagandists sometimes called the new Soviet elite Stalin's falcons. This term could be variously interpreted—not only apologetically but also ironically. An elite began to form surprisingly fast, especially considering the prominence of anti-elitist rhetoric and the repressive measures directed against the former elite during the 1917 cataclysm and long afterward. The new masters of the country formed themselves into a new kind of Communist nobility. Lenin to the end of his political life could see that the social group that had lifted him to the highest layer of society was being rapidly transformed into a kind of Mafia, the members of which were mostly preoccupied with their personal profits and career opportunities. Lenin's last letters and articles produce an impression of hopeless attempts to stop the process of crystallization of a new elite by cursing this revolutionary specter. However, it was impossible to frighten the specter with words of damnation. Fate took bitter vengeance on Lenin for his persecutions and extermination of "the best and the brightest" of the nation. By the mid-1920s, the appearance of the new class became a fact.

During the first stage of the revolution, not only unprincipled climbers but also honest zealots and fanatics of the Communist faith were among the members of this elite. However, those devoted to the cause were numerically a minority of the elite except in its highest ranks. In practice, the revolution was not crafted by fanatical idealists. Its motive force was supplied by people who had no desire to sacrifice themselves for abstract ideals. On the contrary, they sought to realize their own advantage in this life and found that the revolution offered great opportunities.

As the Soviet regime became consolidated and the new ruling elite formed, the share and significance of idealists in the ruling class steadily declined. Leading positions were captured by different kinds of unprincipled opportunists. At the next stage, in the 1930s, the "true Bolsheviks," people with a firm intellectual commitment and with a record of pre-revolutionary service to the party, became the subject of a massive political purge and mostly disappeared from the political elite. Many of the political executioners endangered other executioners and became the victims of execution in the end. An example of these "romantics of Revolution" and their tragic fate, a man of rather attractive personal qualities despite his earlier radical and even blood-thirsty statements, was Nikolay I. Bukcharin.[2] Lenin called him "the Party pet" before Stalin skillfully maneuvered to destroy him. Similarly, in revolutionary France, the political guillotine decapitated those who had first put it to use.

The easy violation of basic moral precepts can be explained by the moral relativism and moral anomie of revolutionaries. This created a further erosion of all kinds of social norms—moral, religious, and legal. The destructive potential of normlessness accumulated during the pre-revolutionary decades and reached its climax during the Revolution. Under the usual conditions of social life, normlessness exists mainly among marginalized groups. In a period of basic social upheaval, the marginalized groups establish the predominant pattern of relationships. In such circumstances, idealists are not able to keep their leading positions and are forced to accede to opportunists.

The "morality" of the new elite was simple and practical. That gave it its vitality. The most important components of their specific "moral code" were:

1. *Total lack of any internal ethical taboos*—that is, moral self-restrictions. Everything practical in terms of the needs of the current situation became permissible. One of the consequences of that view was the widespread ruthlessness that made the Russian post-revolutionary history so tragic.

2. *Unreflecting obedience to the stronger*, the possessors of real power came to prevail. Real power was increasingly concentrated in the hands of two political branches—Bolshevik party apparatchiks and the political police known as the NKVD (the Ministry

of Internal Affairs, which maintained a security force so large that it effectively amounted to a kind of army). The simplicity of this principle was enforced by its universal character. When a person stepped onto the ladder of a Soviet career, the rules of the game sorted out those willing to serve the expedient purposes of those at the upper levels of the hierarchy. The others were eliminated.

3. *Calculated manipulation by ideological slogans and political demagoguery as weapons* in the struggle for power and privileges is characteristic of unscrupulous politicians. In a society in which all forms of property are controlled by the state, these patterns of opportunism became the general route to success.

Let me offer a passing remark in this context concerning the real meaning of ideology for the policies pursued by the Bolsheviks. Many Western and Soviet scholars have treated the ideological clichés of the Bolsheviks too seriously when considering them as a foundation of basic policies. Mistaken assumptions frequently brought scholars to the wrong conclusions. In fact, the so-called ideological dogmas and "basic political principles" were never true articles of faith for the Bolsheviks. They proclaimed these dogmas and principles as "sacred" and were ready to commit massive bloodshed in the name of such principles only so long as these were to their advantage. As soon as any dogmas blocked the Bolsheviks' way, they were quickly abandoned in practice.

Among the socio-psychological features of the new elite, a *one-dimensional perception of the world* was the first to prevail.[3] There were no complexities or objective controversies in their picture of the world. A derivative from that point of view was the lack of any need for critical, reflective self-analysis, which had always had been inherent in the thought processes of "normal" intellectuals. These were people of action, always prepared to struggle and to use any means to achieve their goals of dominance. One other basic socio-psychological peculiarity of the new elite was *a necrophilic type of personality*—a willingness to deal in death. (I use the term not in the accepted sense of a rare sexual perversion but as a psychoanalytical metaphor for a social pathology that characterized a specific category of people and that totalitarian regimes used as an active force.)

The people who managed to seize positions in the new political elite were not political actors but gamblers: they played horrible games with enormous stakes and by rules normally peculiar to the criminal world—to the bottom, not the top, of the social pyramid. They lived mostly by Mafia-style laws and rivalry among "families." Misunderstanding these circumstances was a reason for the analytical mistakes frequently made both by internal and foreign collaborators and critics of the regime. In particular, this was true of the impressive successes of Soviet foreign policy in the 1930s and 1940s. During that period full of events and Soviet gains, only one serious diplomatic failure can be noted in Soviet politics—in its game with Hitler. And to whom the Soviet diplomacy lost out is very remarkable: not to politicians representing democratic societies (they were outsmarted rather easily) but to a similar kind of Mafia not bound by traditional moral precepts.

The majority of members of the upper Soviet political hierarchy under Stalin were people who were poorly educated, bad mannered, and primitive by intellectual criteria. But in terms of the achievement of their purposes, they were smart and shifty fellows. There were quite a few exceptions, members of the elite who adhered to high standards of culture and education. But their fate is noteworthy: they either died out surprisingly quickly, like G. Chicherin, N. Krasin, and A. Lunacharsky, or were shifted to the periphery of the elite and, in most cases, later exterminated, like N. Bukharin, M. Litvinov, and A. Voznesensky. The most pernicious variant was the "intellectual criminal"—those who completely subordinated their knowledge and talents to serving immoral, inhuman purposes, like USSR Procurator-General A. Vyshinsky. This accounts for both the victims of multiple purges and those who always managed to be on the winning team.

There was one more peculiarity of the Stalinist elite. Different from the political elite under normal political regimes, *it was unstable.* One could surge up to the top with lightning speed on a wave of political intrigues and chance. After one wrong step, one could fall back to an even lower level—to the hell of prisons and the Gulag Archipelago. Therefore, the ruling circle does not correspond to the notion of an elite in an exact sense because an elite supposedly maintained a rather high level of personal responsibility and stability within its ranks. Thus this Stalinist ruling circle could be called *a pseudo-elite.*

After Stalin's death, the situation gradually changed. The tyrant's practice of regular purges, accompanied by brutal repressions against former favorites, was abandoned. To the contrary, the ruling strata created for itself, to some extent, a kind of status of immunity. Its composition and the hierarchy of "legitimized" privileges stabilized; its children acquired the status and ambitions of the offspring of nobility. The moral qualities of the elite had not improved; it merely acquired some superficial respectability.

The way this elite governed society did not fundamentally change the modes of the Tsarist regime. The revolutionary cataclysm turned the social pyramid over, totally destroying the traditional doctrine and crushing people who supported the Tsarist throne, but the new elite inherited the basic autocratic principle of rule. They tightened control over society through many new manipulative skills.

First, they mastered *the skill of exploiting the wrong side of human nature.* This skill became apparent during the Revolution and civil war. It was also one of the main features of Stalin's dictatorship. Second, the regime chose its social base carefully, not only realizing what human vices could be exploited but also being aware of who possessed these vices to the utmost. The social upstarts or parvenus became its main force—people obliged to the regime for everything and therefore ready to do everything to preserve it, which coincided with preserving their privileged social status. Under any other regime, these people would have been doomed to stay in the lower part of the social pyramid; the Communist Party autocracy opened incomparable opportunities. This gambling made sense. The song "Internationale"—the Communists' hymn—promised: "The man who was nobody will become everybody." This promise was realized in a monstrous way under Stalin's rule, especially during the periods of purges and reprisals when many vacancies at all level of power became available.

Some of the members of Stalin's elite were true believers in Stalin's divine wisdom and the impeccability of his politics. Some tried to make careers by honest means, and a few even succeeded. But people of this kind were not the regime's "trump card." They were not the ones who advanced its political agenda. On the whole, *the rules of the game were to the advantage not of the best and the brightest but of the worst,* who were promoted regardless of their social origins. The greatest vertical leaps were not made by real representatives of the laboring classes, as Soviet propaganda proclaimed. They were made by people who ostentatiously displayed attributes of their proletarian origin but held no allegiance to their former social background—and who actually betrayed it. Such positive elements of class consciousness as solidarity, collective responsibility, honest work, respect for the labor of other people, and even simple common sense could rarely be found among these parvenus. Other qualities were necessary to succeed. Contrary to Darwin's pattern of natural selection, this pattern could be called counterselection or anti-natural selection. The most successful promoters were the marginals—individuals devoid of class consciousness who abandoned a former code of morality but failed to adopt a new one. Thus in practice the criterion of social origin was not critical. The roots of the person did not matter. Members of the new elite could come from among workers, peasants, the clergy, entrepreneurs, and intellectuals. Their common denominator was lack of any moral code at all. The marginals devoid of social ties consisted of several million people, became the major support of the regime, and passed the baton of their immoral expediency to successive generations of the Soviet pseudo-elite.

FINAL TRAGEDY OF THE INTELLECTUALS—GRASS UNDER THE ASPHALT

The first knots in the tragic fate of the Russian intelligentsia were tied in the 1860s. The culmination of this tragedy occurred at the end of the second decade of the twentieth century. We turn now to the final stage of that tragedy: what happened to the intelligentsia during Stalin's era. As we saw in the course of this book, in Russian culture and history, the word for *intelligentsia* means more than merely qualified professional status. Stalin's policy was directed to eliminating its essential humanistic component, reducing it to a purely professional characteristic.[4]

Let us begin with the most privileged segments. In the early period of the regime's existence, a fairly considerable portion of the intellectuals joined the new ruling elite. They were mostly the radical intellectuals and their ideological successors. However, the course of developments worked against them. Some came to an adequate understanding of the situation and left the elite themselves; others were supplanted by expedient time-servers. A small and diminishing group of intellectuals remained on the periphery of the ruling elite. As soon as true essence of the regime became more obvious, its share of supporters among the intellectuals grew smaller and smaller. But regardless of their motives, all intellectuals who stayed in the elite or nearby had to pay for their standing. And in order to preserve their material conditions or the illusion of active participation in public life, they sacrificed important things, the essential elements of intellectual conscience and morality: the social roles of public conscience and compassion for suffering people, feelings of civic responsibility, and critical reflection about the broader circle of public issues. They no longer found it impossible to echo the powerful voice of authorities or to betray truth for material gain. For the intellectuals, these values were as natural as breathing fresh air. All those elements were sacrificed by the intellectuals of the nomenklatura in order to save their professional positions and status and their access to goods distributed under the strict control of the country's new masters.

In Russia, where the altruistic fulfillment of the functions of critical public thinking and conscience by the intelligentsia was a long-term tradition and a kind of social norm, such conformity to authoritative power was like self-denial. Despite these adverse circumstances, some intellectuals of the nomenklatura managed to preserve some of these important features of their lives. Among these features were the general culture of mind, professional skills, habits of productive intellectual work, creativeness in seeking solutions to nonstandard problems, versatility, and some degree of tolerance for different opinions and views. This branch of the intelligentsia managed to save many of these qualities and even used them for the public good, constrained by political circumstances and an instinct of self-preservation. However, in the context of the Russian tradition, these professional qualities were supposedly necessary but not sufficient for the social role of the true intellectual.

Even in such an emasculated version, the Russian intellectual was not able to survive as a member of the Stalinist elite. If the Tsarist authorities tried to keep intellectuals in the position of learned servants, the Soviet authorities acted more persistently and consistently, making them intellectual serfs. In Stalin's time, the intellectuals were usually tolerated only in specific—qualified but powerless—positions and so far as the machinery of government could not do without them.

In some supreme moral sense, all the blows that fell on the heads of the intellectuals who served in the nomenklatura were not completely unjust because they had been beaten by the rules of a game that they had voluntarily joined and tried to win. Their problems and losses were not comparable with the problems and losses of the major part of the intelligentsia, who lived in poverty and under constant moral pressure. The fate of the majority of intellectuals under Stalin's dictatorship was really tragic. They were subject to humiliation and discrimination and were kept under fear of repression, which never stopped. But the worst of it all was that *the foundations of the intelligentsia's existence—the possibility for the free exchange of thought and their relative material independence—were completely undermined and denied.* The socialist state practically monopolized the status of employer and, consequently, the payment of compensation. This monopolist position over the distribution of material goods was overtly exploited by the authorities in compulsory and manipulative ways. Beginning in Stalin's time, the condition of political loyalty to those in power became a necessary condition for employment. Step by step, the scope and intensity of demands for the expression of this loyalty grew. Tests became more and more sophisticated and the consequences of "excommunication" grew harsher and harsher. At the same time, the material conditions of life for most of intelligentsia were humiliatingly low. For instance, salaries for people in the largest and probably most significant intellectual professions—teachers and doctors—became absolutely miserable.

Concerning the exchange of reflections about public issues, one might say that surveillance of such activities can be compared in its severity (or, to use the language of the epoch, vigilance) only with control over the most dangerous crimes. The whole Soviet intelligentsia was under the intentional, vigilant, and ill-willed observation of the authorities, including the secret police and informers. As a result, such natural qualities of the intellectual mind and way of life as critical and skeptical reflection about social reality, the need to speak out on public issues and to exchange opinions on politically acute questions, and the inclination to create informal groups for discussion of socially significant problems were treated and persecuted as the gravest of crimes.

An additional way to control intellectuals was *to manipulate their attitude on rendering self-sacrificing service* on behalf of the future welfare of the people. This attitude and the feeling of social responsibility were still inherent among Russian intellectuals. The authorities cynically exploited these altruistic qualities when they needed to use the intellectual and creative potential of the intelligentsia. The Stalinist regime, as in its other manipulations, discovered the precise points of vulnerability in the psychology of the intelligentsia. It turned to the advantage of the system the intellectual's drive to be socially useful by all means, even under hostile and incompetent surveillance and without public recognition, material compensation, or any control on further use of their achievements. These considerations did not matter, because the feeling of being of service to the people—though often illusory—warmed the souls of intellectuals and gave them the sense that they were not living in vain. The regime cynically exploited these noble feelings for its inhuman purposes. One of the bitter paradoxes of this situation was that intellectuals, having no chance to do anything serious beyond their professions, in other spheres of public life, escaped into the "canyons" of professional activity in the narrow sense of word, as the only avenue still open to them. Thanks to such concentration of mind, they sometimes managed great achievements and, ironically, effective support of the regime that most of them hatred.

The most characteristic example was in the field of military technology. In a number of other scientific-technological spheres, the regime's power base had also been created to a considerable degree by these well-intentioned intellectuals. In some cases, the fruits of their labors did in the end bring some benefits to the people; in other cases, they brought only harm. The status of the intelligentsia itself and the conditions of its existence were much lower than in Tsarist Russia. The value of intellectuals was determined by only one criterion: whether they served "the Revolution and proletariat"—in practice, whether they served the regime's own purposes and the interests of the ruling elite. Constraining activity to narrow professional canyons, however, did not guarantee the personal safety of intellectuals. Waves of repression reached them and washed them out of their canyons.

This pathological situation was bound to cause serious moral and psychological deformations in the self-consciousness of the intelligentsia. And indeed it did. From the beginning of 1930s, one could observe spreading symptoms of degradation and decline in moral values and of psychological wretchedness among intellectuals. In spite of the considerable decline in the quality and standing of the intelligentsia as a "species," its ethics and the character of its behavior during the worst years of Stalinist repression nevertheless showed a persistent quality not confined to the practical needs of survival or to narrow professional or egoistic interests. For instance, even during the darkest hours of Stalin's rule, some intellectuals retained moral prohibitions against denunciation and against people making their careers via the misfortunes of others. We should not exaggerate the intellectuals' solidarity: individuals motivated by fear and in some cases by personal benefits regularly violated these moral prohibitions. As is well known, intellectuals are also sometimes skillful at inventing self-justifying motivations for their behavior. But taboo violators always exist everywhere.

Neither the devaluation of the intelligentsia's morality nor the pressure of repression was able to prevent intellectuals from fulfilling an important part of their traditional function. First, they saved some of the basic cultural skills and values that are necessary prerequisites for culture and civilization to survive; second, they supported within the society and, critically important, among the youth, some level of interest in perennial cultural values; and third, by so doing, they passed on the cultural baton to more favorable times.

Certainly those functions were often only partially fulfilled, and varying degrees of opportunism entered the mix. However, no other segment of society served those functions. Soviet society, in spite of the extremely unfavorable climate of the epoch, saved some promising intellectual and moral values. This happened mainly through the actions of the semi-underground guardians of intellectual values that had been trampled underfoot by the Revolution.[5]

THE CHURCH BROUGHT TO ITS KNEES

As noted, the Orthodox Church had been "discharged" from state service by the new powers because they had their own ideology, symbols of faith, rituals, and mechanisms to enforce spiritual conformity. Orthodoxy after 1917 not only lost state support for the first time in its existence in Russia but faced a decisive, consolidated foe in power. The time of its true test came: for clergy to defend its doctrine from alternative doctrines aggressively intertwined with the new state; and for the Orthodox flock to support their church in its struggle up to the point of being prepared to suffer for the holy faith of the ancestors. In general, neither the Church nor the flock passed this test.

The Church did not develop its own internal resources for spiritual opposition to aggressive atheism. The supposedly Orthodox nation in its mass did not support its traditional church in this difficult hour. Unfortunately, when the Orthodox Church lost the status of an official state religion and when continued allegiance became a cause for troubles, people quickly and extensively defected from the Church.

In that respect, the USSR differed for the worse from other Eastern European countries. In those countries, when Communists gained power, each regime began its campaigns against the clergy and the faithful following the Soviet pattern. However, they faced resistance so staunch as to include preparedness for self-sacrifice. The Communist regimes quickly abandoned their attacks in favor of some mode of peaceful coexistence.

Some of the terrible details of government repression and its scale have now emerged—confiscation of monasteries and church property, mass imprisonment, and shooting of the clergy—as have details about isolated heroic acts of resistance, like the rebellion of believers in the town of Elets in 1918; the tragic marches of monks with gonfalons and icons against the machine guns and bayonets of special requisition detachments; and the staunch behavior of patriarch Tikhon and several other members of clergy on trial, among other episodes.[6] The peak of reprisals was in 1937, when 85,000 Orthodox clergymen were shot. In 1938 the figure was 21,500; in 1939, 900; in 1940, 1,100; and in 1941, 1,900.[7] By 1941 there were only slightly more than two hundred Orthodox parishes in the territory of USSR and only four bishops who were not imprisoned.[8] Practically all monasteries had been closed. Only "tame" priests completely obedient to secular authorities could expect to get the necessary permission of a special state agency to serve. Similar pressures and tendencies were applied toward all faiths and denominations. Reprisals against the Muslim clergy, for example, were probably even fiercer in their scale and brutality. The regime conducted its most atrocious war against the so-called sectarians: the purpose was to exterminate them completely. However, the most tragic aspect from a historical point of view was the indifference of the overwhelming part of the country's population: they observed passively while the symbols of their religion and the basis of a faith were subject to brutal repudiation. En masse, neither clergy nor parishioners mustered the resources to defend their churches or their freedom of religious conscience.

Certainly, one should not ignore the rather widespread compassion for the persecuted church and the various attempts by the flock to help it somehow. But one also should not ignore the active participation of hundreds of thousands, if not millions, of people in campaigns of awful antichurch persecution that were conducted in large part by people who had been baptized, who were supposedly Christians and members of the Orthodox Church. Beyond the state support of repression, one should recognize that antichurch activists revealed themselves as a much more powerful and better organized group than the church defenders. The history of relationships between the obedient Church and Communist power after direct persecutions ceased is a theme that also has a bitter moral context.

THE VICTORIOUS WAR AGAINST THE PEASANTRY

To consider the fate of Russia's largest social class, the scale of that tragedy made it the greatest crime on the list of Bolshevik crimes. I refer to the peasantry who constituted the overwhelming majority of population and essentially fed the rest of society.

As noted in the previous chapter, as early as in the spring of 1918 the Soviet authorities, in an attempt to get food for starving cities and soldiers, opened a campaign against the peasantry in the form of "appropriating the surplus." In the pursuit of that policy, armed detachments forcibly requisitioned from villages almost all grain and other agricultural products. In response to this policy of state robbery, the peasants, after many unsuccessful rebellions, practically stopped producing food beyond modest family needs. They had lost any economic reason to produce additional food because all the "surplus"—that is, grain available to be sold—was being requisitioned by gunmen from the cities, activists mobilized by the Communist Party. In effect, the peasantry seized power by the throat. It proved to be a more efficient counteraction than any rebellion. Under threat of total starvation, the Communists were forced to retreat. Under the framework of the New Economic Policy, the program of surplus appropriation was abandoned in favor of a "tax in kind" policy. These new rules of economic behavior supported the entrepreneurship of peasants within certain limits.[9] Beyond the early tendencies toward expropriation, the Bolshevik masters of the country initially seemed to peasants to be better than their former masters in some respects: they gave people pieces of land on long-term lease, and they did not intend to take anyone to court for massive robbery of the estates or for other crimes committed by many of the peasants, particularly when dressed in soldiers' uniforms. From the peasants' point of view, some real injustices of the previous regime were corrected in 1917, and peasants were also impressed by the "social proximity" and understandable phraseology of the Bolsheviks. Even under the NEP, using various lawful and quasilawful means, their new masters took too large a share of agricultural production, but that was not unusual for the Russian peasantry; some former masters had taken more and had definitely imposed more severe conditions.

Such semifree conditions of life allowed for the natural processes of differential success among farmers and in patterns of rural economic development. The more skillful and diligent peasants gradually became more prosperous as well. Voluntary agricultural cooperation developed. The NEP quickly influenced the market situation: it stopped starvation and economic devastation and stimulated a significant rise in standard of living, both in the countryside and cities, after the catastrophic plunge during the revolutionary years. Thus a normalization of the situation took place, though not by means of active, energetic party commissars in leather jackets armed with revolvers. When they left villages alone, processes of a normal life were renewed.

However, this did not last long. The new authorities, like most of the rulers in Russian history, could not accept a situation of coexisting with a relatively independent social class. It was not consistent either with Russian tradition or with the character and spirit of the new regime to govern society purely by means of indirect regulation. The Bolsheviks could not relinquish the tools of direct control over the bulk of society because this undermined their power, their concept of resources, and their ideology. In terms of an autocratic logic, any self-constraint made the regime appear weak and was therefore unacceptable. On the other side, independent farmers did not need a system of command and control. A conflict between Bolshevik power and village life was inevitable.

The signs of a new turn of events fatal for the peasantry appeared as early as 1925. The authorities intervened more and more in the economic life of villages and increased the pressure of different forms of taxation and extortion. The major part of this burden was overtly placed on the backbone of the villages—on the most hardworking and consequently relatively successful and well-to-do peasants, known as the kulaks. Simultaneously, there was overt rewarding and promoting of the most marginal people in the villages—that is, the people who were not able to succeed even under privileged conditions of considerable state support. The so-called Committees of Poor Peasants, established in every village and supported by the Bolshevik authorities, gained increasing influence in the different aspects of peasant life. All this was but a prelude to further pillage and plunder of Soviet villages under the slogans of "extermination of kulaks as a class" and "total collectivization."[10]

The economic aspect of the situation grew worse. When nationalized industries were not able to offer the peasantry sufficient goods in exchange for their grain, there were two options for solving the problem: either to supply the industrial products or to confiscate the grain. How to solve this problem became the focus of discussion in the leading circles of the Communist Party. The supporters of moderation, backing policies of meeting economic requirements, proved to be the minority. Instead of the development of a partnership for mutually beneficial economic exchange between city and village, a strategy of massive robbery and enslavement of the peasants was adopted. It was the beginning of a tragedy that brought innumerable human victims and economic losses and became the major source of deformed economic development in Russia.

One of the most terrible paradoxes of Stalin's time was that the country almost failed to notice its own dismemberment. For a long period, almost everyone—at least in cities and beyond the major areas of starvation in the Ukraine, North Caucasus, and Kazakhstan—failed to grasp the true scale and meaning of tragedy and its immediate and distant consequences. It was a triumph for the state in a closed and secret society. Only gradually, a long time after the events, did the truth began to penetrate outside the ruling circle, first through the belles lettres. The exact numbers of victims remains disputable because of the absence of reliable statistics.[11] In the Ukraine alone, different sources have estimated that as many as three to five million people died of starvation in the winter of 1932–33.[12] Many millions of peasants were exiled to subarctic and uncultivated areas of Siberia and were destined to be exterminated; the calculations of those in power were precise—most of those exiled did not survive.

Putting aside for a moment the human cost of this genocide, the massive extent of the violent collectivization of agriculture was nonsensical in terms of political economy. We can scarcely find another example in modern Western history of such extreme neglect of economic considerations for purely political purposes. It looks especially strange at first glance because this action was undertaken by the followers of the Marxian economic-materialistic approach to social life. But in fact it was not strange: Lenin's formula for the unconditional priority of politics over economy served as a practical guide for Soviet rulers. The economic statistics of these years were terrible in absolute terms. For instance, during the winter of 1930, livestock losses in the countryside constituted more than half of the total number of horses, two-thirds of the sheep, and 26 million hogs. Consumption of meat and fat in the cities for 1932 was one-third of the level of 1928.

The "economic determinism" formally proclaimed by the Bolsheviks yielded in practice to an administrative despotism that applied arbitrary authority and terror to a whole social class, the peasantry. The Bolshevik leadership planned the massive collectivization as a true military campaign to force total submission of the rural areas. This campaign was accompanied by all the attributes of war—military force, plunder, devastation of the countryside, mass deportations of the population, governing settlements by special "prefects" with dictatorial powers, organizing a "fifth column" inside the subdued population, puppet administration by local residents, demoralization of the "foe," etc. This campaign was deliberately pursued and it concluded in total defeat of the peasantry. It is noteworthy that the seventeenth Congress of the Bolshevik party held in 1934—the first congress after collectivization—was named the Congress of Victors. The damage to Soviet agriculture and to the work ethic of the rural population has proven to be irretrievable.

Now let us analyze briefly the key factors that contributed to the overwhelming superiority of the autocratic state in this war directed against the class that constituted the absolute arithmetical majority of the population and that supplied the country with food.

We need to begin with the same *stereotype of submissiveness to decisive power.* This basic stereotype in the Russian national consciousness is maximally expressed in the peasant mentality despite the fact that frequent explosions of peasant rebellion and burning of landlords' estates recur throughout Russian history. While serving as an outlet for the periodic discharge of social "steam," paradoxically these spontaneous impulses of outrage and violence have also supported the stereotype of submission. These mainly irrational acts of vandalism have usually stopped spontaneously and have not formed any positive ideals of freedom in Russian mass consciousness. On the contrary, they formed a syndrome of guilt; and in the presence of force, this has only strengthened the stereotype of slavish obedience to the master. The more decisive and stern the master is, the more complete is the obedience. This attitude was exploited in full measure by collectivization.

Second, the role of *direct coercion,* or the real threat of it, as we have seen, was quite significant. Coercion was conducted by two connected forces: by troops of the Ministry of Internal Affairs (NKVD), who served as a secret military force and who conducted direct punitive actions without legal constraints, and by the corps of "twenty-five-thousanders," party commissars sent to rural areas from big cities and endowed with dictatorial powers. The commissars were empowered to use any measures to achieve the "control figures" by dispossession of kulaks, collectivization, and confiscation of tools and food supplies. These control measures were established by the very top leadership.

The third important element of the campaign was *recourse to the support of the poor peasants of each village and also of the so-called activists.* The former category of people, mainly marginals who were insignificant and useless under normal circumstances, were used to fill most front-rank positions in the new power structure. The regime regarded them as the main sponsors of its policy. These people understood that their well-being depended entirely on their readiness to serve the regime in complete obedience. If they were deprived of the regime's support, they had nothing. This understanding of their complete dependence and also their subconscious feeling of their own inferiority determined their slavish devotion to the regime, their capacity to discharge its dirty deeds without hesitation.

The other group of supporters for Bolshevik power in the villages, the activists, were different from the marginal people in one respect. To be an activist under the Soviet regime actually meant to be a meticulous time-server, an active conformist demonstrating maximum servility to authority, trying to gain favor by all means. Usually this trait applied to those people who had high ambitions but were incapable of satisfying these through achievements in their profession (agriculture, in this case) or in other socially prestigious roles. The activist tried to raise his or her status through pseudo-activity by means of a demonstrative zeal for fulfilling the Bolsheviks' orders in the pursuit of collectivization. The authorities rewarded their zeal, mainly by confiscation of the property of peasants. Beyond material incentives, such activists also were driven by envy of their well-off neighbors, by the intoxicating feeling of impunity, and by other similar abstract motives. The Bolsheviks were always skillful in the manipulation of this sort of tool. The ideological factor was not insignificant for activist behavior—*a faith in abstract justice greatly intensifies if it coincides with personal profit.*

Fourth, *the collectivization campaign revived and exploited the ancient traditionalist stereotypes of communal ethics.* From a certain point of view, collectivization with its slogans of common leveling, socialization, and redistribution of the "surplus"—that is, the property of others—had some similarity with the oldest communal peasant traditions. And those traditions, as practiced in Russia in contrast to Switzerland, for example, did not contain any antidotes against the growth of despotism.

Last but not least was the factor of *a massive ideological campaign of socio-psychological pressure and demoralization of the "class enemy."* The aims of propagandist machinery were, on the one hand, to promote ideas about "high justice," expediency, and the irreversibility of collectivization policy; and, on the other hand, to discredit, isolate, suppress, and psychologically disarm any opposition. Therefore, anyone who dared to resist the terrorist force—as the regime was in essence and in the politics of power—was stigmatized as a foe, as an insect or a weed to be removed from the social soil. This ideological campaign succeeded in all its aims: the "enemies" were demoralized and isolated, and the passive majority was paralyzed by fear and the presumed inevitability of events. A certain segment of peasants, especially the youth, were psychologically strengthened by their faith in the veracity of propagandist myths.

The collectivization campaign restored on the territory of the former Russian Empire a regime of serfdom, more sophisticated but no less brutal than its predecessor. The masses accepted the politics of power, including its most cruel repressive actions, more easily than they otherwise might have because it came from a known hand, from people of the same or close social stratum. The illusion of democratic rule existed. Such psychological aberrations considerably increased the stability of this kind of seemingly quasi-democratic but actually pseudo-democratic regimes—both Communist and Fascist.

THE POWER OF WORKERS?

We turn at last to the class of industrial workers. We have already seen that post-revolutionary development of the country brought more evil and misfortune than good to all strata of society except the new class, the elite of the Soviet nomenklatura. But we should remember that the Revolution was made on behalf of the industrial working class. We need to check the hypothesis that all the evils were the price paid for the happiness of "the hegemon of revolution," "the progressive part of society"—that is, first of all, the working class. However, this concept is far from both historical justice and historical truth.

Its claim on justice seems to be undermined by the circumstance that industrial workers before 1917 and for a long time afterward made up only a small minority of the country's population. According to official data, in 1913 there were three million factory workers in Russia, about 2 percent of the population. During the First World War, the Revolution, and the Civil War, this number was reduced by more than half. According the demographic statistics, by 1925 the number of workers was less than two-thirds of the prewar level, only 1.8 million. After a decade of unprecedented and intensive industrialization, by 1937 workers amounted to 10 percent of the total population—17.5 million. In 1928, they contained 12.4 percent and in the census of 1939 (infamous for massive data falsification), 33.5 percent of the population.[13] But as far as we know the custom of Soviet statistics to increase the desired figures, to double and even triple registers of the same persons, to count workers together with their families, this figure looks quite doubtful.

Even if one were to take seriously the Bolshevik claims about the priority of proletarian interests, one should recognize that sacrificing the interests of the overwhelming majority of the country's population to meet the particular interests of this minority can hardly be considered a just policy.

To consider the supposed truth of the slogan concerning "the proletarian state," we need to analyze the internal structure of the class of industrial workers. Before the Revolution, a significant segment industrial workers consisted of experienced, regular workers. However, even then they were not the absolute majority. World War I and the Revolution sacrificed the lives of a major part of the core of the industrial working class. The gradual restoration and, later, spasmodic growth of its numbers mainly involved newcomers from the villages. As a result, those who were factory workers "by birth" became a small minority of the working class.

Most of the newcomers were peasants by birth who migrated to cities either in search of jobs or to escape from the horrors of collectivization. By their culture they were marginals rather than activists: they were not aggressive and unscrupulous but lacking in self-confidence, frightened, and poorly oriented to city life and therefore easily subject to any kind of suggestion, blackmail, or pressure.

Further, it was a commonplace in socialist mythology that it was the hereditary proletariat who always supported the Bolshevik party the most faithfully and treated it as their political representation. At least two kinds of objections to this arise. First, the stratum of hereditary workers included a considerable portion of the so-called workers' aristocracy; that is, the most qualified and consequently most highly paid group of workers. By their style of life and the character of their consciousness, they were closer to the middle stratum of the urban population. They were more or less satisfied with the material conditions of life and frequently possessed some property; therefore, they would be inclined to support social stability and could not be the faithful partisans of Bolshevik policies favoring mass property redistribution. Second, much evidence exists of stubborn organized resistance by a considerable segment of workers to the Bolshevik authorities in the first months and even years after the coup of October, 1917.[14]

These questions need to be elaborated thoroughly, but even on the basis of knowledge we do possess, there are serious reasons to reconsider the cornerstone doctrine of official Soviet historiography—the concept of workers' power. Certainly, a substantial portion of the workers actively supported the Bolshevik regime. However, if all of these circumstances are taken into consideration, the inevitable question arises: Was the social base of regime too narrow to consider it to represent "the power of the people"?

PEOPLE'S FATE IN THE "PEOPLE'S STATE"

One of the ways of legitimizing the political practice of terror was to employ a narrow, limited conception of what constituted the people and the nation. In socialist doctrines, the term *the people* was usually identified with poorly educated manual, industrial, and agricultural workers—the so-called proletarians of city and village. I think there is no need here to treat all this nonsense seriously or to waste time proving the complete falseness of this construction. Unfortunately, this problem was not abstract for the tens of millions of people who were considered outside the range of the true people—who were viewed as an insignificant and harmful part of the nation based on their social origin. Under the umbrella of this theory, the legitimate interests and human rights of a huge number of human beings were sacrificed or neglected. If we follow this terminology for a moment, these are more reasons to suggest that the people were badgered and trampled by new bronze horsemen who relied on the worst part of nation and the worst traits of the national mentality—obedience, submission to a powerful hand, and willingness to march in columns along prescribed routes to the rhythm of ideological drums.

This approach was consolidated even on the constitutional level. The first Soviet Constitution adopted in 1918 proclaimed the right of the socialist state to deprive whole categories of people of their civil rights "in the interests of the Socialist Revolution" (article 23). In article 65, the categories of people deprived of suffrage were enumerated: people using hired labor, people living on unearned income, vendors, trade and commercial commissioners, monks and clergy, and employees and agents of the former police. These categories contained in total almost half of the population. Since elections are not a very important element of life in totalitarian regimes, these restrictions were abandoned in the Constitution of 1936. But other more important ones were established. Even the late Soviet constitutions recognized the political rights of citizens only on condition that they acted "in the interests of working people" or for "the purposes of consolidation of the socialist order" (Constitution of 1936, articles 125, 126); "in agreement with the interests of people and for the purposes of consolidation and development of the socialist order" (Constitution of 1977, article 50); or "in accordance with the purposes of building Communism" (Constitution of 1977, article 51). Those who have spent their lives in Soviet society know all too well what restrictions and repressions are really covered under these formulations.

A Society Intoxicated with Terror

It goes without saying that the machinery of terror was the true foundation of the regime's power. But the theme of terror is not a special topic of this book. It is more important here to examine how and why this society *accepted terror as an appropriate form of government,* and from whom and on what basis the agents of terror developed. Three factors explain these things.

First, the bloody nightmare of Stalinism was not a kind of natural calamity or some isolated episode in the Russian history. It was a continuation of the ancient Russian autocratic tradition of periodic genocide campaigns directed against the Russian nation. The most grandiose of these efforts, each measured by the scale of its own time, would include the *oprichnina* of Ivan the Terrible, the period of Peter I, and the years of the Revolution. However, this is not a full list: dozens of other lesser campaigns, episodes, and situations could serve as examples, when the lives of thousands and thousands of people were sacrificed in an offhand manner or recklessly placed at political risk.

Second, in the course of Stalin's genocide campaign, the offspring of an alternative tradition, the person-centered tradition of liberal democracy—much younger, less widespread, and less deeply rooted—was eradicated almost completely. Stalinism was merely the culmination of the longer-term campaign against this alternative, which began with the October Revolution.

Third, the involvement of millions of people in Stalin's crimes, in one way or another and to different degrees, caused the moral degradation of post-Revolution society as a whole. We know that moral self-destruction follows in the wake of crimes committed both individually and collectively. On a group level, such moral degradation, as a rule, is irreversible within a single generation. It is unclear, though, how many generations will be necessary to remove the stains of Stalinism from public morality. Moreover, the period increases if the virus of Stalinism is reproduced among succeeding generations. The general environment encourages its survival, as recent political events in Russia unfortunately demonstrate. Not only full publicity concerning Stalinist crimes but also public repentance of the nation are apparently needed for the revival of public morality. It seems that the problematic of Stalin's crimes and the catastrophic influence of the Stalinist regime on the fate of Russia and other Soviet nations are inexhaustible fruits of evil in this world. I have merely tried to outline briefly some aspects of their effects in the drama of Russian history.

The Problem of Deceived Generations

Considering the phenomenon of Stalinism, we run the risk of misunderstanding much if we conduct our analysis only on the basis of categories like butchers, victims, and the frightened majority, though these categories reflect an essential core in the march of events. A considerable number of the people who lived then perceived the years of Stalin's rule in other colors. Many people sincerely believed that the regime with Comrade Stalin at its head created conditions for a new and wonderful life. This life would have come about quickly had it not been sabotaged by many different foes and reactionaries who undermined the efforts of Bolsheviks. Therefore, any measure was permissible in the struggle against these dangerous public enemies.

These believers in Stalin's divine wisdom and righteousness, these people who fulfilled the criminal orders of the regime, who worked extremely hard at a backbreaking job, who enthusiastically applauded Comrade Stalin and marched in columns of the faithful during official celebrations, did not suspect that they were puppets being manipulated to perform evil missions. Even in cases where one's mind and conscience were not able to justify especially cruel or unjust actions, subconscious qualms were alleviated with the help of cunning propaganda prompted by the salutary formula: "You can't make an omelet without breaking eggs." This mass aberration, when people do not believe in their own common sense or trust their personal observations but accept shameless, false, and primitive propaganda, seems to be explained on the basis of two major kinds of socio-psychological mechanisms.

The first are the so-called defensive mechanisms of the psyche—displacement and rationalization. Human consciousness is inclined to displace unacceptable information and replace it with false but acceptable conceptions. It is difficult and probably impossible for many people to live with an honest understanding of themselves as mere tools for criminal and immoral purposes. Humans in such circumstances are willing to be deceived or to deceive themselves. They either invent excuses for themselves or allow themselves to accept myths that embellish the use of power and its intentions. People have an urge and prefer to believe in morally appropriate concepts and explanations. It is especially easy to make an accommodation with evil when convenient versions and symbols of faith are actively espoused by powerful and well-orchestrated propaganda machinery.

Socio-psychological mechanisms of a second kind—suggestion and countersuggestion—also come into play here. The influence of these mechanisms was especially strong in the Soviet circumstances because of the lack of any tradition of political nonconformity or of an open public realm. On the contrary, a long tradition of recognizing the supreme authority of official sources weakens the autonomy of independent judgment and one's confidence in public opinion. In such circumstances, mass consciousness has proven defenseless against the impact of official propaganda. Conformity rules. The filters of skepticism, mistrust, irony, and the independent reflection on political questions inherent to Western consciousness began to form in Russian political culture only in the second half of the nineteenth century. For that reason, public opinion was fragile and vulnerable to the impact of massive and aggressive lies. Therefore, we have to think about the subjects of Stalin's empire as a deceived generation.

The Heroism of the Anthill

One of puzzles of Stalin's regime was its steadiness during crises. This cannot be explained solely by terror and deception. Why did such an inhuman system demonstrate such a high degree of effectiveness and will to self-preservation in times of crisis? Why did the people who found themselves in a crisis situation through the fault of their rulers rally so effectively to the support of those rulers? These questions apply to Stalin's industrialization policy and the defense of the Motherland in World War II.

The concept of system-centered patterns of social order, I submit, helps to answer this question. This factor gave additional strength and steadiness to the Stalinist regime. The underdevelopment of individualistic consciousness in a system-centered society, the evaluation of humanity only in terms of the individual's efficacy for a social whole created the ground for an unreflective self-sacrifice for the collectivity. I call this syndrome the heroism of the anthill. This phenomenon appeared in extreme form under war conditions. In economic situations, this phenomenon also occurred when the regime relied on the heroism of workers as a major source of support.

The heroism of the anthill differs seriously, especially in its moral and psychological foundations, from heroism in the traditional sense of sacrificing oneself deliberately. Under such circumstances, a heroic deed is recognized both by oneself and by the social milieu as an act of high self-abnegation. Therefore, it is presumed that the purpose for which such a high price is paid must be significant and that no other solution exists. In other words, heroic self-denial is not a norm but an exception. It is acceptable only in extreme circumstances. We can certainly find many examples of this kind of heroism in Russian and Soviet as well as in Western history.

During Stalinism, however, human self-denial became a social norm, a mode of behavior expected by the social milieu even when the objective circumstances did not demand such a sacrifice. Alas, these sacrifices reflected the low value placed on an individual's life in the system-centered scale of values. Sacrificing the lives of the state's subjects was not considered noteworthy. The heroism of the anthill allowed the regime to use human bodies to plug leaks and fuel engines in the ship of state. It allowed the regime to use human bodies in ways that are not worthy of honor and emulation. Is Russian civilization to reach beyond the system-centeredness of the anthill? That is a crucial test for judgment of changes in post-Bolshevik Russia.

CHAPTER TEN

After Stalin

The System Yields to Fatigue

This is not a book about politics as such. However, in this chapter devoted to the late period of the Bolshevik system, I briefly address the political instruments of the Soviet regime to illustrate that although they were employed in more moderate, less cruel ways during the later stages of the Bolshevik system than at first, the same ethical and socio-psychological mechanisms were at work.

One cannot equate the time of Stalin with that of Brezhnev. The differences are evident even to the unaided eye. Perhaps it is only to the unaided eye that these differences appear to be fundamental. To an observer equipped with a theoretical lens or a practical knowledge of the inner workings of the political machinery, the differences do not seem so substantial. To the contrary, upon examination it becomes clearly evident that the two periods are fundamentally of the same kind. It is more accurate to view them as two phases in the development of essentially the same political regime. The supporting pillars and processes of the political system—the basic structure of power relationships and the principles governing implementation of power—stayed the same.

During the later stages of the Soviet era, society remained ill with the same disease, caused by same virus. The political names of different forms of this virus are Stalinism, neo-Stalinism, and so forth, but ontologically all belong to the deeper layers of social reality—the system-centeredness of the anthill—as reflected in several centuries of Russian history.

BASIC INSTITUTIONS OF THE SOVIET REGIME

Having elsewhere published (in English) detailed descriptions both of the basic institutions of the Soviet regime and of its modus operandi, the mechanics of power in terms of political science, I restrict discussion here to an enumeration of them with brief comments upon each.[1]

Indivisible Hegemony of a Single Organized Force

In Soviet political life it was the vanguard party, built on the principles of rigorous centralism, that ensured political control of practically every aspect of society as well as the effective dissemination and reiteration of commands coming from a single center. The tremendous dehumanizing capabilities of this machine, its lack of mechanisms to prevent mistakes, its capacity to multiply mistakes, and its lack of capacity to promote worthy individuals to the top or at least to block criminal abuses of power became publicly known thanks to *glasnost.* Gorbachev and part of his team made a dramatic attempt to transform this terrible machine into a force capable of leading positive social changes but on the condition of keeping the Communist Party in power.

The unfolding of events has demonstrated clearly that these hopes were completely illusory. A transformation of the system through party mechanisms proved to be unrealistic.

A Leader with Formally Unlimited Powers

Since the days of Stalin, the post of the general secretary had been a key position of power in the Soviet political system. The general secretary's powers were not formally set down in any law. At some point, the concentration of power in the hands of the general secretary came to depend very little on the personal qualities of the person who happened to occupy that position. But unbounded power by no means signified freedom of action. The party apparatus had a wide variety of ways and means to influence its leader. The process of building the nomenklatura and promoting people through its ranks into the positions that served as the real gateways to leading roles was always under the general secretary's control. Control of information and interpretation of guidelines preempted opportunities to take decisions. Thus, the apparatus strove to ensure that its own man was promoted to the role of leader and then served as his eyes and hands. It was able to do this to some degree at all times, in all periods.

Practically Unchecked Party and State Apparatus

If the leader was under the control of the apparatus, the apparatus was for all practical purposes not controlled by anyone. Created by Stalin in the 1920s as a machine to carry out the will of the leader, it gradually became a force unto itself. Its role grew especially large during the post-Khrushchev decades.

Some attempts were made in the Gorbachev years to reduce the influence of the apparatus and to place it under the control of society. However, despite certain structural and personnel changes, it must be acknowledged that the actual results achieved in this respect were a long way from conforming to the clamor of proclamations made on this account. *The obedience of the apparatus extended only to the limits within which there was nothing that threatened its own dominant position.* Its instinct for self-preservation was well developed.

Of course, the apparatus was not homogeneous in human terms. But the general conservative spirit of its corporate structure and its bureaucratic corporate ethics in one way or another bound the whole together. Mechanisms for effective social control of the apparatus were not created. Specifically, perestroika failed to make any cardinal change in the social status of the apparatus or in its composition. A transformation was required for creating agents who could move from being society's master to become servants of society. But that did not happen either under Gorbachev or later in the post-Soviet era.

The Machinery of Coercion and Potential Repression

The historical circumstances under which Soviet power was born and evolved caused it to give primary attention to the tasks of creating machinery for its own physical self-defense. Hence, one of its first concerns was to create of an intricate network of special organs invested with broad powers for the physical repression of real, potential, or imagined political opponents—anyone who did not obediently serve.

This diabolical machinery had moments of supreme intensity and other periods of low-key work; for a time it operated at the very forefront of the state's existence, but then it receded behind the scenes, into the depths. For seven decades, however, it was kept in a state of constant preparedness to be able to strike abruptly at any moment with lighting speed at the first signal of danger.

Ideological Monopoly

For long decades, in the sphere of ideas, there was a consistent orientation toward monopolization of all ideological platforms. Monopoly over the "only true line" had been completely established in the late 1920s. This machinery can be called *the institution of enforced unanimity of thought.* In its general form, the basic law of action characteristic of this machinery may be described as *the principle of the nonfreedom of information.* The system-centeredness of the anthill in human societies depends on control of language, communication, and the flow of ideas and information.

Two-Tier Ideology

This institution was formed later than the others and had no notable prehistory in the pre-Stalinist period. It signifies the existence within the political practice of the ruling party of two fundamentally disparate aspects in the realm of ideas. One aspect, the external one, had a declarative and, in many ways, camouflaging character; the other, the effective, internal one, was exercised by the inner circle of the initiated and reflected the true ideology. In other words, the outer aspect was intended for mass consumption, for propaganda, while the inner aspect was the real policy apparatus. For example, whereas in the external rhetorical realm universal equality was proclaimed, at the internal real level an intricate system of privileges continued to proliferate. Nepotism, protection, and favors took root, and a caste psychology was cultivated. Demagoguery about democracy in its most perfect image was fully coordinated with the practice of cruel suppression of any sprigs of independent thought. Appeals to economize went hand in hand with unprecedented waste; appeals for effectiveness were coupled with unprecedented bureaucratic lethargy engaged in pseudo-activity on a stupendous scale.

After April, 1985, the sphere and the scale of political duplicity shrank substantially. The development of the "new political thinking," glasnost, and the turn to openness of social and political life reduced the possibilities for conniving among the inner circle. What had been secret became increasingly apparent. Nevertheless, essential changes in the realm of deeds rather than words came neither then nor later, not even under Yeltsin's regime.

Total Dependence of the Individual on Authority

The post-NEP Stalinist course toward universal de facto subordination of economic and social life to the state created a situation in which almost all channels for satisfying primary human needs—for obtaining work, education, medical assistance, housing, food, etc.—were under the monopoly control of those in power. The upshot was that individuals found themselves in a situation of total dependence.

The authorities acquired a whole array of ways to influence the individual by providing both incentives and deterrents. A person could be promoted in a job, but it was also possible to create an intolerable atmosphere there, not to mention to fire the individual; a person might or might not be given an apartment; one might be permitted to travel abroad or one might not; a writer's book might or might not be printed. Moreover, one's offspring could be barred from university and drafted into the army. A general ban might be levied on hiring a person, and then three months later criminal charges could be brought against that individual for sponging! In fact, all the threads came together in the same hands.

The other side of the institution of total dependence of the individual on a chastising or rewarding hand was an intricate and rigidly ranked system of distribution of every conceivable privilege. Altogether this system embraced millions of people throughout the country. This hierarchical feeding trough had two objective consequences. On the one hand, it created and sustained an army of palace guards for the regime, and on the other, its influence on public morals was extremely negative, corrupting the insiders and those aspiring to their ranks, and creating and continually rekindling a sense of social injustice among all other people. What is more, the insiders were usually not satisfied with the privileges duly accorded them but endeavored through informal favors to acquire all kinds of additional goods, which merely aggravated mass aversion to the caste of life's masters. This institution had a ruinous influence on public morals as well.

WORKING PRINCIPLES OF THE REGIME

Following this brief review of the basic institutions of power in the regime, we now turn to some of the principles that function in the more dynamic aspects of a system that is undergoing restructuring. These working principles are the processes that govern the way of life.

Preventive Eradication and Suppression of Opposition

The regime invented nothing in this regard but merely adapted, modernized, and continued the tradition of employing police methods to respond to any social discontent. Under the cover of rhetoric about "moral and political unity," the regime cultivated for decades in the public mind universal suspiciousness, blind conformity, and an intolerance of dissent. These features were sustained psychologically by intimidating the ordinary citizen with the specter of external and internal foes, since enemies—whether they were real or imaginary is unimportant for propagandistic manipulations—were always at hand.

Forced Labor

The entire world now knows about the extermination work camps of the Stalin's Gulag, the many millions of persons, their numbers constantly replenished, who erected the great edifices of Communism practically with their bare hands and on the bones of their fellow inmates. The principle of coercion also underlay the use of the labor of soldiers to build civilian projects, the regular mobilization of city dwellers for agricultural work (some such actions were camouflaged as "patronage assistance"), and enforced "voluntary" work on Saturdays.

During all those years, forced labor was an essential component of the Soviet economy. Between the alternatives of an effectively developing society and an obedient society, unqualified preference was given to the latter.

Initiative Discouraged

In every sphere, the system was based not on active, inquiring individuality but on obsequious, obedient agents: even the brightest talent was tolerated only insofar as one remained under control and, better yet, one did not contemplate independence. Today we can see how far and how rapidly Russian society has moved away from the former Stalinist ideal of cogs in the machine. There were roadblocks along the way, but eventually this movement became irreversible.

Manipulation of People's Baser Qualities

One of the most widely manipulated human qualities is envy. It can be evoked by another's talent, success, prosperity, beautiful wife, successful husband, or more capable children. What do people not envy! Envy is based on some or other form of natural inequality, perceived by the envious person as injustice and hence arousing a perverted thirst for revenge. A base desire to see one's rival harmed is, alas, present in many people. In Christian society, the system of moral norms has nonetheless in some measure obstructed at least the cruelest manifestations of envy. The fundamental relativism of the revolutionary morality that pervaded the whole Communist ideological code forcefully contributed to removing all moral constraints, allowing envy to prevail.

The functionaries of the regime included some artful "soul hunters," people who were ready and able to make use of human baseness—to advise scoundrels on what to do and how to suppress the pricks of conscience. For example, envy was one of the viruses stimulating the denunciation of coworkers, bosses, and neighbors, an epidemic that swept through the country in the second half of the 1930s and was openly encouraged by the authorities. The prize to the denouncer might be twofold: material advantage inherited, as it were, from the victim (job, status, housing, or property) and moral satisfaction from exacting retribution.

Another property of the human soul, similar in psychological roots to vanity, is the "hero complex"; that is, the desire to acquire by any means available a reputation one has not rightfully earned. An even more universal tool was the exploitation of fear. The regime knew exactly how to instill fear in the souls of its subjects, how to frighten them.

This mechanism of exploiting every base human instinct—manipulation of envy, vanity, cowardice—operated at all levels of the pyramid of power from the Politburo to collective farms, from the Academy of Sciences to the Gulag. The only differences lay in the prizes. They varied from high titles, top-ranking positions, broad powers, and material abundance to miserable handouts or a chance to even a score with a prison mate or get an extra portion of prison food. But the negative incentives—persecution, deprivation, civic and physical death—varied little no matter what the level; they were more dependent on the era. The forms of temptation and intimidation, and sometimes the set of incentives and threats, varied from Stalinist to Brezhnev and post-Brezhnev times, but the machinery remained much the same at the core.

Negative Nationalism

An important principle of operation for successive generations of Soviet leadership was the exploitation of negative nationalism. It goes without saying that patriotism also has positive and often lofty expressions, but this kind of politicized patriotism was purely an ideological manipulation. The party attempted to keep several different ethnic groups within the Soviet Union hostile to one another. There was always the sense of "us" and "them," encouraged by unsettled historical scores between non-Russian nationalities, especially in such tense and potentially explosive multinational regions as the Caucasus and Central Asia. In relation to the external world, the myth of the West's military threat to the Soviet Union, of the country as a besieged fortress, was exploited. It must be said that this worked effectively on mass consciousness since it was based on the old tradition of regarding the surrounding world as a combination of diverse enemies. Chauvinism as well as old historical scores between different nationalities were exploited on the internal front rather skillfully.

However, ethnic passions are more difficult to control than an atomic reactor: the process sometimes spills over in the most unexpected and dangerous directions. The longer such passions have remained under pressure, the more violent are the eruptions. We now are eating the fruits of a long-standing national policy of the Soviet rulers.

Pseudo-Activity

The regime profligately squandered resources on various forms of pseudo-activity. One was pseudo-democracy, the effort to create an image of highly democratic society, which unfortunately deceived not only the uninformed and manipulated subjects of regime but also many supposedly more informed Western analysts. Another was playing on appearances, whereby the totally programmed nature of the entire system of control in fact strove to achieve not real, useful effects but certain favorable formal showings and indices.

Rejection of the Best People

Clever and honest people, acting on the most sincere patriotic motives, often undertook unselfish attempts to make the system more civilized, more effective, and more humane. They did this in the most varied areas of the economy, science, management, and art. But as a rule the results were negligible. At best, some secondary scraps of improvement were adopted. But the cardinal ideas either got hopelessly mired in the bureaucratic swamp or were emasculated politically. The only exceptions were technical ideas and technocratically dominated social projects and plans.

Why did this happen? It would seem that any power would be interested in strengthening the state through offering constructive assistance to the most active and talented segment of society. But in fact, for some types of power, modernization is dangerous, since it almost always results in a loss by the ruling oligarchy of some of its control over society. The main danger, however, is represented by those who have new ideas. These are usually people with a nontraditional way of thinking and with pronounced individuality, people who are inwardly independent and do not recognize the sanctity of official bureaucratic logic. Hence, such persons represent a threat to the bureaucratic mind. In any event, the risk exceeds the potential benefits. Anything that rises above mediocrity is dangerous for the status quo if it is not kept totally under control.

In the mid-sixteenth century, Archbishop Vassian wrote to Ivan the Terrible: "Do not keep the wisest and best people around yourself if you wish to be an autocrat." How Ivan resolved this problem is well known: He offered them poisoned toasts. But in subsequent centuries as well, power usually gave an unequivocally negative answer to the question of its potential alliance with a liberally disposed intelligentsia, in particular. The damage done to the country by such long-lasting forms of self-evisceration is incalculable.

Promotion of the Worst People (Negative Selection)

Essentially this is the obverse of the preceding principle. Unprincipled careerism was the leading "moral" quality of people who had successfully moved upward in the pyramid of power. Often they did not even bother to camouflage their motives. As a result, the ruling elite of the regime was essentially an anti-elite, for it was formed from the worst segment of each social stratum. Social background does not make any difference for people of this kind; they can derive from any social group. Their crucial feature is lack of a moral code and moral ties to others.

Manipulation of Public Consciousness

This has always been one of strengths of the regime. In the first decades of its existence, it usually relied on an undeveloped consciousness. As time passed, however, it became clear that cries of "hurrah" and "down with," expressions of righteous anger and unanimous approval could be extracted not only from workers but from professors as well. From the standpoint of practical politics, the regime needed cries of down with or death to the enemies more than it needed hurrahs. The main purpose of such campaigns was always an internal political one, regardless of the target of damnation, whether that target was internal enemy (like Andrei Sakharov) or an external one (like "U.S. imperialism").

Perversion of Law

The notion of the law as an instrument of power is usually conceptualized as Asiatic or Byzantine. However, a pragmatically suspicious attitude toward the law—seeing it as no more than an instrument of power rather than a covenant or charter of individual rights—unfortunately has its own roots in Russian society as well.

Most of the laws adopted in the Soviet Union could be classified in one of two categories: declarative propagandistic proclamations and laws with real efficacy. The first category served the purpose of imitating democratic societies. Laws of this sort were formulated with deliberate vagueness. As a result, a considerable portion of them consisted of meaningless phrases and dead norms.

The laws that actually worked were another matter. They were prepared and adopted without broad, showy pseudopublic allusions and were ratified in a truly businesslike manner by decisions of the higher party functionaries, and then rubber-stamped without discussion in the "supreme legislative body." In contrast to the laws that existed merely for show, these were often of a distinctly repressive or prohibitive character, and indeed this applies not only to the Stalinist period but to more recent times as well. It is sufficient just to leaf through the laws of 1983–84, when a number of harsh punitive restrictive acts were adopted in labor legislation at the same time as the declarative Law on Work Collectives was adopted. Even Gorbachev's new era began with a repressive and clearly anti-economic law on nonlabor sources of income.

Use of State Awards as Bait

To further its own interests, the regime also used awards and honors as an important instrument for the manipulation of social consciousness. Admittedly, in order to conceal this, it was necessary to maintain the prestige of awards by giving them not only to its own hangers-on and parasites but to people who truly deserved recognition for their real services to society. But the relative proportion of those who were rewarded for their services tended generally to decrease as time passed. The most deft, those most capable of intrigue, tended increasingly to predominate among the award recipients; at some point, the procedure for nomination and for granting awards turned into a mafialike contest among fawning, parasitical "courtesans" for the favors of the "sovereign."

Exploitation of the Authoritarian Political Tradition

Romanticizing of the "holy fatherland" and of a return to the spirit of the forefathers is a routine technique in the political life of any country. It is resorted to especially frequently in crisis situations when it is necessary to arouse and stimulate the national spirit. What can consolidate the people more easily than common sacred objects and reminders of the unity of their historical destiny? Hence, the historical trustworthiness of these symbols of faith is essential, and it is also important that they be perceived as such.

In Soviet history, this tactic was first adopted as a weapon by Stalin, who exploited the authority of Lenin as the generally accepted leader of the Revolution to create a posthumous cult, which in fact contradicted Marxism, Lenin's own will, and the desires of Lenin's widow. Stalin needed this cult to "sanctify" his own actions with Lenin's authority. This example makes graphically evident that the intellectual core of Marxism had a strictly subordinate, pragmatic significance in symbolic manipulation for the Soviet regime. On the other hand, the institution of ideological duplicity was unambiguously embodied in this principle.

Later, at a moment that was critical for the regime, Stalin did not shrink from shifting ideological accents with cynical design but feigned an emotional appeal to the banner of the great ancestors and other symbols of the holy fatherland, which Stalin himself had earlier profaned and desecrated many times. The effect, it must be said, was considerable. In more recent times, his heirs on the Brezhnev team used Stalin himself, just as calculatingly, as the symbol of a golden age. And, however bitter it may be to acknowledge this, such a course encountered quite broad public support, the age factor playing no decisive role at all. The young neo-Stalinism that came to replace classical Stalinism was in some respects even worse.

All in all, psychological and moral Stalinism chronologically occupies a much broader niche than merely the troubled years of Stalin's actual rule and is alive even now. We have no guarantees that there will be no attempts to make use of the most authoritarian political tradition for momentary political ends.

STEPS LEADING TO THE COLLAPSE OF THE SOVIET SYSTEM

Despite the array of stabilizing mechanisms that held the Soviet system together, it did not remain completely stagnant. Some key transitional steps were taken that gradually undermined the basic principles of the Soviet regime from the high noon achieved during Stalin's rule.

It was Stalin's immediate successor as general secretary of the Communist Party, Nikita Khrushchev, who took the first step. He initiated a critical assessment of Stalin's actions, particularly his repressive actions against "honest Communists" who had been purged as potential sources of opposition and disagreement. These victims were rehabilitated—mostly posthumously. Khrushchev eased, to some degree, the pressure on intellectuals, opened the iron curtain a little to the influence of world affairs, and slightly improved the material conditions and social status of peasants as victims of the second Russian serfdom. His reform measures were limited and his actions were inconsistent.

The system perceived even such small measures to be a threat to its basic principles. Khrushchev was ousted by a kind of palace coup by leading members of the party's Politburo, giving way to the Brezhnev era of complacent defense of the traditional organizing principles of the Soviet regime.

The next cautious move to change the system was undertaken in the economic sphere by Aleksey Kosygin, who served as prime minister during the Brezhnev era. Kosygin was technically concerned about economic performance. His efforts were effectively blocked without any attack against him personally.

The critique of Stalinism, the consideration of economic change, and the relaxation of oppressive police methods meant that the system was becoming less and less rigid and allowed greater latitude in choice and movement as people related to one another in meeting the requirements of life. A greater degree of spontaneity emerged in popular culture as people coped with their ordinary problems. The system became more vulnerable to the possibility of change.

Brezhnev's successor, Yuri Andropov, made a desperate effort to stop the process of contemplating change in the basic principles of the Soviet system. As former head of the KGB, he again tried to mobilize resources to keep in place an efficient way of achieving obedience. He died in office only fifteen months after becoming the general secretary of the Communist Party, and this campaign came to an end.

Mikhail Gorbachev came to power in March of 1985 and conceded it six years and a half years later, In December of 1991 the USSR was disbanded. In his first year and a half, Gorbachev's leadership followed in the Andropov tradition, but he took the turn of advocating both glasnost (openness) and perestroika (restructuring) of the Soviet economy and to some degree of the political institutions as well. He hoped that both openness and reform could be achieved by reliance on the command-and-control mechanism of the Communist Party but with a more liberal bent. His views evolved toward a more social democratic position. When leading elements in the party attempted a coup d'état, the regime collapsed. Those accustomed to obedience were at a loss about where to turn when a crisis of command arose. The step by cautious step relaxation of terror, the acknowledgment of grounds for criticism, and the possibility of change opened the way for collapse of the system before it became ready for the more fundamental transformation from system-centeredness to a more person-centered social order.

Gorbachev made significant steps toward transforming country from a closed to semi-open society. He tried, however, to keep these processes under control, relying upon the levers of power inherited from the classic Soviet mode of rule. It became obvious during his last years in power that this did not work, and he made some inconsistent efforts to expand the old tool kit. But he failed. The principle of formally unbounded power but practically constrained space for action knocked him out of the running. The conservative core of the party-state apparatus rebelled. They did not succeed in their strategic restorative purpose, but the upheaval was enough to destroy the political basis of Gorbachev's authority. The system he tried to reconstruct managed to dispose of him instead.

By historical criteria, "Gorby" was in power only a short time. But those minutes on the watch of history counted for more than decades. He seems the most dramatic and still enigmatic person at the Soviet top, despite a plethora of books about him.[2] By all means, he belongs to history in the high sense of the word. We are still too much in shadow of the time of perestroika and its consequences to evaluate this act of the Russian drama with academic calm and objectivity. One thing is clear, however: Gorbachev pushed the country to a new crossroad and opened another opportunity, at a new level, for making a historic choice between system-centered and person-centered ways of development. People and only people themselves will determine by their own small actions the future path of the country: whether it will proceed along the old beaten authoritarian path, in which the human individual is inevitably relegated to the notorious role of a cog in the machine, or along a democratic path—a person-centered path—in which the rocky road at the beginning creates in people a sense of social responsibility, independence, and dignity. The importance of the position of individuals is markedly enhanced in transitional periods. And history is once again offering us, the generations now living, the opportunity to influence the future of Russia and perhaps of the entire world. We have let the chance slip through our fingers many times before. Perhaps the present will move us toward a new course.

CHAPTER ELEVEN

At the New Crossroad

For Russia, the final fifteen years of the twentieth century proved to be the most unusual, uncertain, and promising. Russia is at a dramatically new crossroads facing both old and new choices, some going far beyond the choice of political leadership and even of political or economic system. It faces a choice about the basic principles of human order. In the final analysis, the choice is between system-centered and person-centered patterns of order. The danger that the wrong public choice could be made is real, in which case the country will again inevitably face a vicious, fruitless cycle of system-centered dynamics in some superficially modernized version. In this context it is important to understand that the so-called Communist revenge was only one version of the wind on its circuits (Eccles. 1:6). As a modern Moscow scholar wrote in the Russian liberal journal *Vestnik Evropy* (European Herald), now reborn after its suppression in 1918 and a leading journal for a hundred years before it was silenced, Communism was a failed attempt to combine traditional values and the stable characteristics of mentality with the task of making society dynamic.[1] The failure of this attempt, however, does not prevent other temptations to create a new version of an effectively governed and socially obedient society.

The chance for a considered choice as a substitute for preemptive patterns of human order is still open. That is why I now examine threats to considered alternatives.

THREATS TO CONSIDERED ALTERNATIVES

Elections are a necessary but not a sufficient institution for a civil society. Certainly, Russia has achieved a certain progress on its way to forming a civil society. However, the present society is too weak to offer effective pressure against the forces resisting and undermining the development of an open civil society.

There are three main sources of these threats. First are the old-style hardhats (including some young people, unfortunately), who overtly or covertly support the antireformist Communist and nationalist parties and movements; that is, organizations incompatible with the ideas and principles of an open civil society. Second, the state bureaucracy at all levels embodies a preemptive system of power relationships and attempts to preserve its privileged position of serving as society's guardian—offering the tutelage of Dostoevsky's famous image of a Grand Inquisitor. Russian bureaucrats are not unique in the possession of these qualities. However, in terms of the Russian-Soviet tradition, there have been more opportunities for the unrestricted development of these qualities beyond all limits inherent democratic countries. That is why the bureaucratic syndrome is a serious threat to successful reforms in Russia. The recent and current struggle around civil service reform confirms these apprehensions. Having been involved in this process as the main author of a democratic project of reform in 1998, aiming to transform the Russian bureaucratic machinery from traditional service to the state into genuinely *public* service, I can testify to this.[2]

And third is the conservative syndrome of mass consciousness that opposes changes at the deeper level of consciousness required of thoughtful citizens. The first and second kinds of threats seem clear enough, so after this brief indication of the dangers from the top, we need to consider the dangers from deep within the society.

THE CONSERVATIVE SYNDROME IN RUSSIAN MASS CONSCIOUSNESS

Alexis de Tocqueville in his analysis of democracy in America stressed the important, sometimes crucial, role of habits of the heart and mind of people in the political order. For better or for worse, this aspect of society finds confirmation in the current drama of events in Russia. The deep structure of Russian psychological conservatism is the psychological constant of mass consciousness.[3] This conservative syndrome is an important obstacle to the true modernization of Russia, but it can be overcome. To underestimate or misunderstand this phenomenon can cripple or distort even the best plans of reformers. Moreover, neglecting it may provoke actions by forces hostile to reforms and encourage reactionary political forces. Unfortunately, we have faced this aggressive counter-reformism several times during the post-Communist years.

The first feature of this conservative syndrome is *an impersonal social attitude* expressed in the notorious Soviet slogan "everybody can be replaced." The extremely brutal forms of this orientation manifested themselves under Stalinism and were usually associated with the Gulag Archipelago and forced collectivization of the peasantry. Actually this phenomenon has a much broader historical and cultural background. This inhuman anti-personalism runs directly counter to the person-centered spirit of Western civilization. The essence of this attitude is to reject any measure of autonomy reflected in the independence of the individual. Aggressive anti-individualism has at least two basic characteristics: a leveling psychology (pseudo-egalitarianism) and a compulsive pseudo-collectivism. Pseudo-egalitarianism is masked as social justice; and pseudo-collectivism is based on a dramatically anti-personal stereotype of "all together," implying situations in which, irrespective of the will of the individual, one is involved in a sectarian joint activity where one's personal opinion is subordinated to collective considerations. The person is sacrificed, victimized in a vulgarized notion of unity and conformity. The social price of this sacrifice is that when those people who are unusual and critical-minded are removed from normal social life—they were removed from physical life in Stalin's period—they no longer have the potential for affecting changes in society. The result of this principle of selection is a deficit of people skilled in practical fields of activity.

The second feature is a counter-rational *social inferiority complex and fear of change.* This is found at various levels of consciousness and social strata and derives from the intersection of two controversial components. On the one hand there is a sense of dissatisfaction and lack of prospects concerning the dominant social system, and on the other hand there is an awareness of one's own organic kinship with this system by virtue of which even a change for the better seems to threaten the routine "harmony" and order of things. What is curious is that this complex persists even among the poor and underprivileged. Change is feared even by many of those who would seem to have little to lose and much to gain. Practically all sections of society maintain thick amorphous layers of people who in a perverse way are comfortable with the status quo ante. Here, we are obviously faced with a stereotype the historian N. M. Karamzin noted when he said: "We are less sensitive to the evil we know than to a new good we do not believe at all."

The third feature is *lack of moral regulators of social behavior.* The traditional system of moral values earlier predominant in Russia gradually weakened and then failed within the period from the mid-nineteenth century to the mid-twentieth century. The traditional system of morals outlived itself, and its decay was inevitable. However, no other equally universal and legitimate system of moral regulators ever replaced the old one. The attempt to cultivate a new Communist morality failed because of its false, hypocritical character. As a result, society has reached a state of moral anomie—a moral vacuum—marked by a lack of internal moral standards. The notable growth of crime in the country is only one symptom of it.

The fourth feature, closely related to the third, is *the inadequate development of a work ethic.* For centuries, labor in Russia was mostly forced labor—either through serfdom in agriculture or through a considerable degree of noneconomic pressure, control, and compulsion in industry and trade. Many categories of laborers were alienated from the results of their own work and had no positive incentives to increase their efficiency. As a consequence, work—with some exceptions, such as work within the home or for the family—was psychologically regarded as a kind of unprofitable conscription enforced from above. At the beginning of the twentieth century, many things started to change for the better in this respect. The process continued until 1917 and even during the early post-revolutionary years. But the totalitarian appropriation of the fruits of human labor in practically all fields, particularly forced collectivization and the extensive exploitation of prison labor, nearly brought an end to this process of forming a new—liberated—work ethic. Moreover, the unwritten Soviet law that reigned in public opinion was expressed in informal rules of leveling, and punishing initiative, encouraging passive obedience, servile loyalty, and further retreat from the spirit of free and productive labor relations. The Soviet regime relied not on social efficiency but on total control over the population.

The thought patterns of the past, including the Communist era, were totally opposed to the liberal Protestant ethical tradition of responsibly choosing what to make of one's life. Popular Russian proverbs like "hard work is for a fool" reflect the alienation of labor. The catastrophic condition of the work ethic in the field of so-called collective agriculture (still not reformed) is a remarkable example of it. Work for direct family needs and frequently for physical survival at tiny vegetable gardens and new cottage industry or at small-scale local markets was the exception, merely confirming the general rule. This lack of faith in honest labor as a reliable source of well-being and lack of respect for the property rights of others represent the deeper roots of the high incidence of criminality in Russian entrepreneurship.

The fifth feature is the conviction that *the strong hand of authoritarian state power* is the main, if not the sole, foundation on which the whole social superstructure can be maintained. I submit that in the 2000 election, the overwhelming victory of Vladimir Putin, who proclaimed the priority of centralized "order," was based to some extent on this trait of mass consciousness. Its main attributes are lack of confidence in law as an effective instrument for the protection of human rights, fatalistic obedience to any instructions coming from above, identification of the state as the guardian of society, and formalized patriotism.

A further feature, one of the pillars of authoritarianism, is *fear of chaos and anarchy,* a fear that inevitably goes hand in hand with faith in the strong hand of authoritarian state power. The idea of freedom is displaced in popular consciousness by the frightening idea of disorder. For people who have spent all their lives as subjects of an omnipotent state, the condition of freedom seems unusual and dangerous, especially if it is accompanied by economic troubles, as inevitably happens when reform measures are undertaken. In reality, people fear the necessity of making personal, independent decisions about their own lives. The course of reform can be conducted only by persons who are freed from the false idea that a powerful central agency is the sole guarantee of a country's welfare. In this context, the great degree of continuity in personnel, attitudes, and modes of actions among public employees inside the machinery of government inherited from the past creates threats to the reform process. The place of the Russian bureaucracy in the politics of reform needs to receive serious attention.

The seventh feature is *nationalism.* This is too large and painful a problem to be discussed in this brief outline of the conservative syndrome. I draw attention to only one aspect of it. As a rule modern nationalism, including great-power chauvinism, has in its psychological roots an inferiority complex, heavily camouflaged and often not recognized by the people themselves. The ideology of false consciousness built on that complex is always smeared with tar and feathers, with witch-hunting prejudices—the witch is somewhere else and someone else. There is a passion to put the blame for one's troubles and bad luck onto evil strangers and foreign influences instead of looking for it in one's own mirror.

These features are not unique to Russia. They are also inherent, to some degree, among all human beings in different patterns of social and political order. But the problem is that in Russia (and the USSR) these modes of mind and behavior have been encouraged for centuries by the system of political morality and by authoritarian political regimes. Any opposing system of norms has been treated as a sort of dissident counterculture, with the expected repressive consequences. And now the conservative syndrome constitutes a set of shackles. Moreover, one can see that society contains serious potential for opposing transformation. In some circumstances that potential tends to turn into terrible destructive energy—like the systematic threats, discrimination, and even planned arson directed against the few individual farmers achieving economic success. This kind of sabotage has become almost routine in Russian rural areas and has effectively buried the efforts of entrepreneurially minded people to become their own masters.

Fortunately, the conservative syndrome is an important but not the only form of Russian public consciousness. The spores of an alternative system of social morality and psychology, the person-centered counterculture, have survived in spite of all repression, and now, in more favorable circumstances, they are sprouting and developing rapidly.

Instead of compulsory collectivism based on system-centeredness in traditional patterns of order, a newer and higher form of collective action based on the voluntary association of people willing to assume personal responsibility for viable and innovative patterns of development is critical to the dawn of a new era in Russian civilization. Progress in this respect is the source of cautious and moderate optimism about the future of Russia.

PARADOXES OF THE YELTSIN ERA AND BEYOND

I need to address the meaning of the turbulent political events of the Yeltsin era in relation to the analysis offered about the drama of Russian political history. We frequently repeat the cliché that Russia is currently living through troubled times, dangerous times, difficult times. Optimists like myself, following Confucius, cautiously call them interesting times. All this is true, but it is only one aspect of the truth. These years for Russia have also been the most promising decade since 1881 and the best chance to tackle what was left to be done at that time. For the first time in this long period, we have a real opportunity to change the long-term trajectory of the Russian historical way—its very paradigm; the key principle of its development.

The last decade of the twentieth century and the opening of a new millennium seem to be a crucial but extremely turbulent and dangerous juncture, a crossroads opening up new patterns for public choice about the country's course in history. The character of choices people make in Russia will determine their future for many decades ahead—and not only for Russia. I am far from making an existentialist or Pan-Slavic overestimation of the mystical meaning of Russia for the rest of world. But the Russian factor, in one variant or another, will be an important component of the global processes of change. It will be there whether the Russian course of development is favorable or catastrophic. Other peoples of the world also confront serious challenges of a comparable kind. Peoples everywhere face difficult challenges about the future. We can learn from one another's failures and successes.

Like the great historical French and American experiments, the less successful Russian experience has had a considerable general significance for the rest of world for several reasons. One, largely of analytical importance, is that Russian history and modern life have been and still are the arena of persistent struggle between two fundamentally different patterns of social order, of dramatic attempts and repeated failures to change the politically dominant pattern. What were the reasons for these repeated failures?

Many analysts, both Russian and Western, are inclined to consider the Yeltsin era through a dark lens. For instance, Stephen Cohen, a distinguished American specialist on Soviet and Russian politics, has systematically enumerated all conceivable wrongs that occurred during this period and tends to hold the president personally responsible for the mistakes and even for unpredictable side effects.[4] I agree with portions of his critique. But I cannot accept a one-sided approach when achievements that are unquestionable (particularly in view of the almost catastrophic starting point and the limited maneuvering room) are ignored. Probably this is at least partially a problem deriving from excessive expectations, and I would be the last to fault anyone for an attitude initially too optimistic. We have not yet reached a point from which we can take a distanced, balanced, and impartial analytical view. But this is no excuse for avoiding an attempt at judgment of recent developments.

Indeed, some serious mistakes have been made, but there have also been successes, especially considering the Soviet legacy and the social breakdown brought on by that system. Russia in the 1990s made a rather heroic attempt to reconsider and change its historical trajectory. This is an extremely difficult and dangerous task, and all the more so in that the incentives were solely internal, not including an army of occupation or other kinds of pressure or support from outside to stimulate the process, as has been the case in some other countries. It is sad that there are few people either inside or outside Russia who really understand this.

How do we analyze recent controversial political and social processes in Russia? I have come to the conclusion that it is not the usual logic of step-by-step analysis that counts but the bizarre problems of social dilemmas and fundamental paradoxes that pose the analytical problems. In this section I attempt to clarify some of the paradoxes that have become manifest in the 1990s and beyond.

1. *The circumstance that the Communist regime fell so easily, almost without serious resistance, created a threat for democracy because it allowed many features of the old regime to be preserved almost untouched.* The legacy of Communism is still the essential feature of contemporary Russian political life. In the romantic period of perestroika, many people hoped that as soon as they managed to destroy the CPSU-KGB monster (the CPSU is the Communist Party of the Soviet Union), everything could be rearranged somehow. But as in 1917, this kind of hope proved an illusion. The system was able to persist, denying people's expectations.

The collapse of the Bolsheviks' political system and mythology has not provided automatically for the victory of democracy and an essentially new historical course for Russia. The preexisting style of social relationships, in a general sense, again demonstrated its persistence and capacity to adapt and to reorganize in accordance with old principles under new circumstances. It once more brought to bear its capacity to sacrifice ideological symbols in order to preserve its core essence—an anti-individualistic orientation.

Thus the core of this paradox is that it might have been better if the Communist system of power had resisted more stubbornly because in that case: (a) it could have been destroyed and reconstructed much more thoroughly than has actually happened; (b) its institutions and actors would have discredited themselves in the process of this struggle and would have had no chance to gain new legitimacy in the people's eyes; and (c) a new mode of leadership for coping with problems of everyday life—people with both democratic values and skills in practical affairs—could gradually have formed in the process of struggling with the Communist apparatus. In the absence of such preparatory classes, most of our democratic activists proved to be unprepared to govern. As a result, we have too great a degree of continuity of institutions in power, of persons in power, and of principles of government. Even in the best case scenario, the result of a fuller struggle would be rather gradual cultural change. But more decisive substitution of political landscape could alleviate this process and make it less controversial and dramatic. The denazification of Germany after World War II is a lesson that should not be neglected.

2. *In the autumn of 1993, the dismissal of the Supreme Soviet and shooting on the streets of Moscow were not the actions against a democracy but actions directed to protect a weak democracy from mortal danger.* Many people concluded that this action was the destruction of parliamentary democracy and the victory of dictatorship. But the problem was that the Supreme Soviet had never been a parliament. During the Bolshevik coup, the Soviets, meaning "councils," were among the instruments for the seizure of power. Later they were used as "democratic" camouflage for an antidemocratic regime. After 1991, and especially in the case of the Supreme Soviet, they had become quasilegal bodies that manifested the group interests of regional Communist elites and tried to block reforms by all means. In the end, the Supreme Soviet, this pseudo-parliament, provided an umbrella for a Fascist-Communist putsch. I spent those days on the streets of Moscow near the focal point of events observing what took place and was able to consider what might have happened had the

putsch been successful. Recourse to military force was the only way to stop a real counterrevolution and prevent a bloodbath in Moscow.

3. *President Yeltsin, despite his Communist background, bad manners, and controversial actions, was for several years, an effective icebreaker for creating Russian democracy.* He coped successfully with two attempts at totalitarian restoration. Liberal economic reforms began under his patronage. He did what neither Gorbachev nor other reformists dared to do.

The paradox is that the decisive use of central power proved to be an effective instrument to create the beginnings of a market economy and to pursue the democratization of society. Unfortunately, the dynamics of institutional development relate to the personal qualities of people in power, containing their own negative peculiarities: power corrupts. The logic of "court life" gradually outweighed Yeltsin's original democratic orientation. Liberal aspects of reform were abandoned even before they were tried; they developed late and as a result were not well rooted in his personal attitudes. Yeltsin's physical degradation had bearing as well. The combination of Kremlin authoritarian traditions and intrigues prevailed.

A derivative paradox of this situation was that the president tried to compensate for his loss of political will by means of demonstrative, decisive gestures. The most tragic of such gestures was the beginning of what became the Chechen war. In terms of a broader perspective, I believe that the pattern of extensive presidential authority fixed in the current Constitution has nearly exhausted its positive potential. It now risks being transformed from an instrument of reform into an instrument of conservatism in support of traditional relationships and priorities. Until this pattern can be overcome, we will constantly face the danger of pseudomodern gestures, new in form but traditional in deep essence and political tricks. This has happened more than once in Russian history.

4. *The post-Soviet, reformist political leadership inherited the old bureaucratic machine and tried to use it as a tool for the conduct of liberal and democratic reforms, in spite of the entrenched and conservative character of that machine.* Members of the bureaucracy had no other option and one cannot fault

them for being there. Their political responsibility is that they obviously underestimated or neglected the dangers of the "no action alternative." The inherited administrative command-and-control system quickly recovered from the shock and continued to work as it had before. Because of its very logic and regardless of the honest intentions of some bureaucrats, the administrative system either resists real changes or tends to distort their spirit, and it ignores the intent of the changes. Opinions about capitalism being bureaucratic and anti-liberal in post-Soviet Russia have substantial merit. An analysis of the activities of the post-Soviet ministries could provide many examples of bureaucratic entrenchment. However, in conducting such an analysis now, one would face technical difficulties similar to those in the Soviet times because the system is no longer open to researchers.

The administrative machinery not only preserved most of its preexisting defects but has acquired new ones. The most obvious shift is the decline in the qualification level of the state apparatchiks because the most skilled and talented have moved to commercial endeavors. Another less obvious but probably more crucial factor is the decline of administrative morality, loss of a bureaucratic code of behavior, in favor of personal advantage. This kind of normlessness has been amplified by the great temptation to convert administrative power into private property rights through privatization of state enterprises. This was probably inevitable: the process of destruction always leaves behind assets to be salvaged. But that does not make the process acceptable to citizens or serve as a sufficient explanation for those who suffer from corruption and red tape. The resulting remarkable and, at first glance, discouraging scale of people's alienation from a supposedly democratic state is a natural human reaction to the extensive bureaucratic abuses prevailing in Russian society.[5]

5. *Pro-liberal domestic policies have not met with an adequate response among the majority of the country's population: people have either abused the unusual degree of freedom available to them or are frightened by it.* Productive private initiatives have not prevailed as liberal policy makers had hoped; instead, anomie has prevailed. I call this phenomenon the released-prisoner syndrome of consciousness. It is characterized by a loss of

orientation to life under new conditions of supposedly unrestricted freedom. The new rules of the game made the previous experience with the conditions of life inappropriate to successful adaptation and created a kind of moral vacuum instead.

As a result we faced: (a) criminalization of business with a lack of respect for law and property rights, even among the new rich and successful proprietors, the so-called new Russians; and (b) nostalgia about Soviet times, when people were not expected to take initiatives but merely to serve as obedient subjects of an omnipotent state. Certainly, this idealized vision of the Soviet times is distorted and wrong. The Soviet state was never a kind and compassionate ruler, a benevolent patron of the nation. But people view reality through their own subjective filters, particularly older people, who are frequently inclined to idealize past times and to react negatively to new challenges. That is why the current moment looks dangerous and critical. Data from surveys of mass attitudes indicate that the normal social basis for liberal policy—liberal individualism—enjoys much less influence than its opposite, several variants of anti-personal collectivism or nonliberal individualism. The latter is an important phenomenon with influence among different social groups.

6. *The pro-Western foreign policy of the late Soviet Union and the early Russian Federation (1992–93) has not met with an adequate response from the West.* For many years, the West tempted the USSR with ideas of European integration, a "common European house," an alliance of civilized nations to address global problems. The USSR responded to such campaigns negatively and has been justly criticized for that from both inside and outside. One of paradoxes is that in the end, during perestroika, all this phraseology ironically laid the foundation for what was called a doctrine of new political thinking. In the beginning, during the early Gorbachev era, it served mostly manipulative purposes of a political game on the world political stage.

However, ideas usually have their own logic of development. Gradually this doctrine grew popular and was transformed into a basic policy concept. In particular, under the direct influence of this concept, the Kremlin abandoned its geopolitical ambitions and voluntarily surrendered its "outer empire" and, later, its "inner empire." This was a huge, almost unprecedented gesture, the meaning of which went far beyond the needs of practical politics and has not yet been carefully considered. It was the demonstration of a complete break with a centuries-long imperial political tradition and an invitation to reconsider the whole system of international relationships. It can probably be compared to some degree with the dissolution of the British Empire after the Second World War.

Nobody expected these developments. Most analysts feared that the Soviet monster, armed to the teeth, would desperately resist, defending the borders of its empire with terrible consequences. But this has not happened. The new Russia sincerely offered to rearrange relations with Western partners on a new foundation. The paradox is that the most Western politicians proved not to be ready to follow their own slogans to meet this challenge. The traditional geopolitical approach and short-term, narrow political calculations prevailed. This undermined the political positions of the democrats—the natural allies of the West—and gave unexpected support to the bearers of the Russian imperial tradition. It gave an impetus to the revival of the "great power syndrome," of some traditional Pan-Slavic and Pan-Russian orientations. In my opinion, the West also bears a share of responsibility for the revival of old imperial attitudes in Russian politics and social life.

7. *The Russian patriotic movement works not for but against the true interests of the people living in the Russian homeland.* The so-called Russian patriotic movement is manipulating: (a) elements of the conservative syndrome in mass consciousness, particularly imperial and chauvinistic aspirations; and (b) the feeling of national humiliation provoked by both real and imaginary problems in Russia and of the ethnic Russians outside Russia proper. One can hope that this nervous and even hysterical neo-nationalism is only a temporary reaction that will be supplanted by a more balanced paradigm integrating both national and universal values. But we have come through and not entirely left behind an alarming, dangerous period in that respect.

The main danger is not the revival of the Communist regime, and I hope that the extreme nationalistic parties do not find serious opportunities for gaining power either. The real danger is some version of pseudo-modernization of the country. By this I mean a situation in which the same or a similar system-centered ethos survives or revives behind a renovated institutional facade. The only reliable guarantee of avoiding that scenario would be the development of independent institutions in civil society. Democratic reforms cannot be carried out by the government alone. Governments can facilitate the process, taking the initiative in sponsoring opportunities that can only be brought to realization by relying on the self-organizing and self-governing capabilities of people in the context of their own relationships with one another. The character of a free market economy and of a civil society depends as much on the self-organizing and self-governing capabilities of people as on the policy initiatives of the government—or more so. It is in this context that the phenomenon of Vladimir Putin must be considered. The purely political aspects of his line are not our subject here, but I want to draw attention to one paradox.[6] President Putin is seemingly inclined to semiliberal politics in relation to the economy and a pro-Western line in international affairs. But unlike Yeltsin, he does not believe that changes can be accomplished other than by the strong hand of centralized rule. His major administrative ideas involve rebuilding vertical command-and-control power and putting personally devoted figures in key positions in the pyramid. In terms of my concept, these look like steps toward enforcement of system-centeredness. Restoration of such old Soviet symbols as the hymn and military banner seem to play to the same theme. He probably considers all this an appropriate price to pay for economic transformation. But taking into account the enormous inertia of authoritarian, bureaucratic rule and, more important, the inevitable contradiction inherent in such discord between means and ends, it may prove a miscalculation.

We can also consider the results of general elections as a kind of paradox. The Communists did the worst damage to the country during their seventy-eight years of rule. They were responsible for victimizing tens of millions of people and for the ruin of a country potentially one of the richest in the world. Yet they maintained considerable support among the electorate. The conservative system-centered syndrome is still an essential component of mass consciousness. This list of paradoxes could be continued; I have merely chosen the examples given because in my opinion they help to identify the core of the current Russian situation.

CONCLUSION

Returning to the image of a new junction or crossroad in history, Russia looks like a traveler at the dividing marker, cautiously testing different paths with a walking stick. The final public choice has not yet been made. Karl Popper revealed the key in *The Open Society and Its Enemies* when he observed that the fear and tension inherent in movement from a closed to an open society dominate "the greatest moment in the history of any civilization." We are probably facing the greatest moment in the history of Russian civilization.

Beyond that, I believe the drama of Russian history holds significance much broader than merely for those who have a special interest in Russia itself. The tragic Russian experience contains not only negative traits to be avoided by the rest of world; it also needs to be critically reconsidered in all its aspects in light of perverse symptoms manifest in the development of the Western democratic system of order. It is not by chance that some of the most acute Western analysts warn of dangers facing Western democracies in the twenty-first century. V. Havel, president of the Czech Republic, writes about the hopes, prospects, dangers, and tasks facing a new Europe.[7] The Russian nation, as part of European civilization, has paid a huge price for lessons that need to be appreciated and understood. This experience has many aspects. On the one hand, there were unsuccessful attempts to create a brave new world by using the instruments of state power to try to transform society. The attempts yielded a bizarre combination of new manipulative social technologies and autocratic repression. However, there have also been surprisingly successful efforts by responsible individuals working in association with one another to save and even to develop spiritual and intellectual resources, including positive skills of collective life, under very unfavorable circumstances.

Second, the dynamics of the conditions of human life in Western countries seem to suggest the idea that humankind needs to move toward a new synthesis of individualism and collectivism as the best prospective pattern of human order, and to search for ways to overcome problems that I view as clashes between system-centeredness and person-centeredness. Admittedly some acute problems, like terrorism, must initially be addressed by military force and law enforcement. But the only way to reach the roots of such problems is through readiness and openness for broad dialogue. We may find new ways of creating collectivities grounded in voluntary associations of individuals and in their capacity to cooperate on the basis of both personal and property rights, with freedoms and justice, in connection with democratically organized self-governing entities. The collectivism grounded in tribal associations or autocratic dominance is what we have observed so frequently and so clearly on this intellectual journey through Russian history. Those ways need yield to a higher kind of collectivity based on voluntary association and self-governing capabilities. There are plenty of challenges and difficulties to be faced along this path. And they cannot be resolved solely by decisions at the top or by a single public choice made by a nation as a whole.

A key problem we all are forced to consider is the problem of change through time.

To end this intellectual journey through the drama of Russian political history over the last four centuries, I wish to quote from an old German poem written by Paul Fleming early in the seventeenth century, after the devastation of the Thirty Years War.[8] These lines symbolize for me the position we face in the exercise of intellectual courage to consider the meaning of human experience as a complement to God's Creation in the emerging patterns of human civilization.

Missing Time
Man, you live in time yet time you do not know;
You humans do not know from what you come and in what you are.
Yet one thing you do know: that you were born in a time
And that you will be lost in a time as well.
But what is this time that once had you conceived?
And what will this time be when it will make you wither?
Time, it is both, something and nothing, and so is man.
But man still ponders this very something and this nothing.
Time dies in time and is conceived in time as well.
It comes from me and you, and you and I come from it.
Man, he must live in time; and time, it lives in man,
Yet man must cede while time still goes on being.
Time is what you are, and you are what time is,
Yet still, you are much less than time will ever be.
Alas! Why does not come a time that has no time at all
To take us from these times into its time,
To take us from ourselves, so that we once might be,
As He now is, like a time, that does not ponder time.

Notes

FOREWORD

1. Henry Sumner Maine, *Ancient Law* ([1861] 1864), 165.
2. Alexis de Tocqueville, *Democracy in America,* 2 vols. ([1835, 1840]; reprint, New York, Knopf, 1945), 1:434.
3. Tocqueville, *Democracy in America,* 2:291.
4. Tocqueville, *Democracy in America,* vol. 2, chap.6, book 4, 318–19.
5. Harold Berman, "World Law," 1995, 1617.

CHAPTER 1: ON METHODOLOGY AND GENERAL CONCEPTS

1. Ironically, the collapse of socialist regimes in Eastern Europe, where this kind of monism acquired almost sacred status as the official and the only "fair" doctrine, has not brought the ideology of economic determinism to an end. Moreover, as a prominent English scholar notes, a version of economic determinism has lately been disseminating in Western thought that could give Marxism chance of resurrection. See Larry Ziedentop. *Democracy in Europe* (Allen Lane, Penguin Press, 2000). In his introduction to the Russian edition of this book he wrote: "European political thought became a victim of the phenomenon I call 'economism,' which can be considered a symptom of belated influence of Marxism on liberalism. A dangerous delusion resulted: the assumption that just as economic behavior can be modified rather rapidly (through taxes, the interest rate, by means of advertisements, etc.), political foundations and habits also can be changed fast. But it is not true. The principles and habits of free people are formed only gradually" (reverse translation from author's introduction to the Russian edition, *Demokratiya v Evrope* [Moscow: Logos, 2001], xxxix–xl). On the other hand, in Russian academic circles we have had discussions that are interesting from a methodological standpoint on the significance of the subjunctive mood. Problems of alternative paths and possibilities and the role of occasional (fortuitous) events in the course of history were specifically addressed. For example, at the Round Table at the Institute of Universal History, I gave a paper about historical junctions as a topic of alternative history. See *Odyssey. Chelovek v istorii. Istoriya v soslagatel'nom naklonenii?* (Odysseus. Man in history. The subjunctive mood in history?), (Moscow: Nauka, 2000), 5–85.
2. See, for example, Vamik D. Volkan, *Bloodlines: From Ethnic Pride to Ethnic Terrorism.* (New York: Farrar, Straus and Giroux, 1997).
3. Reverse translation from the Russian edition, F. Manuel, "O pol'ze i vrede

psikhologii dlya istoriiII Filosofiya i metodologiya istorii" (On the advantages and disadvantages of psychology for history), in *Philosophy and Methodology of History,* (Moscow: Nauka, 1977), 288.

4. Different aspects and manifestations of this kind of dichotomy are among the perennial and most acute subjects of social and political thought. Moreover, it became a critical point for dividing them on two incompatible (intransigent) visions of world. Thus in the nineteenth century we can see a liberal "camp," including people like John Stuart Mill, Wilhelm von Humboldt, and Herbert Spencer, and a collectivist camp occupied by Karl Marx, his followers, and other socialist and anarchist ideologists. In the twentieth century the most aggressive and, unfortunately, most influential wing of collectivist ideology made a remarkable shift toward the coercive side of collectivism; that brought to the political arena different versions of totalitarian and authoritarian regimes. On the other hand, liberals like Henry Bergson, Karl Popper, and Milton Friedman enriched and developed the intellectual basis of the liberal concept by categories of open and closed societies and many other conceptual innovations; see Henry Bergson. *Les deux sources de la morale et la religion* (1932); Karl R. Popper, *The Open Society and Its Enemies* (London: Routledge and Kegan Paul, 1966); Milton Friedman, *Capitalism and Freedom* (Chicago: University of Chicago Press, 1982). More practical in aspect and closer to the central object of this book, efforts to support the open society forming in post-Communist Eastern Europe and Russia must be noted. In particular, the multidimensional programs of the Open Society Institute, created and sponsored for many years by George Soros, made a contribution to this process. (I can affirm this as a long-term participant in projects of this institute.) As readers will understand, lists of names, books, and actions might be extended greatly from what I present here, but that would be beyond the purposes of this book. One thing must be clarified here: *my construct of person-centeredness versus system-centeredness focuses not at the political level but at a deeper, more fundamental level of the dichotomy under consideration.*
5. Certainly it would be incorrect simplification to connect Christianity or any of its denominations directly with liberalism. A mutual dependence of these phenomena is much more complicated. However, a certain positive correlation between them definitely exists. I agree with Larry Ziedentop, who wrote: "Undoubtedly, in a certain sense liberalism can be considered as a secular form of Christianity developing initial elements of Christian moral values by means of making distinction of public and private spheres." Siedentop, *Democracy in Europe,* XLII (reverse translation from Russian). See also Emil Durkheim, *The Elementary Forms of the Religious Life* (New York: Free Press, 1995).
6. Nicolai A. Berdyaev. *Filosofiya neravenstva: Pis'ma k nedrugam po social'noy filosofii* (The philosophy of inequality: Letters to foes in social philosophy), (Paris: Ymka-Press, 1970), 143.
7. Emil Durkheim, *Sociology and Philosophy* (Glencoe, Ill.: Free Press, 1953). For an interesting concept of three patterns of human associations—atomistic/contractual, organic/functional, and mutual personal—see Frank G. Kirkpatrick, *Community: A Trinity of Models* (Washington, D.C., 1986).
8. Vincent Ostrom in several of his works has analyzed that phenomenon using as examples the French and Communist pretenders who exercised leadership on behalf of the proletarians as a whole or on behalf of the oppressed part of soci-

ety as a whole. See Vincent Ostrom, *The Meaning of Democracy and the Vulnerability of Democracies: A Response to Tocqueville's Challenge* (Ann Arbor: University of Michigan Press, 1997), chapter 3, "Newspeak and Doublethink," and chapter 9, "Comparing African and European Experience." See also his *The Meaning of American Federalism: Constituting a Self-Governing Society* (San Francisco: ICS Press, 1994).

9. See the monograph study of these problematics: Elinor Ostrom, *Governing the Commons: The Evolution of Institutions for Collective Action* (New York: Cambridge University Press, 1990).
10. See, for example, studies by a leading American political psychologist who successfully applied his psychiatric experience, psychoanalysis in particular, for analysis and practical projects in the field of international conflict resolution. Vamik D. Volkan, *The Need to Have Enemies and Allies: From Clinical Practice to International Relationships* (London: Jason Aronson, 1988).
11. Alexis de Tocqueville, *The Old Regime and the French Revolution* (Garden City, N.J.: Doubleday, 1983), 210.
12. There are several partial translations of this course into English. We shall address them all, as can be seen in references to following chapters.
13. Alexander L. Yanov, *The Origins of Autocracy: Ivan the Terrible in Russian History* (Berkeley: University of California Press, 1982).
14. Yanov, *Origins of Autocracy,* 11.
15. Richard Pipes, *Russia under the Old Regime* (New York: Scribner, 1974).
16. The notion of *intelligentsia* was first introduced in the 1860s by Russian novelist P. D. Boborykin. This word is actually an attempt to combine two different social and linguistic phenomena: (1) the social group of brain workers—that is, people with a certain level of education and whose activity is professional in character; and (2) people of the certain worldview and moral position, those "who produce new purposes and new knowledge, who take the role of bearer of critical thought, of historical, moral, and other self-consciousness and self-changeability"; L. M. Batkin, *Italianskie gumanisty: stil' zhizni, stil' myshleniya* (The Italian humanists: Style of life, style of thought), (Moscow: Nauka, 1978), 17. This second meaning corresponds closely with the Latin word *humanitas,* which covers both virtue and erudition, and the meaning of which conjoins education and profession. There are also some modifications of this second meaning. The German sociologist E. Wien treats critics and linguistic creative work as a vocation, with a sense of self-conscious existence as an intellectual. He wrote: "People belonging to the intellectual strata become intelligent only if they fulfill their critical function"; E. Wien, *Intellectualle in Politic und Gesellschaft* (Stuttgart: Enke, 1971), 89. But on the whole, one can speak about two different (probably complementary) traditions in the understanding of the words *intelligentsia* and *intellectuals*—the more instrumental Anglo-Saxon approach and the more moral and humanitarian Italian-Russian approach.

    This ambivalence of terminology has frequently produced and continues to produce a lack of mutual understanding and even direct distortions of meaning. I use the word *intelligentsia* mainly in its humanistic meaning. In the Russian situation, the intelligentsia was the vigorous but practically the sole possessor of person-centered orientation. In the West, we do not see a similar opposition because there person-centeredness had become widespread among different social groups from the beginning. In Russia, to be intellectual was a sort of vocation, frequently involving great self-sacrifice. This fundamental difference is expressed in the word *intelligentsia* in the Russian language, implying some emotional tension and noble traits. But this concentration of person-centeredness mainly at the margins of one social stratum is the source of the tragedies that have followed.

17. See the extremely interesting documentary film "Let History Judge," produced in 1960 in Leningrad. Vasiliy Shulgin as a hero of the film has benevolent and edifying conversations for ninety minutes with people who were well-known opponents of Shulgin from the pre-revolutionary period, with the former top-rank Communist Party official F. Petrov, and with several of his ideological successors. Shulgin treats them as not very well brought-up or wise but diligent followers of the system-centered ideals of his younger years. The appearance of this film presents a remarkable indication of the continuity of autocratic power in Russia in spite of the complete change in its "revolutionary" facade.

CHAPTER 2: THE TIME OF TROUBLES

1. L. N. Gumilev, *Searches for an Imaginary Kingdom: The Legend of the Kingdom of Prester John* (Cambridge: Cambridge University Press, 1987).
2. V. O. Kliuchevsky, *A History of Russia,* trans. C. J. Hogarth (New York: Russell and Russell, 1960). 1:308–309.
3. V. O. Kliuchevsky, *The Rise of the Romanovs,* trans. Liliana Archibald (London: Macmillan, 1970), 13–14.
4. Niccolo Machiavelli, *Florentine History,* with introduction by Harley C. Mausfield (Princeton, N.J.: Princeton University Press, 1988).
5. V. O. Kliuchevsky, *A Course in Russian History: The Seventeenth Century,* trans. N. Duddington (Chicago, Quadrangle Books, 1968), 53.
6. Kliuchevsky, *Course,* 11–12.
7. Kliuchevsky, *Course,* 12.
8. Kliuchevsky, *Course,* 12.
9. Kliuchevsky, *History of Russia,* 3:65.
10. Kliuchevsky, *Course,* 28–29.
11. Kliuchevsky, *Course,* 53.
12. Marina V. Razhbaeva and Vadim E.Semenkov. "Istoriya Russov: ideologiya kasachestva i ego mesto v istorii Ukrainy i Rossii" (The history of Russes: The ideology of Cossacks and its place in the history of Ukraine and Russia), ONS *(Social Science Today),* no.3 (1998): 188–92.
13. The notion of sublimation originated from psychoanalysis. Sigmund Freud considered it one of mechanisms of psychological defense, a way to overcome internal neurotic conflict. It assumes that the energy of the human individual tends to be switched (sublimated) from some socially forbidden realm to another realm that is socially more appropriate. (See his classic, many times reissued works *Beyond the Pleasure Principle* and *The Ego and the Id.*) More recently this notion has been incorporated into certain branches of social psychology; see, for example, Eric Fromm. *The Anatomy of Human Destructiveness* (New York, 1973), and Shibutani Tamotsu, *Society and Personality: An Interactionist Approach to Social Psychology* (Englewood Cliffs, N.J.: Prentice-Hall, 1967).
14. M. Bloch, *Feudal Society* (Chicago: University of Chicago Press, 1961), 107.

15. Bloch, *Feudal Society,* 110–11.
16. Kliuchevsky, *Course,* 316–17.
17. Kliuchevsky, *Course,* 38.
18. Kliuchevsky, *Course,* 41–42.
19. The popular modern Russian historian Alexandr Panchenko even affirms that, unlike in Western Europe canons, "pretending" did not exist in Russia until the seventeenth century, being considered a mortal sin. Alexandr M. Panchenko, *O russkoy istorii i kul'ture* (On Russian history and culture), (St. Petersburg: Azbuka. 2000), 28–31.
20. Kliuchevsky, *Course,* 32.
21. Lev I. Mechnikov, *Protivniki gosudarstva na Rusi* (The opponents of state in Russia), (Reprint edition of *Kolkol.* Moscow: Nauka, 1978), 93–98. Ruslan G. Skrynnikov, *The Time of Troubles: Russia in Crisis, 1604–1618.* (Gulf Breeze, Fl.: Academic International Press. 1988). Sergei M. Soloviev, *The Time of Troubles: Tsar Vasily Shuysky and the Interregnum 1606–1613;* ed., trans., and with an introduction by G. Edward Orchard (Gulf Breeze, Fla.: Academic International Press, 1989).
22. Tocqueville, *Old Regime;* see especially part 2, chapter 9.
23. Kliuchevsky, *Course,* 48.
24. Based on the Polish text from the second edition, Adnrzhej Frycz-Modzhevsky, *O Poprawie Rzeczypospolititei* (Warsaw, 1953); originally translated from Latin by Cyprian Bazylik for the first (1577) Polish edition. This translation and bibliographical inquiries made by courtesy of Roman Frawkowski.
25. Martin C. Rady, *Russia and the Ukraine 1462–1725.* (London: Hodder and Stoughton, 1990); Daniel B. Rowland, Muskovite Political Attitudes as Reflected in Early Seventeenth Century Tales about the Time of Troubles, Ph.D. thesis, Yale University, 1976; *Polacy w zyciu kulturalnym Rosji: praca zbiorowa (pod redakcja Ryszarda Luznego)* (Wroclaw: Zaklad im. Ossolinskich, 1986); Konstantin V. Kharlampovich, *Polskli wplyw na szkolnictwo ruskie w XVI i XVII st.: Z niedrukowanego oryginalu rosujskiego przelozyl i wstepem zaopatryl A. Wanczura* (Lvov, 1924).
26. Kliuchevsky, *Course,* 278.
27. Kliuchevsky, *History of Russia,* 369.
28. Kliuchevsky, *Course,* 350–53.
29. Kliuchevsky, *Course,* 390.
30. The Polish ambassador Neville, who left the detailed description of Golitsin's plans, gave him this title.

CHAPTER 3: THE DEVASTATING COURSE OF PETER'S "MODERNIZATION"

1. See, for example, Robert K. Massie, *Peter the Great: His Life and World* (New York: Knopf, 1980); Evgenii V. Anisimov, *The Reforms of Peter the Great: Progress through Coercion in Russia* (Armonk, N.Y.: M. E. Sharpe, 1993).
2. *The Memoirs of Princess Dashkova, Written by Herself,* 3rd ed. (Leipzig, n.d.; in Russian), 125. What seems to be quite remarkable is that in a late Soviet edition, this passage of her notes, originally written in French, is presented in another translation, much milder in tone. See Ekaterina R. Dashkova, *Zapiski 1743–1810* (Notes 1743–1810), (Leningrad: Nauka, 1989), 127.
3. Modest Hofmann and Andre Pierre, *By Deeds of Truth: The Life of Leo Tolstoy,*

trans. from French by Ruth Whipple Fermaud (New York: Orion Press, 1958), 161.

4. V. O. Kliuchevsky, *Peter the Great,* trans. Liliana Archibald (New York: St. Martin's Press, 1958), 16, 54.
5. Kliuchevsky, *Peter the Great,* 29.
6. Kliuchevsky, *Peter the Great,* 46–47.
7. See Nina B. Golikova, *Politicheskie protsessy pri Petre 1* (The political trials under Peter I), (Moscow: Izdatel'stvo MGU, 1957), 14–15.
8. Kliuchevsky. *Peter the Great,* 54–55.
9. Kliuchevsky. *Peter the Great,* 55.
10. Kliuchevsky, *History of Russia,* 4:373.
11. Kliuchevsky. *Peter the Great,* 270.
12. Kliuchevsky. *Peter the Great,* 271.
13. Kliuchevsky. *Peter the Great,* 263.
14. Kliuchevsky. *Peter the Great,* 155.
15. Kliuchevsky. *Peter the Great,* 120.
16. Kliuchevsky. *Peter the Great,* 145–46.
17. Kliuchevsky. *History of Russia,* 4:244–46.
18. Kliuchevsky. *History of Russia,* 246.
19. Let me clarify the differences between the two strata of the Russian nobility. Boyars constituted the upper section of the ruling class, next in rank below the ruling princes until the abolition of this class by Peter I; gentry *(dvorianstvo)* were the lower part of the same class, having originally received their status with appropriate estates and serfs on condition of their service (military, as a rule) to the crown.
20. Peter B. Struve, "The Historical Meaning of the Russian Revolution." In *Out of the Depths (De Profundis): A Collection of Articles on the Russian Revolution,* trans. and ed. W. F. Woehrlin (Irvine, Calif.: C. Schlacks, Jr., 1986), 206.
21. Struve, "Historical Meaning," 207.
22. Alexis de Tocqueville, *The Old Regime, and the French Revolution.* (Garden City, N.J.: Doubleday–Anchor Books, 1955), 98.
23. Tocqueville, *Old Regime,* 98–99.
24. See the introduction to a collection of her works: Oleg N. Mikhailov, "Ekaterina II: imperatritsa, pisatel', memuarist" (Catherine II: empress, writer, memoirist), in *Sochineniya Ekateriny II* (Works of Catherine II), (Moscow: Sovetskaya Rossia, 1990), 3–20. On Catherine's contribution to the origin of liberalism in Russia, see Leonard Shapiro, "Liberalism in Russia," in his *Russian Studies* (London: Collins Harvill, 1986), 48.
25. Kliuchevsky, *History of Russia,* 5:93, 98.
26. Kliuchevsky, *History of Russia,* 5:98.
27. Kliuchevsky, *History of Russia,* 5:117–18.
28. Kliuchevsky, *History of Russia,* 5:108–109.
29. See, for example, Mark Raeff, *Origins of the Russian Intelligentsia: The Eigtheenth-Century Nobility* (New York: Harcourt, Brace and World, 1966).

CHAPTER 4: ROMANTIC DECEMBRISTS AND PESSIMISTIC PHILOSOPHERS

1. There are whole libraries of books on Decembrism. One of the classic works in English is Mark Raeff, *The Decembrist Movement* (Englewood Cliffs, N.J.: Prentice-Hall, 1966).
2. See, for example, Philip Pomper, *The Russian Revolutionary Intelligentsia* (Wheeling, Ill.: H. Davidson, 1993).
3. Kliuchevsky, *History of Russia,* 5:172.
4. Alexandr A. Lebedev, *Chaadaev* (Moscow: Molodaya gvardiya, 1965; in Russian), 111–12.
5. Vilhelm K. Kukhelbeker, *Puteshestvie, dnevnik, stat'i* (Journey, diary, articles), (Leningrad: Nauka, 1979), 15.
6. Ivan D. Yakushkin, *Zapiski, stat'i, pis'ma* (Notes, articles, letters), (Moscow: Izdatel'stvo sotsial'no-economicheskoy literatury, 1951).
7. Natan Y. Eidelman, *Lunin* (Moscow: Molodaya gvardiya, 1965), 40.
8. Lebedev, *Chaadaev;* Raeff, *Decembrist Movement;* Eidelman, *Lunin,* 101; V. O. Kliuchevsky, *Sochineniya* (Works), 8 vols. (Moscow: Izdatel'stvo sotsial'no-economicheskoy literatury, 1958), 5:244–45. Various forms of Catholic influence can be seen in Russia during most of the nineteenth century. An example of formally entering upon Catholisism was Pecherin, who became a priest in Dublin but kept his ties with Russia. Another way was to incorporate some elements of Catholic views into Orthodoxy; Peter Chaadaev can be considered an the example of this. A third way, turning to ecumenism, is best personified in Vladimir Soloviev, the great philosopher of the last quarter of the century. See V. A. Tsimbaeva, *Russkiy katolitsism: Zabytoe proshloe rossiyskogo liberalisma* (Russian Catholicism: A forgotten past of Russian liberalism), (Moscow: Editorial URSS, 1999).
9. Yakushkin, *Zapiski,* 15.
10. Eidelman, *Lunin,* 197.
11. Kukhelbeker, *Puteshestvie,* 291.
12. Mikhail Lunin. "A Look at the Secret Society in Russia (1816–1826)," in *The First Breath of Freedom,* compiled by N. Eidelman (Moscow: Progress, 1988; in English), 12–14.
13. Alexander Pushkin, "The Bronze Horseman" (translation by D. M. Thomas).
14. See A. Herzen, in *Voices in Exile: The Decembrist Memoirs,* compiled by G. R. V. Barratt (Montreal: McGill-Queens University Press, 1974), 48.
15. Fedor Tiutchev, "December 14, 1825," in *On the Heights of Creation: The Lyrics of Fedor Tiutchev,* translated from the Russian with introduction and commentary by Anatoly Liberman (Greenwich, Conn.: Jai Press, 1993), 44.
16. A. Herzen, "On the Development of Revolutionary Ideas in Russia," in *The First Breath of Freedom,* 312.
17. The first English-language edition of the Marquis de Custine's *Russia,* translated from the French, was published in the middle of the nineteenth century (New York, 1854), half a century before the abridged and "politically corrected" Russian edition.
18. Astolphe Marquis de Custine, *Custine's Eternal Russia,* ed. and trans. Phyllis Penn Kohler (Miami, Fla.: Center for Advanced International Studies, University of Miami, 1976), 52, 136.

19. Custine, *Russia,* 53, 203–204.
20. *My Past and Thoughts: The Memoirs of Alexander Herzen,* 6 vols., authorized translation from Russian by Constance Garnett (London: Chatto & Windus, 1924), 2:271.
21. Natan Y. Eidelman, *Conspiracy against the Tsar: A Portrait of the Decembrists* Moscow: Progress, 1985; in English), 7.
22. Quoted in Eidelman, *Conspiracy,* 74.
23. Eidelman, *Conspiracy,* 311.
24. Petr Y. Chaadaev, "Philosophical Letters," in *Russian Philosophy,* 3 vols. (Chicago: Quadrangle Press, 1965), 1:109, 112, 113, 120.
25. Kliuchevsky, *History of Russia,* 5:153.
26. See Mark Raeff, *Michael Speransky, Statesman of Imperial Russia, 1772-1839* (Westport, Conn.: Hyperion Press, 1979); Petr A. Zayonchkovsky, *Pravitel'stvenny apparat samoderzhavnoy Rossii v XIX v* (Governmental apparatus of autocratic Russia in the nineteenth century), (Moscow: Mysl', 1978).

CHAPTER 5: A DECISIVE JUNCTION

1. I believe that one of the most interesting and provocative recent books on this problematic is Larry Ziedentop's monograph *Democracy in Europe,* especially chapters 2, 3, 6, and 9; it is especially interesting to consider his ideas in comparison with the classic works of Milton Friedman; see also C. B. Macpherson, *The Life and Times of Liberal Democracy* (Oxford, Oxford University Press, 1977); K. Minogue, "How Critical Is the 'Crisis of Liberalism'?" *Encounter* (London) 63, no. 1 (1984): 199–207; G. F. Gaus, *The Modern Liberal Theory of Man* (London: Croom Helm, 1983).
2. Among a number of publications on this subject, note the classics: Isaiah Berlin, *Russian Thinkers* (New York: Penguin, 1979); James Billington, *The Icon and the Axe* (London: Weidenfeld & Nicholson, 1966); Richard Pipes, *Russia under the Old Regime*; Mark Raeff, *Understanding Imperial Russia: State and Society in the Old Regime* (New York: Harcourt, Brace and World, 1984); and Victor Leontovitsh, *Geschichte des Liberalismus in Russland* (Frankfurt am Main: Vittorio Plostermann, 1957). A good anthology of the eminent nineteenth- and twentieth-century Russian thinkers' selected works has been published recently in Moscow: *Opyt russkogo liberalisma: Antologiya* (The experience of Russian liberalism: An anthology), (Moscow: Kanon, 1997).
3. *Golosa iz Rossii* (Voices from Russia), 4 vols. (Moscow: 1974–1976, fascimile edition).
4. Georgiy V. Plekhanov, *Revolyutsionnoe dvizhenie semidesyatykh godov* (The revolutionary movement of the seventies) in *Sochineniya* (Works), 30 vols. (Moscow and Leningrad, 1927), 5:126. See also Arthur P. Mendel, *Michael Bakunin: Roots of Apocalypse* (Eastbourne, U.K.: Holt-Saunders, 1982), and Aileen Kelly, *Michael Bakunin: A Study in the Psychology and Politics of Utopianism* (Oxford: Clarendon Press, 1982).
5. Darrell P. Hammer, *The USSR: The Politics of Oligarchy,* 3d ed. (Boulder, Colo.: Westview Press, 1986), 62.
6. Leonard Shapiro, "Lenin's Intellectual Formation and the Russian Revolutionary Background," in his *Russian Studies,* 202.

7. Hammer, *The USSR*. See also Philip Pomper, *Peter Lavrov and the Russian Revolutionary Movement* (Chicago: University of Chicago Press, 1972); *Russian Intellectual History: An Anthology*, ed. and comp. Mark Raeff, with an introduction by Isaiah Berlin (New York: Humanity Books, 1999).
8. For a classic English-language work on this topic see Nicholas Riasanovsky, *Russia and the West in the Teaching of the Slavophiles* (Cambridge, Mass.: Harvard University Press, 1952).
9. Robert E. MacMaster, *Danilevsky: A Russian Totalitarian Philosopher* (Cambridge, Mass.: Harvard University Press, 1967), 208.
10. MacMaster, *Danilevsky*, 191.
11. MacMaster, *Danilevsky*, 257–58.
12. F. M. Dostoevski, *The Diary of a Writer*, vol. 2, translated and annotated by Boris Brasol (New York: Farrar and Rinehart, 1949), 780.
13. Dostoevski, *Diary*, 636–37.
14. Dostoevski, *The Diary*, 661.
15. Dostoevski, *The Diary*, 669.
16. G. S. Pomerants, "Dolygaga doroga istorii" (The long road of history), *Znamya*, no. 11 (1991): 185.
17. On the history of the Narodnaya Volya organization and its spiritual ideological ties with Bolshevism, see Leonard Shapiro, "Lenin's Intellectual Formation," 202–18.
18. For a comprehensive and well-documented study of this subject, see Mikolay A. Troitskiy, *Tsarizm pod sudom progressivnoy obchshestvennosti: 1866–1895* (Tsarism under the trial of the progressive society: 1866–1895), (Moscow: Mysl', 1979), 239–81.
19. See, for example, Egor A. Perets, "Dnevnik gosudarstvennogo sekretarya" (Diary of the secretary of state), in *Aleksandr II: Memuary, dneivniki (Alexander the II: Memoirs, Diaries)* (St. Petersburg: Pushkinskiy fond, 1995), 346.

CHAPTER 6: AFTER THE CATASTROPHE

1. See R. Hastie, Vladimir Galaktionovich Korolenko: The Writer and the Liberation Movement, 1853–1907. Ph.D. dissertation, 1979, 425.
2. Albert Schweitzer. *Kultura i etika* (Culture and ethics), (Moscow: Progress, 1973), 61.
3. Georgiy V. Plekhanov, "Tsarstvovanie Aleksandra III" (The reign of Alexander III), in *Sochineniya* (Works), 30 vols. (Moscow and Leningrad, 1927), 24:163.
4. Boris N. Chicherin, *Vospominaniya* (Memoirs), (Moscow: Izdatelistvo sabashnikovyukh, 1934), 42, 279.
5. I had the opportunity to describe in detail the dramatic history of this social group in the nineteenth century in *Gosudarstvennaya Sluzhba* (The public service), edited and co-authored by A. Obolonsky (Moscow: Delo, 2000), 56–84.
6. P. Zayonchkovsky, *Pravitel'stvennyi apparat samoderzhavnoi Rossii v XIX veke* (The autocratic Russian government's apparatus in the Nineteenth century), (Moscow: Mysl', 1978), 186–87.
7. A. P. Chekhov, "The Peasants," in *Anton Chekhov: Five Great Short Stories* (New York: Cover, 1990), 66–68.
8. Georgiy V. Plekhanov, "K psikhologiii rabochego dvizheniya (On the psychology of the labor movement), in *Sochineniya* (Works), 24:258.

9. See P. Kropotkin, *Rechi buntovshchika* (Speeches of a rioter), (St. Peterburg: Golos Truda, 1921).
10. *Uncle Vanya,* in *Monologues from Chekhov,* trans. Mason W. Cartwright (Toluka Lake, Calif.: Dramaline Publications, 1983), 22.
11. David Patterson, ed. and trans., *The Gospel According to Tolstoy* (Tuscaloosa: University of Alabama Press, 1992), xxv.
12. Leo Tolstoy, "Patriotism and Government," in *The Complete Works of Count Tolstoy,* 24 vols. (Boston, 1905), 20:147, 162.
13. "Christianity and Patriotism," in *Complete Works of Tolstoy,* 20:476.
14. "Patriotism or Peace," in *Complete Works of Tolstoy,* 20:438.
15. Ibid, in *Complete Works of Tolstoy,* 20:452–53.
16. Ibid, in *Complete Works of Tolstoy,* 20:450, 457.

CHAPTER 7: THE EVENING GLOW

Epigraph Source: *Complete Poetry of Osip Emilevich Mandelstam,* trans. Burton Raffel and Alla Burago (Albany: State University of New York Press, 1973), 91.

1. Among the plentiful literature, see for example Peter Waldron, *Between Two Revolutions: Stolypin and the Politics of Renewal in Russia* (Dekalb: Northern Illinois University Press); and Melissa K. Stockdale, *Paul Miliukov and the Quest for a Liberal Russia, 1880–1918* (Ithaca, N.Y.: Cornell University Press, 1966).
2. *The Memoirs of Count Witte,* trans. and ed. by Sidney Harcave (Armonk, N.Y.: M. E. Sharpe, 1990), 369, 387–88, 479, 483–84, 489, 595.
3. *Memoirs of Count Witte,* 375.
4. For detailed analysis of these questions, see Aron Ya Avrech, *P. A. Stolypin i sud'by reform v Rossii* (P. A.Stolypin and the fate of the Russian reforms), (Moscow: Politizdat, 1991), 234–53.
5. Leonard Shapiro, "Stolypin: Most Controversial Russian Statesman," in his *Russian Studies,* 93–99.
6. See David Kerans, *Mind and Labor on the Farm in Black-Earth Russia, 1861–1914* (Budapest: Central European University Press, 2000); Judith Pallot, *Land Reform in Russia, 1906–1917: Peasant Responses to Stolypin's Projects of Rural Transformation* (Oxford University Press, 1999).
7. See Corinne Gaudin, "No Place to Lay My Head: Marginalization and the Right to Land during the Stolypin Reforms," *Slavic Review* 57, no. 4 (1998).
8. Avrech, *P. A. Stolypin,* 265.
9. Vasiliy V. Shulgin, *Dni* (The days), (Leningrad: Priboy, 1927), 55.
10. See, for example, Roberta Manning, *The Crisis of the Old Order in Russia,* (Princeton, N.J.: Princeton University Press, 1982); Peter Waldron, *The End of Imperial Russia, 1855–1917* (New York: St. Martin's Press, 1997).
11. *Memoirs of Count Witte,* 413.
12. Tocqueville, *Old Regime,* 155–56.
13. Fedor K. Sologub, *The Little Demon,* trans. John Cournos and Richard Aldington (New York: Knopf, 1916), 261.
14. Sologub, *Little Demon,* 491.
15. Sologub, *Little Demon,* 98–99.
16. *Memoirs of Count Witte,* 515–16.
17. *Memoirs of Count Witte,* 517.
18. For the perspectives of the Vekhi see Nikolai Berdyaev et al., *Vekhi—Land-*

marks: A Collection of Articles about the Russian Intelligentsia, trans. and ed. Marshall S. Shatz and Judith E. Zimmerman, with foreword by Mark Raeff (Armonk, N.Y.: M. E. Sharpe, 1994).

19. Tocqueville, *Old Regime,* 143.
20. See Pomper, *Russian Revolutionary Intelligentsia.*
21. *Memoirs of Count Witte,* 397.
22. *Memoirs of Count Witte,* 595.
23. Andrey Bely, "The Crisis of Consciousness and Henrik Ibsen," in *Petersburg,* translated by Robert Maguire and John Malmstad (Bloomington: Indiana University Press, 1978); Andrey Bely, *Spirit of Symbolism,* ed. John E. Malmstad (Ithaca: Cornell University Press, 1987), 139–40.
24. Vladimir E. Alexandrov, *The Major Symbolist Fiction* (Cambridge: Harvard Univeristy Press, 1985), 130.
25. Ibid., 131.
26. Andrey Bely, *Petersburg,* 203.
27. *Complete Poetry of Mandelshtam,* 36.
28. Innokentiy Annensky, *Poetry* (St. Petersburg, 1910)
29. Marina Tsvetaeva, *Art in the Light of Conscience: Eight Essays on Poetry,* trans. Angela Livingstone (Cambridge, Mass.: Harvard University Press, 1992), 162–63.
30. Alexander A. Blok, *Selected Poems.* (Moscow: Progress, 1981), 108.

CHAPTER 8: THE INVERTED PYRAMID

1. Tocqueville, *Old Regime,* 5.
2. The notion of anomie was introduced by Emile Durkheim in *The Division of Labor* (Glencoe, Ill.: Free Press, 1933), 169; see also David E. Apter, *Introduction to Political Analysis* (Cambridge, Mass.: Winthrop Publishers, 1877), 388–90.
3. S. A. Askol'dov, "The Religious Meaning of the Russian Revolution," in *Out of the Depths.* (Irvine, Calif.: C. Schlaks, Jr., 1986), 30. This collection of articles on the Russian revolution written by the group of Russian intellectuals called the vekhovtsy (from the word *vekhy,* landmarks), appears to be the first serious attempt to give the events of 1917 philosophical and moral explanation.
4. Hammer, *The USSR,* 33.
5. Nikolai Berdyaev, "The Specters of the Russian Revolution," in *Out of the Depths,* 56.
6. Stefan Zweig, *Joseph Fouche: Sochineniya* (The complete works), 6 vols. (Moscow: Hudozhestvennaya Literatura, 1963), 4:421.
7. S. A. Pokrovsky, "The Curse of Perun," in *Out of the Depths,* 196.
8. See Erich Fromm, *The Anatomy of Human Destructiveness* (New York: Holt, Rinehart and Winston, 1973); and his *Escape from Freedom,* (New York: Farmar and Rinehart, 1941).
9. The term *necrophilic* is not used in the common sense—to signify a sexual perversion. Instead, it is used here as a psychoanalytical metaphor for a social pathology that characterized a specific category of people and that totalitarian regimes used as an active force.
10. A. A. Minin, "Dukh razrusheniya v russkoi revolyutsii: Sotsial-no-psikhologicheskii etyud" (The destructive spirit in the Russian Revolution: A social-psychological essay), in *God ruskoi revolyutsii* (The year of the Russian Revolution), (Moscow: Zemlya i Volya, 1918), 27–39.

11. Karl Marx in his *The Eighteenth Brumaire of Louis Bonaparte* described such a movement as the declassed mobs of people thirsting for redistribution of the national wealth in tips, grants, and other benefits.
12. Pokrovsky, "Curse of Perun," 195, 202
13. N. A. Berdyaev, "The Specters of the Russian Revolution," op. cit., 36.
14. B. Pil'nyak, *Golyui god* (The naked year). *Selected Works* (Moscow: Hudozhestvennaya literatura, 1976), 104.
15. M. Gorky. *Peterburgskiye tipy* (Types of Petersburg), in *The Complete Works* (Moscow and Leningrad: Gosudarstvennoe izdatel'stvo, 1930), 19:166.
16. Minin, "Dukh razrusheniya," 38.
17. Dmitriy A. Volkogonov, *Lenin*, book 2 (Moscow: Novosti, 1994). Alexandr N. Yakovlev, *Po moshcham i eley* (Such balm as relics are—Eccl.) (Moscow: Evraziya, 1995). This strange title originated in a phrase of Patriarch Tichon, voiced after Lenin's first temporary mausoleum was flooded by sewage in 1923. Yakovlev was a leading member of the Politburo, Gorbachev's "right hand" during the perestroika years; in the 1990s he was chairman of the Presidential Comission on Rehabilitation of Victims of Political Repression. His small book contains hundreds of horrible illustrations and excerpts of previously top secret documents from many Soviet archives. Also see Stephane Courtois et. al *The Black Book of Communism: Crimes, Terror, Repression*, trans. Jonathan Murphy and Mark Kramer (Cambridge: Harvard University Press, 1999). This collection of essays on all Communist regimes of the twentieth century and the tragic consequences of their rule. It was published in twenty countries; in Russia, for example, 100,000 copies were printed.
18. P. D. Kondrat'ev. "God revolyutsii s economicheskoi tochki zrenija" (The year of the Russian Revolution from the economic point of view), in God ruskoi revolyutsii, 218.
19. Berdyaev, "Specters of the Russian Revolution," 46–47, 63.
20. *Lenin i Vchk* (Lenin and Vcheka), (Moscow: Politizdat, 1975), 503–504.
21. V. I. Lenin, *Zapugannye strakhom i borjushchiesja za novoe* (The frightened and the struggling for the new). *Complete Works*, 55 vols. (Moscow: Gozudarstrennoe izdate listro politicheskoy literatury, 1962) 35:21.
22. M. Voloshin, "Bourgeoisie," in *Twentieth Century Russian Poetry: Silver and Steel—An Anthology*, ed. Albert C. Todd and Max Hayward, with Daniel Weissbort (New York: Doubleday, 1993), 41.
23. M. Gorki, *On S. A. Tolstoi* (On S. A. Tolstaya), in *Complete Works*, 22:153.
24. Tocqueville, *Old Regime*, 154.
25. P. Fabrichny, *Pechat'* (The press).
26. *Dekrety Sovetskoy vlasti* (Soviet power decrees), 2 vols. (Moscow: Politizdat, 1957), 1:432.
27. *SU RSFSR* (Collection of Laws of the Russian Federation), 1918, no. 28, clause 362. The system of suffocating an independent press was already evident. Changes over the last seventy years merely perfected the arrangements: the structure has been improved, private publishing houses were abolished, all exceptions from the common order of censorship were canceled, and the existence of a supervising body (Glavlit) became top secret.
28. M. Voloshin, "Red Guard," in *Twentieth Century Russian Poetry*, ed. Todd and Hayward, 35–36.
29. Lenin, *Complete Works*, 35:189.

30. Yakovlev, *Po moshcham i eley,* 36.
31. See, for instance, documentary evidence in *Krest'yanskoe vosstanie v Tambovskoy gubernii v 1919-1921 g.* (The peasant revolt in Tambov guberniya in 1919–1921), (Tambov, 1994), 178–79, 163.
32. *SU RSFSR,* 1918, no. 47, cl. 559.
33. *SU RSFSR,* 1918, no. 27, cl. 350–60.
34. *SU RSFSR,* 1919, no. 50, cl. 488.
35. Lenin. *Complete Works,* 35:157–58.
36. M. Voloshin, "Terror," in *Modern Russian Poetry: An Anthology with Translations,* ed. Vladimir Markov and Merrill Sparks (Indianapolis: Bobbs-Merrill, 1967) 519.
37. *Lenin i Vchk,* 57.
38. See, for example, Alexander I. Solzhenitsyn, *The Gulag Archipelago,* vol. 1 (New York: harper and Row, 1973.
39. *Marx Karl, Engels Fridrih: Sochinenya* (The works), 50 vols. 2d ed. (Moscow: Politizdat, 1964), 33:45.
40. See *Lenin i Vchk,* 417–18.
41. In formulating the purposes of the new politics, Lenin said frankly and definitely that Bolsheviks should regroup before their new attack against "the class enemy." In other words, he considered this partial return to common norms of regular society to be a forced and temporary measure. Thus, everything that developed later was done according to Lenin's precepts.
42. Mikhail I. Gernet, *Prestupnost' i samoubiistva vo vremya voiny i posle neje* (Criminality and suicides during the war and after), in *Selected Works* (Moscow: Yuridicheskaya literatura, 1974), 463–64.
43. M. I. Gernet, "Predislovie k rabote *Prestupnyi mir Moskvy*" (Preface to the work *The Criminal World of Moscow*), in *Selected Works,* 424.
44. Berdyaev. *Filosofiya neravenstva,* 26.
45. Berdyaev. *Filosofiya neravenstva,* 104–105.
46. *Tsypin V. Istoriya Russkoy Pravoslavnoy Tserkvi, 1917–1990.* (History of the Russian Orthodox Church, 1917–1990), (Moscow, 1994), 34.
47. *Samizdat* literally means self-publishing. Politically sensitive materials were most often self-published (usually in typescript), as they would otherwise not have been produced by the state publishing houses, which maintained a monopoly on publication in the Soviet Union.
48. *Izvestiya TsK KPSS* 1990, no. 4, 191–93.
49. Yakovlev, *Po moshcham i eley,* 83–98; *Kommunisticheskiy regim i narodnoe soprotivlenie v Rpossii, 1917–1991* (The Communist regime and popular resistance in Russia, 1917–1991), (Moscow: Posev, 1997), 17.
50. Among many books on this subject, one that seems especially provocative is Andrei D. Sinyavsky, *The Russian Intelligentsia* (New York: Columbia University Press, 1997).
51. Lenin, *Complete Works,* 35:48, 173, 193.
52. Lenin, *Complete Works,* 54:220–21.
53. Cited in Solzhenitsyn, *Gulag Archipelago,* 1:321.
54. Vladimir Kirillov, "We" (1917), in *Twentieth Century Russian Poetry,* ed. Todd and Hayward, 189–90.
55. Vladimir V. Mayakovsky, "Left March" (1918), in *Selected Verse* (Moscow: Raduga Publishers, 1985), 77–79.

56. Mayakovsky, "Ode to Revolution," in *Selected Verse,* 78–79.
57. Anna Akhmatova, "Requiem" (1918), in *Modern Russian Poetry,* 279.
58. Osip Mandelshtam, "The Twilight of Freedom" (May 1918), in *Modern Russian Poetry,* 21–22.
59. Osip Mandelshtam (1918), *Selected.* (New York: Farrar, Straus and Giroux, 1975), 22.
60. Mandelshtam, "My Time" (1923), *Selected,* 21–22.
61. M. Voloshin, "Russia," in *Twentieth Century Russian Poetry,* 41–42.

CHAPTER 9: STALINISM

1. For example, Martin Malia, *The Soviet Tragedy: A History of Socialism in Russia, 1917–1991* (New York: Free Press, 1994); Richard Pipes, *Russia under the Bolshevik Regime* (New York: Random House, 1995); Sergey P. Melgunov, *Krasny terror v Rossii* (Red terror in Russia), (Moscow, CP PS, 1990); Robert Conquest, *The Great Terror* (New York: Macmillan, 1968).
2. See Stephen F. Cohen, *Bukcharin and the Bolshevik Revolution: A Political Biography, 1888–1938* (New York: Knopf, 1983).
3. The notion of "one-dimensional man" was introduced by Herbert Marcuse in his famous book of that title published in 1967.
4. See note 16 to chapter 1 for fuller discussion.
5. Once again I recommend Sinyavsky, *The Russian Intelligentsia.*
6. In addition to sources provided in the previous chapter, I might also offer the following books: *Pospelovskiy Russkaya pravoslavnaya tserkov' v XX veke* (The Russian Orthodox Church in the twentieth century), (Moscow: Respublika, 1995); *Krestny put' tserkvi v Rossii 1917–1987* (The cross way of the Church in Russia 1917–1987), (Moscow: Posev, 1988); Patrick Egan, "Christians under Communism," *Pastoral Renewal,* January, 1984; Alexander I. Solzhenitsyn, *The Gulag Archipelago,* vol. 2 (New York: Harper and Row, 1974).
7. Yakovlev, *Po moshcham i eley,* 94–95.
8. *Kommunisticheskiy regim i narodnoe soprotivlenie v Rossii 1917–1991,* 18.
9. See detailed analysis on this subject, for example in: Sheila Fitzpatrick, Alexander Rabinovich, and Richard Sites, eds. *Russia in the Era of NEP: Explorations in Soviet Society and Culture* (Bloomington: Indiana University Press, 1991).
10. For a detailed study of collectivization and its tragic consequences see Robert Conquest, *The Harvest of Sorrow: Soviet Collectivization and the Terror-Famine* (London: Overseas Publications Interchange, 1988).
11. Based on indirect calculations, Conquest indicates loss of 14.5 million human lives in rural areas of the country during 1930–37, including 6.5 million direct victims of "de-kulakization"; *Harvest of Sorrow,* 445.
12. For a comprehensive demographic study of this subject see Maksudov Sergey, *Poteri naselenia SSSR* (Losses of population in the USSR), (Benson, Vt.: Chalidze Publications, 1989).
13. *Bol'shaya Sovetskaya Entsiklopedya* (The big Soviet encyclopedia), (Moscow: Sovetskaya encyclopedia, 1975), 21:315, 316, 318.
14. See, for example, the Yakovlev and Solzhenitsyn works already indicated, and *Kommunisticheskiy rezhim i narodnoe soprotivlemie v Rossii 1917–1991,*

CHAPTER 10: AFTER STALIN

1. Alexander V. Obolonsky, "The Kind of Political System We Inherited," in *Russian Politics and Law* 31, no. 2 (Armonk, N.Y.: M. E. Sharpe, 1992): 6–26; Obolonsky, "Power and Control in the USSR Prior to Perestroika: Or, What System Are We Restructuring," in *The Global Failure of Socialism,* Champions of Freedom, Ludwig von Mises Lecture Series, vol. 19 (Hillsdale, Mich.: Hillsdale College Press, 1992), 119–132; Obolonksy, "Russian Politics in the Time of Troubles: Some Basic Antinomies," in *Russia in Search of Its Future,* ed. A. Saikal and W. Maley (Cambridge, Cambridge University Press, 1995), 12–27.
2. As the most comprehensive and well balanced study on that subject, with the fullest bibliography, I recommend the Archie Brown's monograph *The Gorbachev Factor* (Oxford: Oxford University Press, 1996).

CHAPTER 11: AT THE NEW CROSSROAD

1. Igor' G. Yakovenko, "Rossia v Evrope" (Russia in Europe), *Vestnik Evropy* (European Herald), no. 1 (2001), 75.
2. See Alexander V. Obolonsky, "The Modern Russian Administration in the Time of Transition: New Challengers versus Old Nomenclature Legacy," *International Review of Administrative Science* 65, no.4 (December 1999): 569–78.
3. For the more extended version of this concept, see Obolonsky, "Russian Politics in the Time of Troubles," 12–26.
4. Stephen F. Cohen, "Russian Studies without Russia," *Post-Soviet Affairs* 15 (1999): 37–55.
5. See Vladimir E. Guliev and Andrey V. Kolesnikov, Otchuzhdennoe gosudarstvo (The alienated state), (Moscow: Manuscript, 1998).
6. For Putin's political program see, for example, Eugene Huskey, "Political Leadership and the Center-Periphery Struggle: Putin's Administrative Reforms," in *Gorbachev, Yeltsyn, Putin: Political Leadership in Russia's Transition ed. Archie Brown et al. (Washington, D.C.: Carnegie Endowment for International Peace, 2001), 113–32.*
7. *See, for example, V. Havel, "The Hope for Europe," New York Review,* June 20, 1996.
8. Paul Fleming, "Missing Time," translated by Erich Ritter, Faculty of Indiana University, courtesy of Nancy Boerner, who connected us. See *German Verse,* introduced and edited by Leonard Forster (Baltimore, Md.: Penguin Books, 1957), 119–20.

Bibliography

Amalrik, Andrei. 1970. *Involuntary Journey to Siberia.* New York: Harcourt Brace Jovanovich.

Berdiaev, Nikolai. 1948. *The Origin of Russian Communism.* Trans. R. M. French. London: G. Bles.

Berdyaev, Nikolai et al. 1977. *Landmarks: A Collection of Essays on the Russian Intelligentsia, 1909.* Ed. Boris Shragin and Albert Todd. Trans. Marian Schwartz. New York: Karz Howard.

Brown, Archie. 1996. *The Gorbachev Factor.* Oxford: Oxford University Press.

Conquest, Robert. 1968. *The Great Terror: Stalin's Purge of the Thirties.* New York: Macmillan.

———. 1986. *The Harvest of Sorrow: Soviet Collectivization and the Terror-Famine.* New York: Oxford University Press.

Crankshaw, Edward. 1976. *The Shadow of the Winter Palace: Russia's Drift to Revolution, 1825–1917.* New York: Viking Press.

Custine, Astolphe Marquis de. 1976. *Custine's Eternal Russia.* Ed. and trans. Phyllis Penn Kohler. Miami, Fla.: Center for Advanced International Studies, University of Miami.

Davis, Nathaniel. 1995. *A Long Walk to Church: A Contemporary History of Russian Orthodoxy.* Boulder, Colo.: Westview Press.

Dunlop, John B. 1993. *The Rise of Russia and the Fall of the Soviet Empire.* Princeton, N.J. : Princeton University Press.

Edgerton, William, ed. 1993. *Memoirs of Peasant Tolstoyans in Soviet Russia.* Bloomington: Indiana University Press.

Florinsky, Michael T. 1953. *Russia: A History and an Interpretation.* 2 vols. New York: Macmillan.

Hammer, Darrell P. 1990. *The USSR: The Politics of Oligarchy.* 3d ed. Boulder, Colo.: Westview Press.

Hosking, Geoffrey A. 1973. *The Russian Constitutional Experiment: Government and Duma, 1907–1914.* Cambridge: Cambridge University Press.

Kaminski, Antoni Z. 1992. *An Institutional Theory of Communist Regimes: Design, Function, and Breakdown.* San Francisco: Institute for Contemporary Studies Press.

Karamzin, Nikolai M. 1959. *Memoir on Ancient and Modern Russia.* Trans. Richard Pipes. Cambridge: Harvard University Press.

Katkov, George. 1967. *Russia 1917: The February Revolution.* New York: Harper and Row.

Knight, Amy W. 1993. *Beria: Stalin's First Lieutenant.* Princeton, N.J.: Princeton University Press.

Laqueur, Walter. 1993. *Black Hundred: The Rise of the Extreme Right in Russia.* New York: Harper Collins.

Lenin, V. I. [1917] 1932. *State and Revolution.* New York: International Publishers.

———. [1902] 1932. *What Is to Be Done?* New York: International Publishers.

Massie, Robert K. 1980. *Peter the Great: His Life and World.* New York: Knopf.

Medvedev, Roy A. 1971. *Let History Judge: The Origins and Consequences of Stalinism.* Trans. Colleen Taylor. New York: Knopf.

Ostrom, Vincent. 1997. *The Meaning of Democracy and the Vulnerability of Democracies: A Response to Tocqueville's Challenge.* Ann Arbor: University of Michigan Press.

Patterson, David, ed. 1992. *The Gospel According to Tolstoy.* Trans. D. Patterson. Tuscaloosa: University of Alabama Press.

Perlmutter, Amos. 1981. *Modern Authoritarianism: A Comparative Institutional Analysis.* New Haven: Yale University Press.

Pipes, Richard. 1974. *Russia under the Old Regime.* New York: Charles Scribner's Sons.

Pobedonostsev, Konstantin P. 1965. *Reflections of a Russian Statesman.* Trans. Robert Crozier Long. Ann Arbor: University of Michigan Press.

Remnick, David. 1993. *Lenin's Tomb: The Last Days of the Soviet Empire.* New York: Random House.

Shapiro, Leonard. 1960. *The Communist Party of the Soviet Union.* London: Eyre and Spottiswoode.

Schumpeter, Joseph A. 1942. *Capitalism, Socialism and Democracy.* New York: Harper and Brothers.

Solzhenitsyn, Aleksandr I. 1973–74. *The Gulag Archipelago, 1918–1956: An Experiment in Literary Investigation.* 7 books in 3 vols. Trans. Thomas P. Whitney. New York: Harper and Row.

———. 1991. *Rebuilding Russia: Reflections and Tentative Proposals.* Trans. Alexis Klimoff. New York: Farrar, Straus and Giroux.

Stickle, D. M., ed. 1992. *The Beria Affair: The Secret Transcripts of the Meetings Signalling the End of Stalinism.* Trans. Jeanne Farrow. New York: Nova Science Publishers.

Trotsky, Leon. 1972. *The Revolution Betrayed: What Is the Soviet Union and Where Is It Going?* Trans. Max Eastman. New York: Pathfinder Press.

Tucker, Robert C. 1973. *Stalin as Revolutionary, 1879–1929: A Study in History and Personality.* New York: Norton.

———. 1987. *Political Culture and Leadership in Soviet Russia: From Lenin to Gorbachev.* New York: Norton.

———. 1990. *Stalin in Power: The Revolution from Above, 1928–1941.* New York: Norton.

Vitte, Sergei. 1967. *The Memoirs of Count Witte.* Edited and Translated by Sidney Harcave. Armonk, N.Y.: M. E. Sharpe, 1990.

Woehrlin, William F., ed. 1986. *Out of the Depths: A Collection of Articles on the Russian Revolution.* Trans. William F. Woehrlin. Irvine, Calif.: C. Schlacks, Jr.

Index

ISBN 1-58544-224-0

90000

9 781585 442249